PUBLICATIONS OF THE ISRAEL ACADEMY
OF SCIENCES AND HUMANITIES
SECTION OF HUMANITIES

———

SPINOZA — HIS THOUGHT AND WORK

Entretiens in Jerusalem, 6–9 September 1977

INTERNATIONAL INSTITUTE OF PHILOSOPHY

ENTRETIENS IN JERUSALEM

6–9 September 1977

SPINOZA
HIS THOUGHT AND WORK

Edited by

NATHAN ROTENSTREICH

and

NORMA SCHNEIDER

JERUSALEM 1983

THE ISRAEL ACADEMY OF SCIENCES AND
HUMANITIES

This *Entretiens* was the third in the series of Jerusalem Philosophical Encounters convened by the S.H. Bergman Centre for Philosophical Studies of the Hebrew University of Jerusalem

ISBN 965-208-055-1

PREFACE

THE INTERNATIONAL INSTITUTE of Philosophy held its annual *Entretiens* in Jerusalem in 1977. This *Entretiens,* which commemorated the three-hundredth anniversary of Spinoza's death, was sponsored by the Israel Academy of Sciences and Humanities and the S. H. Bergman Centre for Philosophical Studies of the Hebrew University, Jerusalem.

These Proceedings contain the papers presented at the *Entretiens* and the prepared interventions of the interlocutors; the volume does not include the open discussion that followed each presentation and intervention. Also not included are the papers of Prof. Raymond Klibanski, who summed up the *Entretiens* but was not able to prepare his paper for publication, and that of Prof. G. H. von Wright, who spoke on Wittgenstein's relation to Spinoza.

On the occasion of the publication of these Proceedings, I wish to thank once again my colleagues and collaborators for the devotion with which they organized this *Entretiens* in Jerusalem. My special thanks are also due to the co-editor of the Proceedings, Ms Norma Schneider, for her conscientious contribution in preparing the manuscripts for publication.

Nathan Rotenstreich

CONTENTS

E. E. URBACH

Jerusalem

Professor von Wright, Ladies and Gentlemen,

I extend to all of you, to the members of the International Institute
of Philosophy and to all participants of this *Entretiens*, the heartiest
welcome on behalf of the Israel Academy of Sciences and Humanities.
Before continuing with my short remarks, I have a sad task to
fulfil, and call upon you to rise and honour the memory of Professor
Chaim Wirszubski, a member of the Local Organizing Committee of
this *Entretiens*. Professor Wirszubski was an outstanding scholar in
the field of Classics. At the same time, he worked for many years on
the influence of Jewish mysticism in the period of the Renaissance.
He completed an extensive work on Pico de la Mirandola, which will
no doubt shed additional light on the question of how Neoplatonism
influenced Spinoza, whose *Tractatus Theologico-Politicus* Professor
Wirszubski translated into Hebrew.
Your resolution to have this Annual *Entretiens* in Jerusalem, under
the auspices of the Academy, the S. H. Bergman Centre for Philosophical Studies and the Van Leer Jerusalem Foundation, is in itself
gratifying. In addition, the theme to which you will be dedicating your
deliberations — *Spinoza, His Thought and Work* — is of interest not
only to professional philosophers, but also to a wide range of people
participating in the cultural life of this country.
The specific Jewish interest in Spinoza and his System during the
nineteenth century was mainly concerned with the Jewish sources of
his thought and his attitude towards them. The only exceptions were
S. D. Luzzato and Hermann Cohen, the two most formidable Jewish
opponents of Spinoza in modern times.
With the emergence of the modern Jewish National Movement,
people turned to Spinoza to find in him support for their own ideol-
ogies. For some he even became the prototype of the secular Jew.
It is surely not mere chance that leading ideologists of the Zionist
movement, like Klatzkin and Sokolov, have written extensive works

on Spinoza, and that the first Prime Minister of Israel, David Ben-Gurion, was a great admirer of Spinoza and the initiator and sponsor of the Hebrew translation of his *Tractatus Theologico-Politicus.*

The Anglo-Jewish philosopher Samuel Alexander concluded his lecture, held in 1921, on "Spinoza and Time", with the following words: "I have been more concerned with the gloss than with the text, but a great man does not exist to be followed slavishly, and may be more honoured by diversion than by obedience. As for Spinoza himself, it is too late a day to express unbounded admiration. Moreover, no courage is required to praise him, for the admirer there is no risk. The Jews will not excommunicate me for my veneration of Spinoza, neither will the gentiles denounce this lecture as infamous."

Today we no longer need even these apologetic sentences. The process of auto-emancipation which we try to attain in this country allows for a free approach both to the personality of Spinoza and to his System. His personality and his fate are a chapter or, one may say, only a paragraph in Jewish history. They should be treated in the same way as the histories of other personalities; however, his philosophical system has to be considered and appreciated in the framework of the history of philosophy.

I am fully convinced that the lectures and discussions in this *Entretiens* will provide a significant contribution towards the advancement of our understanding of Spinoza and his ideas. I wish you success in bringing forward their excellence.

G. H. VON WRIGHT

Helsinki

LADIES AND GENTLEMEN,

It is my privilege, as President of the *Institut International de Philosophie*, to thank our Israeli hosts for having invited the Institute to hold its *Entretiens* in Jerusalem and for their labours in preparing the meeting. I know on the basis of a year's correspondence that Professor Rotenstreich and his associates have spared no efforts to ensure the scholarly success of the conference and the high quality of its social programme. I also wish to thank the three institutions whose sponsorship has secured the locale and the necessary material basis for our meeting: the Israel Academy of Science and Humanities, the S. H. Bergman Centre for Philosophical Studies and the Van Leer Jerusalem Foundation. We much appreciate that Professor Urbach, Vice-President of the Academy, has honoured this inaugural session by his presence.

I understand that these *Entretiens* of the I.I.P. are at the same time the third in a series of encounters of the centre which bears its name in memory of Hugo Bergman. I met this grand old man of Israeli philosophy when, thirteen years ago, I presided over another international organization which held its congress in Jerusalem. He made an unforgettable impression. The humanity and wisdom he embodied seemed to me symbolic of a great tradition of Jewish thought which we hope will for ever be allowed to flourish in the regained homeland of the Jewish people.

This year philosophers all over the world are celebrating the tercentenary of the death of Spinoza. The *Institut International de Philosophie* is happy that it can render homage to this sage by holding its *Entretiens* on the thought and work of Spinoza here in Jerusalem. The place befits the theme, one could say. The handsome little volume of preprints of papers which are going to be discussed here conveys an impression of the multiform relevance of Spinoza's philosophy to contemporary thinking. I should like to mention here two Spino-

[11]

zistic themes, the importance of which is not limited to the circle of professional philosophers but concerns all mankind.

The first is the theme of tolerance. Spinoza's own time was certainly not an age of tolerance. It was rather an age of factitious intolerance, dogmatism, and mutual hatred which followed the split in the unity of beliefs brought about by the Reformation. But without this split the soil would not have been prepared for the seeds of tolerance sown by Spinoza, himself an outcast from the community into which he was born and an alien in the one in which he went to live. It took about two hundred years for the seeds to grow to maturity, and after a short flowering the plant is again threatened by suffocation. Intellectuals cannot do much, I am afraid, to change the climate of brutality and violent hatred which prevails in our world. But they may do something to debunk the hypocrisy of intolerance in disguise. There is a trend to rest content with what is termed the peaceful coexistence of different ideological creeds. But this sentiment is not likely to promote tolerance and mutual understanding; it rather fosters indifference to injustice and coolness to human suffering. Tolerance worthy of the name springs from the insight, beautifully professed by Spinoza in the very title of the *Tractatus Theologico-Politicus,* that freedom of thought "not only may be granted without prejudice to piety and peace of the republic, but also [they] may not be withheld without danger to the peace of the republic and to piety itself". The rulers who do not understand this are blinded to the good of the sociopolitical units over which they rule. To call their attention to this and try to enlighten them requires courage — and sometimes the great courage which involves the sacrifice of one's own freedom and even one's life. Those who make this ultimate sacrifice, like our colleague and fellow member Jan Patočka, have to an eminent degree fulfilled the philosopher's calling. It is not only my hope but my conviction that their sacrifice will in the end promote the cause for which they had to suffer evil.

The other theme I wanted to mention here is the idea *Deus sive Natura.* It can be contrasted with a philosophical anthropology which sees in man the master of nature, "lord and commander of the elements" to quote Marlowe's drama *Doctor Faustus.* This view was the ethos of the scientific-technological revolution which made possible modern industrialized society. The crisis which this form of social organization now experiences and which involves suicidal threats to mankind is basically a crisis in man's relation to nature as a whole. The exhaustion of natural resources, the progress of erosion, the disappearance of wildlife, is the revenge which nature takes on man

[12]

for upsetting the equilibrium of his biosphere. I do not think that secularized man can revert to a state where he lets awe of the divine keep his aspirations in check, including planned interference with nature. The check can only come from an enlightened collective self-interest, from a realization that the complex web of interconnected principles which govern natural processes cannot, without detrimental consequences to all, be meddled with merely to satisfy the whims and wishes of a few — be they private enterprizers or chauvinistic nations. Spinoza's pantheistic identification of God and the world may have features which are either obsolete or have lost their appeal to modern intellectual man. But the wisdom contained in his view of man's unity with the "all-nature" and his subordination to its laws continues to be a source of inspiration for those who think, with Professor Arne Naess and his fellow philosopher-ecologists, that the human race can avoid major threats against its continued existence only if the technocratic attitude prevalent in the industrial states is changed.

Ladies and Gentlemen, this is not the place to dwell on the special problems of our organization. They will be discussed at the General Assembly and at the meetings of the various *Commissions*. But I should like to mention here that, as President of the I.I.P., it has caused me concern to notice that the future of the *Institut* is not unproblematic. We depend for our activities on financial support from UNESCO, granted by its council for human sciences (CIPSH) and administered to us with the International Federation of Philosophic Societies (FISP) as intermediary. It is my urgent hope that, in the relevant quarters, there will continue to exist an understanding, not only for the particular needs of our current bibliographical enterprise, for our continuing survey of contemporary thought, the *Chroniques,* and for our annual scholarly conferences, the *Entretiens,* but also for the existence of the *Institut* as an authoritative body of individual philosophers who feel a critical concern for the cultivation and flourishing of true philosophy — and who may, when needed, voice an opinion on this. May the *Entretiens de Jérusalem* live up to the scholarly standards by the satisfaction of which the *Institut International de Philosophie* will show that this hope is worthy of fulfilment.

NATHAN ROTENSTREICH

Jerusalem

The System and Its Components

I

WE ARE ASSEMBLED HERE in Jerusalem for the annual *Entretiens* of the International Institute of Philosophy. Welcoming you here on behalf of our Organizing Committee, I take the opportunity of thanking the Institute for its resolution to convene in Jerusalem. I express my gratitude to the Israel Academy of Sciences and Humanities, the Hebrew University and its S. H. Bergman Centre for Philosophical Studies, and the Van Leer Jerusalem Foundation for their joint effort in arranging the *Entretiens* and making our meeting possible. I thank my colleagues and staff members, Miss Aubert and Mrs Hyam, for their devotion and cooperation. I express my thanks to the President of the Institute, Prof. von Wright, for his continuing cooperation and guidance.

We meet here both *sub specie temporis* and *sub specie aeternitatis*. The three hundredth anniversary of Spinoza's death is for us an occasion or an occasional cause — *causa occasionalis,* if such term is permitted vis-à-vis Spinoza — for giving our attention to a great philosophical system formulated in the past. Our reverence for a thinker takes the shape of studying the various facets of his system in their inner logic as well as in their impact on the formulation of philosophical thought or accentuation of philosophical problems.

Sub specie aeternitatis, again if this metaphor is admissible, connotes an attempt to understand, at least partially, the nature of philosophic systematic thinking. In this regard Spinoza's system serves our exploration as a kind of score — *"Partitur"* — for our investigation of the nature of systems, even when we are critical of his particular system or express some doubts about the possibility of formulating rounded philosophical systems. We are aware of Frege's statement, namely that in history we have development, in a system we have rigidity. In a way every formulation has as its corollary a rigidity. But the question still remains open to what extent a formulation, though unable to reach finality, encompasses enough to contain a variety of aspects pertaining to philosophical interests. Sometimes the system even contains clashes between interests and their intended direction and resolution, to the point where the clashes themselves serve to overcome the alleged rigidity as well as to open vistas for reformulations of that which has already been formulated. Thus a system has a kind of immanent dynamic and gives momentum to development and history. While being rounded makes the system finished, this quality does not necessarily imply a rigidity in the system.

Let us now say a few words related to the general character of systems, obviously having in mind Spinoza's system, which is the focus and the point of departure of this consideration. A system is certain order or an ordering activity. This feature of it derives from the etymology of the term *systema,* but also from some examples of systems, like, for instance, the organism in the medical sense of the term. A system in the philosophical sense presents an order between different activities of men, like, for instance, knowing and doing, or between different principles, like being and truth or goodness. A system is not a kind of a dictionary of these activities or principles, but presents an interconnection between them as well. In addition, a system is not confined to the presentation of thematic interconnections between partial activities or principles, but raises the question, and *pari passu* attempts to answer it, as to the organizing order which comprises all activities and principles. It does so either by suggesting a meta-principle, for instance the principle of goodness or practical reason, or by presenting a meta-structure, for instance the totality of being in Spinoza's sense. If we take the latter example, we come to the conclusion that the disclosure of the structure of being or reality is essentially also the disclosure of the structure of the human activities, which both emerge from and converge in that structure. When we speak from the point of view of human knowledge, we may reach the position formulated by Kant in his well-known statement that philosophy is a science of all the relations of all knowledge to the essential ends of human reason, and thus philosophy is *teleologia rationis humanae.* A philosopher is not an artificer in the field of reason, but himself the lawgiver of human reason.[1] For Spinoza, even where there is a trace of a teleology of human reason, mainly from the point of view of *amor dei intellectualis,* philosophy cannot be seen in its totality as a teleology

---

[1]   *Kr. d.r. Ver.,* B. 867, Kemp Smith's translation, pp. 657–658.

of that reason, and *a fortiori* the philosopher is not a lawgiver of reason. In a sense the philosopher is neither an artificer nor a lawgiver, but a reader of human reason, and as a reader he sees reason as essentially embedded in the structure of being; thought is one of the attributes of being or God.

Let us make a comment, before going into details related to the papers of our lecturers, on an additional aspect of systems in general, and of Spinoza's system in particular. In the well-known controversy which goes by the name of *"Pantheismusstreit"*, the major contention by Jacobi has been that the only possible system of reason is pantheism, but this would unavoidably lead to fatalism. In our previous juxtaposition of the teleology of human reason as a system, with a system as structure of being and guiding human activities, we have seen that there are more possibilities, typologically speaking, than that which goes by the name of pantheism. But at this juncture we have to observe that fatalism, as assumed in the controversy, is not that unequivocal a feature of the system as is implied in Jacobi's polemic. We refer here to Kant, who also attributes fatality (*Fatalität*) to Spinoza's system as its accredited author, though it is to all appearance much older. Fatalism is related to the necessity of the nature of the being and the world unity flowing from that nature.[2] Again, fatalism is described both as a blind natural necessity in the coherence of nature itself, without a first principle, and as a blind casualty of this principle itself.[3] As the reader of the papers before us can observe, the assumption that Spinoza's system is indeed characterized by the concept of fatality or fatalism is, to say the least, not to be taken for granted.

II

With your permission, I shall now attempt to present a synopsis of some of the major issues raised in the papers before us.

Since our concern is with philosophical systems as an idea, and with their concrete formulation by Spinoza, we begin with a comment against systematization in general, as expressed by Kierkegaard, who said in his Journals: "In relation to their systems most systemizers are like a man who builds an enormous castle and lives in a shack

2   *Kritik der Urteilskraft,* English translation by James Creed Meredith, Oxford Clarendon Press, 1964, Part II, p. 43.
3   *Prolegomena,* Lewis White Beck's translation, Liberal Arts Press, Indianapolis 1950, p. 112.

close by ; they do not live in their own enormous systematic buildings.
But spiritually that is a decisive objection. Spiritually speaking, a
man's thought must be the building in which he lives — otherwise
every thing is topsy-turvy".[4] One cannot be oblivious of the metaphoric,
and excessively so, use of language expressed in that objection. As
to the essence of the argument, it has to be observed that to think
about the structure of being is not to dwell, in the existential or
domestic sense of the term, in that structure ; existence is by its very
nature limited in terms of time, space and actual horizon, while thinking by its very nature goes beyond the limitations of actual existence
or even of experience as encounter. There is no contradiction between
being limited and still transcending that limitation by way of thinking
or knowledge, though we cannot leave aside the question whether the
transcending is asymptotic or reaches its focus. Spinoza did not live
in his enormous systematic building, but the building had an impact
on his life and thinking, as we shall see to be the case in some of the
analyses before us in our *Entretiens*. We may mention an additional
objection by Kierkegaard, where he says, and this is pertinent to our
theme: "God can no more prove his existence in any other sense
than he can swear ; he has nothing higher to swear by".[5] But this is
precisely the point, namely that any proof presented for the existence
of God, whether valid or not, is presented from the perspective of
human thinking and knowledge and not from the perspective of the
divine realm. It is a proof to convince man and is thus involved in
human reasoning and its logic. This emerges from the paper by Mr
Bar-On, who is concerned with the ontological proof, and who shows
Spinoza's version of that proof as expressed in the following syllogism :
if anything exists, then God as an infinite substance exists necessarily. It is absurd to assume that nothing exists, and therefore God
as an infinite substance exists necessarily. The very relationship between the *reductio ad absurdum* argument and the ontological proof
proper as shown by Mr Bar-On is again an indication of the inner
relationship pertaining between human modes of thinking and argumentation and the application of those modes to the issue of the
existence of God and the ontological hard core, namely that essence
involves existence. Again to prove the existence of God is an exercise
within human boundaries, despite the fact that the concern is, the-
matically or noematically speaking, with God as a necessary being.

---

4   *The Journals of Sören Kierkegaard*, A selection edited and translated by
     Alexander Dru, London–New York–Toronto 1938, 583, p. 156.
5   *Ibid.*, 268, p. 72.

Because we start at the human end, and this would be trivial were it not for the criticism of the systematic attempt in general, it is important to see the main theme of the analysis by Mr McKeon in his paper on the background of Spinoza. Spinoza has undertaken to demonstrate by synthesis what Descartes discovered and demonstrated by analysis. The Cartesian distinction between the order and the manner of demonstrating becomes central in this context, even when Spinoza moves to an analytical discovery of God as cause of himself and of all that which follows causally from him. Moreover, while descending from the existence of God to minds and bodies, Spinoza transformed the visible material world of Descartes's principles into the affective, cognitive-emotive world. Thus, if we may so describe it, he brought into the structure different moments of reality and *pari passu* of human behaviour. Here again it has to be observed that, from the point of view of the method, i.e. from the point of view of the human way of knowing the world in all its variety, the first step of the method is to distinguish and to separate the true idea from other perceptions. Along with this will come the restraint of the mind from confusing fictitious, false and doubtful ideas from true ones. It is in this sense that the trend or direction towards improvement as *emendatio* is inherent in the system. Thus the system has an essentially ethical dimension which is elaborated in some of the papers before us. It is only consistent that the emphasis placed on the perfection of the mind raises questions as to the relationship between mind and freedom, or between the state of perfection and the free position of the mind.

The structure of reality as a totality posed the question as to the presence of variety and multiplicity in the total universe. As we know from the correspondence between Spinoza and his peers, this issue loomed large and became central, as is shown in Mr Yovel's paper. If focuses on the transformation of Spinoza's system in the German philosophy of the nineteenth century, and mainly in Hegel. Hegel saw Spinoza's version of philosophizing as a point of departure, but not as a point of culmination for philosophical thinking. Parallely, as it were, he argued that God, rather than being absolute and eternal from the outset, has to be placed as the outcome of the process of self-constitution and self-mediation. Thus the argument presented by Hegel can be understood, following Mr McKeon's distinction, as a new version of the method of synthesis, where the synthesis is not only a method of discovery but at the same time also the mode of self-development of reality. Hegel criticized Spinoza, arguing that the moment of self-consciousness in being is lacking in Spinoza's structure.

We might say that the lack of the historical dimension in Spinoza, as Mr Yovel shows, is an additional expression of the position of substance in Spinoza, as against the position of spirit. We could comment at this juncture that self-consciousness is related to the human mind but not to the attitude of thought as such, and there is no dialectical development from the attribute of thought to self-consciousness. Mr Yovel himself does not project self-consciousness into the structure of being, making the critical comment that coherence is not the ultimate criterion : observing the limits of human rationality is more important than consummating its speculative potential.

At this point we touch on the issue between man and the universe, or the being, as seen through the papers of Mr Kołakowski and Mr Strawson. Mr Kołakowski formulates the inner tension in Spinoza's system as one between the moral affirmation of individuality, on the one hand, and the immersion or development in the direction of the universe, on the other. The tension here pertains between the principle of self-maintenance and the destruction of individuality. In a broader context, and against the basic problem of Neoplatonism, the question of subjectivity is related to that of the ontological status of the finite things in the world. According to Mr Kołakowski there is no way that these two trends can be brought to an internal congruence or harmony within the system. Therefore this tension gave birth to the polemic which in turn was already elicited in Spinoza's lifetime, and eventually to the two main trends related to Spinoza's system : the German Pantheistic trend and the French free-thinking trend. At this point Mr Kołakowski enlarges his analysis by taking Spinoza's system, and we opened with this comment, as a paradigmatic case of a philosophical system *par excellence*. The failure of this system is in turn characteristic of the state of philosophy in general, and is what might be termed 'a fruitful failure'.[6]

Mr Strawson's paper deals more specifically with the aspect of freedom, but it is obvious that this topic is related to the position of individuals as well as to the position of the mind in and vis-à-vis the universe. Let us precede this part of our commentary by referring to the fact that freedom in the philosophical tradition is imbued with several meanings. For instance, it is understood as self-initiation or as absence of impositions — that which is sometimes called 'negative freedom'. It is also understood as positive freedom, as *libertas deter-*

---

6   As to the Neoplatonic background, consult now Gershom Scholem's introduction to Abraham Cohen Herrera, *Das Buch* שער השמים *oder Pforte des Himmels,* Frankfort on Main 1974.

minationis, and Kant's interpretation of freedom as self-initiated under-
taking of obligations is probably one of the most prominent examples
of this particular interpretation of freedom. There are two additional
interpretations of the concept, mainly domination of sensuality and
following one's own essence. When these last two interpretations are
included in the scope of the meaning of freedom we can see that
Spinoza's understanding of the concept can be viewed as following
within the last two connotations. Mr Strawson points out that since
we find in ourselves desires and preferences, our sense of freedom is
related to experiencing ourselves and, in turn, to our attributing the sense
to others. This falls within the realm of phenomenology of the sense
of freedom. The fact that we are faced with a tension between the
reign of causality and the holding of moral attitudes as they are
related to this sense of freedom may force us to conclude that there
is something inherently confusing about moral attitudes. We come
back to the opposition between individuality and immersion in the
universe, which in a way is also present in our awareness of the tension
between the sense of freedom and moral attitudes, on the one hand,
and the principle of causality, on the other. In this regard Spinoza is
taken as representing a paradigmatic system by way of the analysis
of a situation, rather than as representing a solution to the dichotomies
and tensions. To see human behaviour as consisting merely of physical
movement would of itself exclude the status of attitudes and feelings.
But eventually such an exclusion or reduction is impossible, as any
vision of the world is bound to contain a certain broad and sympathetic understanding of human nature. In this sense we see in the
various presentations before us the extent to which the approach of
the being *sub-specie aeternitatis* can be accomplished at all, or, in a
more mitigated form, to what extent human behaviour does or does
not erase the status of the individual or of the mind in its intentionality and freedom.[7]

This issue leads us to the political implications of the concept of
freedom, which Mr Hampshire discusses in his paper. To use his
distinction, we refer here to the relation between the ultimate goal,
which amounts to salvation for the individual, and the political implications related to good government. Emphasis is placed on the
fact that the main justification for advocating freedom of expression,
which is indeed freedom within the social and political context, is
based on the natural desires and needs of individuals. Moreover,

---

[7]   See Martin Heidegger, *Schellings Abhandlung über das Wesen der menschlichen Freiheit* (1806), Tübingen 1971, p. 106.

conatus is interpreted as the striving of living organisms to preserve an individual character; in psychological terms it is related to the individuality of the thinking person. Hence, from the standpoint of the agent, even aggressive and egotistical behaviour has to be seen as grounded in the drive to establish one's own freedom and identity. But precisely at this point an additional aspect of individuality as well as of freedom comes to the forefront, namely the ability to reflect on the causes and objects of one's desires and beliefs. It is this reflection that opens the possibility of changing them. One could say that this is a limited freedom because it is related to the reflection of the limited individual. But, just the same, it is a real freedom which is mainly due to the essence of reflection or to the essence of the ideas of ideas. One of the social manifestations of the presence of reflection is that man, divided by conflicting loyalties, eases that conflict by reflection. This again is the kind of conversion of desires which does not uproot the individual from his belonging to the universe, but mitigates to some extent the natural forces prompting his behaviour. In the long run there can be no peace, nor civilized societies, as long as men are divided by doctrines instead of by interests which they recognize and conceive in common terms. Hence we come back from the position of freedom in general vis-à-vis necessity and freedom within the limits of the socio-political context to a tension between the position of man in his finitude, on the one hand, and in his belonging to the universe at large, on the other. The reality of reflection and freedom have their impact within the limits of finitude and thus in a way create a sphere between drives, which belong to nature, and the totality of substance, which is of course broader than natural drives.

There is an obvious difference between the position of being immersed in nature, the position and attitude of belonging to it, and the awareness of caring for it. Nature is the main theme of Mr Naess's paper, in which he takes Spinoza's view that man belongs to nature as his point of departure for what we today call relevance for the international ecological movement. In this case the tendency is marked by an attempt to interpret the system and at the same time to reconstruct it. The philosophy of Spinoza is now viewed as a vast source of inspiration, however not in the direction of *Gott-trunkener Mensch* as some trends in the nineteenth century had it, but in the direction of investing value and holiness in Nature, though Spinoza would probably take exception to this terminological transplantation. The main principle of Mr Naess's reconstruction of the orientation of the system is rendered in the statement that although humans have the right to self-fulfilment, in the free and rational state they will desire the same for all life forms. In a way we are back at the question of taming desires in and through reflection, though reflection now does not connote only the second order of thinking but also intentionality towards the universal dimension in terms of world loyalty. The structure of all-embracing reality is turned into a principle of human behaviour and a corresponding response to that reality.

III

The diversity of themes in the papers presented and the variety of views expressed should not obscure the basic fact that the question of the structure of the system and *pari passu* the problem of approaching reality in its totality from the human perspective is the *Leitmotiv* of our gathering. The motto *sub specie aeternitatis* cannot obscure the fact that such an exploration is accompanied, if at all, *sub specie homini,* with all the nuances and difficulties which are implied in this mode of thinking. The duality of these two perspectives and their interconnection is the starting point for the exploration to which we devote our *Entretiens.*

An attempt has been made in the present synthesis to outline the variety of aspects inherent in the topic before us, i.e. Spinoza's system, as well as to present some problems connected with the nature of philosophic systems in general, and at the same time to sum up the lectures before us against the systematic background. I hope that no injustice has been done to either frame of reference.

Let us mention again the issue of the nature of the system and the alleged necessity to identify Spinoza's system with fatality or fatalism as Kant put it. It seems to emerge now that Spinoza does not represent a position that can be viewed as leading to the assumption that blind necessity prevails in nature. On the contrary, if there is necessity it is a rational necessity that can be discerned not in terms of the functional relation obtaining between the parts of the universe, but in terms of a structural necessity grounded in the, at least partially, transparent order of the universe. Hence the affirmation of the universe is not an affirmation of incidental factual context, but an affirmation, as Spinoza says, like that which the idea of a triangle must involve, namely that its three interior angles are equal to two right angles. Such an affirmation belongs to the essence of the idea of a triangle. Ultimately, will and understanding are one and the same, and a distinction has to be maintained between desire and will or choice and will. Hence we have to distinguish between rationality as referring to truth and rationality in the domain of usefulness and *pari passu* between will as consent given to the structure and will as desire related to man's natural right to exist and work without injury to himself or others. The problematic character of the system is grounded, among other things, in the structure of components as well as in man's approach to the universe from the point of view of his needs, and of his cognitive affirmation, which becomes more than cognitive in the limited sense of the term. This analysis, which has been elicited by the explorations as presented in the papers of our lecturers, is an attempt to come to grips with the complexity of the system.

Welcoming you once more, I wish to add to the words of greeting a word of invitation following the verse in Psalm CXXII : Ask for the peace of Jerusalem שאלו שלום ירושלים.

RICHARD McKEON

Chicago

The Background of Spinoza

THE 'BACKGROUND' of Spinoza's philosophy may be sought in ante-cedents of doctrines which have been attributed to him or in circumstances of his life which may have influenced what he thought about and how he thought about it. Masterly studies of the *sources* of Spinoza's philosophy, like those of Harry A. Wolfson, have enriched our understanding of Spinoza's philosophy by relating the ideas and terminology he used and the problems and topics he considered to those of ancient Greek and Roman, and mediaeval Hebrew, Arabic and Latin philosophers. To know the sources of a man's philosophy, however, is not to know what he thought to be distinctive in it and in the uses to which he put the conclusions and arguments of other philosophers. I shall examine the background of Spinoza in the *circumstances* which influenced him in the formation of his particular philosophy rather than in the statements which he repeated or echoed in his treatment of old common problems and in his application of new accepted methods. The circumstantial background of Spinoza's philosophy may be reconstructed from (1) social, political and cultural interactions; (2) intellectual synchronisms; (3) scientific and philosophical changes; and (4) matters and means in life and thought: possibilities of freedom and determinations of necessity.

I. SOCIAL, POLITICAL, AND CULTURAL INTERACTIONS

The background of Spinoza was the seventeenth century, which White-head has called the century of genius, and the Golden Age of the Netherlands, from the beginning of the Twelve Years' Truce in 1609 to the Peace of Utrecht in 1713. It was a century in which the Netherlands secured its independence from Spain and became a republic, and in which it fought wars with Spain, France and England, and made alliances with each of them against one or more of the others. The oppositions between the countries were religious and political — between Catholics and Protestants and among sects of Protestants, between advocates of monarchical and of democratic rule and of centralized, federated or democratic forms of government. The same differences divided the southern provinces, which were later to form Belgium, from the northern provinces, from which the modern Netherlands were to develop; in the Netherlands itself republicans opposed the monarchical tendencies of the House of Orange, and statesmen who sought to provide a polity in which Catholicism might co-exist with Protestantism found themselves opposed by statesmen who sought to form a Protestant, or even a Calvinistic state, and who found themselves in turn thwarted by the bitter antagonisms that grew up between two sects of Calvinists, the Arminians and the Gomarists. Yet the United Provinces established their independence and became a republic, built up naval and military power, accumulated commercial and colonial wealth and became an example of freedom and democracy and a centre of tolerance. Jews and Marranos from Spain and Portugal and later from central Europe, Protestants from Antwerp and from other parts of the Spanish Netherlands, and Huguenots from France found refuge there. Spinoza's father and grandfather came to Amsterdam from Spain or Portugal.

The Twelve Years' Truce of 1609 to 1621 was a pause in the Eighty Years' War (1568–1648), during which the Netherlands secured independence and recognition of its independence. William I of Orange, the Silent, had been a moving force in the war of liberation. He had been raised a Catholic in the court of Spain. He was appointed commander of the army in the Netherlands and governor of Holland, Zeeland and Utrecht, and fought in the war against France. In 1563 he petitioned against the persecution of the Protestants. In 1566 he resigned his offices and proclaimed himself a Protestant. The Low Countries combined in the Union of Utrecht in 1579, but the southern provinces were soon reconquered. The seven northern provinces, the United Provinces, declared themselves a republic independent of Spain in 1581. William was made the stadholder of the republic. He sought to rejoin the northern and southern provinces and to establish a regime of tolerance of all religions. He was assassinated in 1584 by a Catholic zealot. In 1585 the provinces of Holland and Zeeland appointed William's son Maurice stadholder. He rebuilt the army and consolidated the northern provinces. France and England made peace with Spain in 1598 and 1604, respectively. After 1588 the existence of the new republic of the United Provinces was gradually recognized. The Netherlands entered into the Twelve Years' Truce in 1609 in part because of internal religious and political strife between Calvinist sects and between Orangist monarchists and republicans. Maurice refused to extend the Truce, and the war was resumed in 1621 and continued to 1648. Maurice died in 1625 and was succeeded by his half-brother, Frederick Henry, as stadholder of five provinces and as captain-general and admiral-general of the union. Frederick Henry was an able general and ruler, and tolerant in religion. The economy flourished, and the court took on royal splendour. In 1641 he married his fourteen-year-old son, who was to become William II, to Mary the daughter of Charles I of England, but the English Civil War (1642–1651) and the Commonwealth turned what might have become an alliance with the royal house of the Stuarts to an opposition against a regicide republic. Frederick Henry died in 1647. He had opposed the peace negotiations which had begun in 1646 and were concluded in 1648 in the Treaty of Münster, in which the Spaniards acknowledged Dutch independence for the first time.

Frederick Henry was succeeded in all his offices by his son William II in 1647. His political and military ambitions, alliance with France against Spain and assistance of the Stuarts against republican England, brought him into conflict with the rulers of Holland, the wealthiest and most powerful of the provinces. He died of smallpox in 1650, and his son, who was to become William III, was born posthumously. The five leading provinces did not appoint a successor to William II, and the 'stadholderless' period extended from 1650 to 1672. Jan de Witt was appointed Pensionary of Dordrecht in 1650 and Grand Pensionary of Holland in 1653. He continued in that post until his death in 1672. He concluded a treaty with Cromwell which ended the Anglo-Dutch war of 1652–1654. After the restoration of Charles II in 1660, commercial rivalry and the royal interest in the house of Orange led to a second war (1665–1667). In 1667 the Dutch fleet sailed up the Thames and the Medway and destroyed the English shipyards and fleet. John Dryden's *Annus Mirabilis*, published in 1667, describes the Dutch War and the London fire of 1666. In 1667 Louis XIV invaded the Spanish Netherlands, and the United Provinces formed the Triple Alliance with England and Sweden against France, but Louis XIV persuaded Charles II to join him in a war against the United Provinces. William III was made commander-in-chief and later stadholder in 1672, and Jan de Witt resigned and was lynched by an Orangist mob. Spinoza had been a friend of de Witt. In 1673 Spinoza twice visited the French army

[26]

in Utrecht and is said to have refused a pension for dedicating a book to Louis XIV. William III of Orange married Mary Stuart, the daughter of the future James II, and in 1688 William and Mary jointly accepted the throne of England.

The years of Spinoza's life, 1632–1677, were a period of political, economic, religious and philosophical change, during which Spinoza moved from city to village to city, discussed philosophy, religion and politics with people of different religious sects and political persuasions, and met and corresponded with statesmen and scientists. Like other Jews, he had freedom of religion, but the Jews of Amsterdam excommunicated him from their synagogue. He had freedom of thought in forming his philosophy, but he was blocked and hindered by restrictions and prohibitions in publishing it. Freedom was a principle and a cause in his philosophy, but experience taught him to distinguish kinds of freedom and conditions essential to their realization and, therefore, to divide philosophy into three sharply distinguished parts determined by those distinctions : ethics, politics and religion.

Spinoza's early education was in the school established by the Jewish community of Amsterdam in 1638. There he laid the foundations of the wide knowledge of the tradition of mediaeval Jewish philosophy shown in the *Ethics* and the *Tractatus Theologico-Politicus*. He studied under Rabbi Saul Morteira, who is said to have marvelled at his acumen at the age of fifteen, and Rabbi Manasseh ben Israel, who, in 1632, published the *Conciliator* in which he sought to reconcile apparent contradictions in Scripture and whose *Hope of Israel,* published in 1650, was dedicated to the wardens of the school. Spinoza's father had been elected warden several times. A copy of the *Hope of Israel* is listed in Spinoza's library. In 1655 Menasseh went to England to address a plea to Oliver Cromwell for the readmission of Jews to England. Morteira presided over the court of rabbis which pronounced a ban of excommunication against Spinoza on 27 July 1656, when Spinoza was twenty-four years old. Thereupon the Dutch authorities banished him from Amsterdam. In 1656 he went to live in Ouwerkerk, a village south of Amsterdam, but he returned shortly to the city.

Spinoza began his secular studies — Latin, mathematics, physics, medicine and the philosophy of Descartes — in Amsterdam. He may have studied Latin first with a German scholar, Jeremiah Felbinger. In 1652 he entered the school of Francis van den Enden, an ex-Jesuit, ex-diplomat and ex-bookseller, who was suspected of atheism. He may have acquired some knowledge of Greek, since a copy of Scapula's *Lexicon* is listed in the catalogue of his library. On his return to Amsterdam Spinoza began his career as a lens grinder and probably became the leader of a small philosophical circle. The *Short Treatise of God, Man, and His Well-Being* resulted from these meetings. The original text of the lessons was in Latin and was translated into Dutch by Jarig Jelles. Two manuscripts of the Dutch translation were found in 1860, and the first edition of the work appeared in 1862.

From 1660 to 1663 Spinoza lived in Rijnsburg, a small village northwest of Leyden. There he expounded Descartes's philosophy to his pupil and pensionary, Casearius. The *Principles of the Philosophy of René Descartes Demonstrated in the Geometrical Manner (More Geometrico Demonstratae)*, with an appendix, *Metaphysical Reflections (Cogitata Metaphysica), in which the more Difficult Questions which turn up in General as well as in Special Metaphysics, are briefly Explained* (i.e. general questions concerning Being and its Affects, and particular questions concerning God, his Attributes and the Human Mind), was published with an introduction by Dr Louis Meyer in 1663. It is the only work published under Spinoza's name in his lifetime.

From 1663 to 1670 Spinoza lived in Voorburg, near The Hague, at the house of a painter named Daniel Tydemann. He continued work on the *Ethics*, which he had probably started in 1661. At Voorburg he met Jan de Witt, who was a mathematician as well as a statesman, and who wrote on probability, jurisprudence and political theory. De Witt became a protector of Spinoza and gave him an annual pension of 200 florins. He is said to have sought Spinoza's advice. Spinoza also met Huygens, Hudde and the group of Dutch mathematicians who wrote the Latin translation of, and commentaries on, Descartes's *La Géométrie*, as well as Vossius, Saint-Evremont and Saint-Glain, who translated the *Tractatus Theologico-Politicus* into French. In 1665 Spinoza interrupted work on the *Ethics* to write a treatise on freedom of thought and expression, possibly at the request of de Witt. At Voorburg he lived in the midst of debates of Calvinists and non-Calvinists, Remonstrant and Counter-Remonstrant Calvinists, and republicans and Orangists. In 1670 he published the *Tractatus Theologico-Politicus*, anonymously and with a false place of publication, Hamburg, instead of Amsterdam, and a false name of publisher. Three other editions appeared with the date 1670, some of which may have been pre-dated because the *Tractatus* was synodically condemned as early as 1671 and banned by the Dutch States-General in 1674, after the death of de Witt. An edition, *'ab authore longe emendatior'*

[28]

was published in 1674 by Dr Louis Meyer, to which he added his own *Philosophy — Interpretor of Sacred Scripture.* The French translation by Saint-Glain appeared in three editions in 1677 and 1678, under three titles: *Clef du Sanctuaire; Reflexions Curieuses d'un Esprit des-Interessé sur les Matières les plus Importantes au Salut, tant Public que Particulier ;* and *Traité des Cérémonies Superstitieuses des Juifs tant Anciennes que Modernes.* An English translation appeared in 1689. Despite the anonymous and clandestine publication, Spinoza was recognized and criticized as the author. Despite the prohibition of its publication, it continued to be published.

Spinoza lived in The Hague from 1670 to 1677, after 1671 in the house of the painter Hendrik van der Spyck. Leibniz has left us an account of his reaction to the assassination of the de Witt brothers in 1672. During his visit with Spinoza in 1676, Spinoza told him that on the day of the murder he felt impelled to go out in the evening and exhibit in the neighbourhood of the crime a poster with the words "Lowest Barbarians !", but that his landlord had locked the door to prevent his intervening and incurring the risk of being torn to pieces. During the invasion of Holland by Louis XIV, Spinoza was invited, in May 1673, to visit the camp of the Prince de Condé in Utrecht. He returned a second time in July, when he met the Marshall of Luxembourg. In 1673 he was offered the Professorship of Philosophy of the University of Heidelberg by the Elector Palatine, with the assurance that he would have "the utmost freedom of philosophizing", which the Prince was convinced he would not misuse to disturb the publicly established Religion (Letter XLVII). Spinoza declined the invitation because teaching would interfere with the developing of his philosophy and because he did not know within what limits freedom of philosophizing ought to be confined to avoid the appearance of wishing to disturb the publicly established religion, for schisms arise not so much from love of religion as from men's various dispositions or the love of contradiction, which Spinoza writes he had already experienced while leading a private and solitary life (Letter XLVIII). The French seized Heidelberg in 1674 and closed the University. In 1675 Spinoza went to Amsterdam to arrange for the publication of his *Ethics,* but he decided to postpone publication, he writes to Oldenburg (Letter LXVIII), because a rumour was spread that a book of his about God was in press, in which he tried to show that there is no God. Certain theologians, who may have started the rumour, brought complaints against him before the Prince and the magistrates, and the stupid Cartesians, to dissociate themselves from him, denounced his opinions and writings everywhere.

On Sunday, 21 February 1677, he died with his friend and physician Dr G. H. Schuller in attendance. In November of the year of his death his unpublished works were published under the title *B. de S. Opera Posthuma*, edited by his friends Jelles, Meyer and Schuller. This work contained the *Ethics,* the *Political Treatise,* the *Treatise on the Improvement of the Understanding,* the *Letters* and the *Hebrew Grammar.* All names and identifying marks were removed from the correspondence. The editors' names, the name of the publisher and the place of publication were not given. A Dutch translation by Jan Hendriksz Glazenmaker, *De Nagelate Schriften van B. D. S.,* appeared in the same year.

II. INTELLECTUAL SYNCHRONISMS

The occasional circumstances are coloured by atmospheric circumstances which were marked off by synchronisms of changes in science and philosophy and which determined stages in Spinoza's life. Spinoza, Locke, Pufendorf and Thomas Stanley, who pioneered in the history of Philosophy, were born in 1632. Descartes published his *Discourse on Method* in 1637, substituting it for the publication of his *De Homine,* after the condemnation of Galileo, preferring to present a method by which any one could make like discoveries, rather than conclusions which might be condemned, and with three appended essays to illustrate the method: the *Dioptrics,* the *Meteors* and the *Geometry.* The teaching of Cartesian philosophy was prohibited in Jesuit colleges in 1640. Jansen published his *Augustinus, seu Doctrina St. Augustini de Humanae Naturae Sanitate, Aegritudine, Medicina,* in the same year. Descartes's *Meditations on First Philosophy* was published in Paris in 1641. In 1642 Galileo died; Hobbes published the *De Cive;* and the teaching of Cartesianism was prohibited at Utrecht. In 1643 A. Heereboord's *Parallelism of the Aristotelian and Cartesian Natural Philosophy* appeared. Spinoza was doubtless acquainted with late Scholastic philosophy from the works of Burgersdijck, Professor of Philosophy in Leyden (died 1632), and his successor Heereboord (died 1659). In 1643 Jansen's *Augustinus* was condemned by the Pope. In 1645 the Royal Society was founded in London. In 1647 the philosophy of Descartes was attacked at the University of Leyden. In the same year the *De Imperio Summarum Potestatum circa Sacra* of Grotius was published; Grotius had been arrested by Maurice of Orange in his struggle with Holland and the Counter-Remonstrants in 1618, had been sentenced to life imprisonment in 1619, but had escaped a few years later; he died in 1645. Descartes published his *Principles of Philosophy* in Amsterdam in 1644; the French translation by Picot appeared in Paris in 1647. In 1649 Descartes published his *Treatise on the Passions*. He left his refuge in Holland for Stockholm in September 1649 and died in 1650, the year in which Hobbes published his *Leviathan*. A great many Dutch works of Cartesian philosophy were published in the decade after his death.

The French original of Descartes's *Geometry* appeared as an appendix to the *Discourse on Method* in 1637 when Spinoza was five years old. The Latin translation of Frans van Schooten was published in 1649 when he was seventeen. In 1659, when he was twenty-seven, an enlarged second edition appeared in two volumes, which contained, among other essays, two letters of John Hudde, one on the reduction of equations and the other on *maxima* and *minima*; an essay by Jan de Witt on the elements of curved lines; and three pieces by van Schooten: a commentary on Descartes's *Geometry*, a redaction of his own lectures, 'Principles of Universal Mathematics or Introduction to the Method of Cartesian Geometry' by his pupil Erasmius Bartholinus, and his *Tractatus de Concinnandis Demonstrationibus Geometricis ex Calculo Algebraico*.

In 1655 Gassendi died, and Hobbes published the *De Corpore*. In 1656 the first works of Christian Huygens were published. Heereboord's *Meletemata* was published in 1654, and his *Rational, Moral, and Natural Philosophy* in the same year. Spinoza criticized Heereboord in the *Cogitata Metaphysica* published in 1663. In 1661 Spinoza began a long correspondence with Henry Oldenburg, Secretary of the Royal Society, in part of which Oldenburg served as intermediary for Robert Boyle. In 1662 Pascal died. The *Political Balance* (*Polityke Weegschall*) of Pieter de la Court (P. van Hove), published in 1662, contains two chapters by Jan de Witt. Spinoza cites "that highly prudent Dutchman V. H., *prudentissimus Belga V. H.*" in the *Tractatus Politicus*. In 1663 Spinoza published the *Principles of Descartes's Philosophy* and the *Metaphysical Reflections*. At that time Geulincx, a Cartesian from Louvain, was a refugee in Leyden. In 1666 Louis de la Forge published the *Traité de l'Esprit de l'Homme*; Cordemoy, the *Discours sur la Distinction de l'Ame et du Corps*; Leibniz the *De Arte Combinatoria*; Locke the *Essay on Toleration*, and Newton performed experiments on the decomposition of light. In 1669 Huygens published the *De Motu et Vi Centrifuga*. The *Pensées* of Pascal and Spinoza's *Tractatus Theologico-Politicus* were published in 1670. In 1671 Leibniz published the *Hypothesis Physica Nova*; in 1672 Pufendorf the *De Jure Naturae et Gentium*. Malebranche's *Recherche de la Verité* was published in 1674. Leibniz probably invented the calculus in 1676, the year in which he first visited Spinoza, four months before Spinoza's death, and asked questions about lenses and the *Ethics.* Later in Paris he asked Tschirnhaus to write to Dr Schuller for Spinoza's permission to show him a copy of the *Ethics* (Letter LXX). Spinoza refused (Letter LXXII), saying that he thought he knew the Leibniz of whom Tschirnhaus wrote, but was suspicious of a visit Leibniz had made to Paris when he was Councillor of Frankfort, and he therefore considered it imprudent to entrust his writings to him so soon. In 1677 Spinoza died and the *Opera Posthuma* was published. Schuller had considered selling the manuscript of the *Ethics* to Leibniz to defray the expenses of publishing these *Posthumous Works,* but another anonymous source of funds was found.

III. SCIENTIFIC AND PHILOSOPHICAL CHANGES

The changing background of Spinoza's life influenced his choice of both subject matter and method in his philosophy. The changes are marked clearly by a series of pairs of terms which have long been commonplaces in philosophical discussion — analytic–synthetic, objective–subjective, true–adequate, *a priori–a posteriori* — which have altered and sometimes reversed their meanings and applications since the seventeenth century. For Spinoza and his contemporaries analysis was the passage in inference from particulars to principles, and synthesis the passage from principles to consequences. After Kant's Copernican turn, analysis became the decomposition of wholes into parts, and synthesis the composition of parts into wholes, and the elemental parts of analytic and synthetic processes of thought became judgements or propositions whose truth is self-evident, and synthetic judgements or propositions whose truth depends on evidence. In the seventeenth century, and for Spinoza, the *objective* status of things was found in minds *lying opposite* to the *subjective* things *underlying* thoughts. After the Critical Philosophy based on the forms of judgement or of thought, the subjective ideas of the mind became the beginning point for the search for objective realities opposite them in the phenomenal or the noumenal world. For Spinoza there was no difference between a true and an adequate idea, except that 'true' refers to the agreement of an idea with its ideatum, and 'adequate' refers to the nature of the idea itself. For idealists and realists alike, since the end of the eighteenth century, adequacy and truth are properties of propositions rather than ideas, and adequacy is sought in references while truth is established by proof. In the seventeenth century *a priori* was demonstration of effects from causes, and *a posteriori* was examination of causes in possible effects. More recently *a priori* has come to mean reasoning from an abstract formula to a concrete instance, and *a posteriori* generalization from concrete experiences to precepts or laws. The stages of the development of Spinoza's conception of the geometrical method may be traced through four conceptions of geometry and mechanics in which these commonplaces operate in the formulation of mathematical and mechanical methods of discovery and proof as applied to philosophical matters: (a) his adaptation of Descartes's geometry; (b) his conversion to the method of van Schooten, Huygens and the Dutch mathematicians; (c) his own use of geometry in ethics, politics and religion; and (d his opposition of universal mathematics *v.* universal mechanics.

a. *Descartes's Geometry : Methodical Discovery and the Geometric Method of Proof*

Spinoza's first encounter with the mathematical method was in the study of Descartes's use of the geometric method in philosophy. Dr Louis Meyer explains what Spinoza tried to do in his *Principles of Descartes' Philosophy,* in terms of analysis and synthesis. Meyer was convinced, he says in his Preface, that philosophy would achieve certainty only by use of the mathematical method. Descartes's philosophical writings contain a mathematical technique and order of demonstrating (*mathematicam demonstrandi* ratio *ac* ordo). It was not the method found in Euclid's *Elements,* however, in which propositions and their demonstrations are subjoined to premises, definitions, postulates and axioms, but another which Descartes called 'analytic' and characterized as the best way of teaching (*ad docendum* via). For he recognizes two techniques or ways of reasoning in demonstrating apodeictically (*duplex . . . apodicticè demonstrandi* ratio), one by analysis which shows the true way (*via*) by which a thing is methodically and as it were *a priori* discovered, and the other by synthesis which uses a long series of definitions, premises, theorems and problems, so that if anything is denied in the consequences, it is immediately shown to have been contained in the antecedents. According to Meyer, Spinoza's *Principles of Descartes' Philosophy* is a synthetic demonstration of what Descartes discovered analytically.

Descartes makes the distinction between analysis and synthesis in his Responses to the Second Objections in the *Meditations,* which Mersenne had collected from a number of theologians and philosophers. Descartes replies to their advice that he set forth his arguments in the geometrical manner or according to the method of geometers (more *geometrico,* or in the French version, *selon la* méthode *des Géomètres*) in order that they might be perceived by the reader in a single apprehension (*unico velut intuito*); that he distinguishes two things in the writings of geometers, the order (*ordo*) and the technique or reasoning (*ratio*) of demonstrating. There are two ways of reasoning in demonstrating: by analysis or resolution, and by synthesis or composition. "Analysis shows the true way by which a thing is discovered (*inventa*) methodically and as it were *a priori*" (the French version translates *"a priori"* by "shows how effects depend on their causes"), so that "if the reader wishes to follow it and pay attention to all that it contains, he will understand the thing demonstrated no less perfectly and will make it no less his own than if he had discovered it himself". Synthesis proceeds by the opposite way or *a posteriori,* that is, by examining causes by their effects (although proof in synthesis is often more *a priori* than proof in analysis), and it demonstrates clearly what is concluded, using definitions, postulates, axioms, theorems and problems, so that if the reader denies any consequence he can be shown that it is in the antecedents. The most obstinate and opinionated reader can thus be convinced; but synthesis is not as satisfactory as analysis to those who wish to learn, because it does not teach the method by which the thing is discovered.

Descartes was convinced that ancient geometers were not ignorant of analysis, although they used only synthesis in their writings, and that they reserved it for themselves as an important secret. He says that he followed only analysis in his *Meditations* because it is the true and best method of teaching, whereas synthesis, which his critics seem to recommend and which is properly placed after analysis in the treatment of geometrical things, cannot be so readily employed in these metaphysical questions, for the *first notions* which are presupposed in demonstrating geometrical things are readily admitted by any one, because they are in agreement with what is perceived by the senses, but it is difficult to perceive *first notions* in metaphysical questions because they seem to be in disaccord with many prejudices based on the senses to which we have been accustomed since infancy. Descartes doubtless derived this conception of analysis and synthesis from Pappus of Alexandria, who described analysis as the way to what must be assumed if what is sought is posited, and synthesis as inference from what is assumed to what is sought. Pappus attributed the distinction to Euclid, Apollonius of Perga and Aristaeus the Elder. Spinoza's library did not contain a copy of the *Collection* of Pappus, but it did contain a copy of six of the thirteen books that have survived of the *Arithmetica* of Diophantus of Alexandria, and Spinoza was doubtless acquainted with Diophantine analysis by which equations are resolved in integers.

Dr Meyer's distinction between analysis and synthesis repeats the words used by Descartes, but the demonstration *more geometrico* of Descartes's *Principles of Philosophy* differed radically from Descartes's application of the distinction. Descartes argued that the synthetic method was well adapted, after principles had been established by the analytic method, to geometry, but not to metaphysics. Meyer and Spinoza, on the contrary, were convinced that synthetic demonstration or demonstration *more geometrico* not only could be used in metaphysics but would remove the difficulties which readers experienced in understanding Descartes's analytic demonstrations. Meyer reports in the Preface that Spinoza had already written the entire second book and part of the third of the *Principles*, "demonstrated in the geometric manner" (*more illo geometrico demonstratas*), and was willing to accede to the request that he redact the first part in the same order (*ordo*). Meyer is careful to point out that the first part prepared by Spinoza does not correspond to the first part of Descartes's *Principles*, but that much of it is derived from the *Meditations*. The change is an indication of a change in conception of method and subject matter. As Descartes used the terms, he used synthetic demonstrations in the *Principles* and analytic demonstrations in the *Meditations*. Descartes states the principles of human knowledge in Part I of the *Principles* and then derives the consequences of those principles in the physical world; Part II is on the principles of material things and treats the laws of motion; Part III is on the visible world and treats cosmology, using a hypothesis based on experience and not reason (iii. 46); and Part IV is on the Earth and treats problems of physics like gravity and light. The *Meditations on First Philosophy* uses analysis to discover the principles of all knowledge and of all things in six meditations: (1) on universal doubt, (2) on the nature of the human mind and that it is better known than the body, (3) on God and proof of his existence, (4) on the true and the false, (5) on the essence of material things and further proof of the existence of God, (6) on the existence of material things and on the real distinction of the mind from the body.

At the end of the Second Responses Descartes sets forth reasons (*rationes*) proving the existence of God and the distinction of the soul from the body disposed in geometric manner (*more geometrico dispositae*), that is, synthetic demonstrations. The first three propositions are proofs of the existence of God. The first is an *a priori* proof

[35]

that "the existence of God is known from the simple consideration of his nature". The second is an *a posteriori* proof from our idea of God: "The existence of God is demonstrated *a posteriori* from this alone, that there is in us an idea of him". The third is *a posteriori* from our existence: "The existence of God is demonstrated also by the fact that we who have an idea of him exist". Spinoza's demonstration *more geometrico* of Descartes's *Principles* begins with an exposition of the universal doubt, which Spinoza does not put in the geometrical order (*ordo*) to avoid the prolixity of such a statement, then proceeds to definitions and axioms which serve as foundations for four self-evident propositions establishing that *ego sum* (which Spinoza has argued is the significance of *cogito ergo sum*) is known first and *per se,* not in so far as we are corporeal things but in so far as we think. Then follow eight axioms which Spinoza has reformulated from Descartes and Descartes's four propositions, three proving God's existence and one proving that mind and body are really distinct. The remainder of Part I is devoted to propositions about the nature of God and two final propositions on God's pre-ordination of all things from eternity and on extended substance.

The geometrical *manner* is clearly the Euclidean mode of deriving propositions from a set of definitions and axioms. For Descartes it is not the same as either analysis or synthesis, for his *Geometry,* in which the analytic method is used, is not expounded in the geometrical *manner,* nor is his *Principles of Philosophy,* in which the synthetic method is used. Spinoza also identified the geometric *manner* with the Euclidean manner of proof, but he differed from Descartes in thinking it suitable to metaphysics as well as to mathematics and physics and to the restatement of analytic as well as synthetic demonstrations, and he therefore joined the reformulation of the second and third parts of the *Principles* with the statement of the metaphysics of the *Meditations* in the geometrical manner. Meyer explains how Spinoza made the changes from the analytic statements of Descartes to the geometric manner simply by putting Descartes's definitions first and inserting propositions of his own and by making like omissions and changes in order.

Spinoza also requested Meyer to explain that he was merely expressing the opinions of Descartes, not his own opinions or opinions with which he agreed. He makes a like statement to Oldenburg in Letter XIII, in which he explains why he allowed the publication of the treatise. His reasons throw light on the constraints under which he wrote and on the distinctions he made between moral and political freedom. He published the work in the hope that people might

[36]

want to see other things he had written which he acknowledged as his own, and that they might make it their business to see that he would be able to publish them without the risk of trouble. If that does not happen, he continues, "I shall be silent rather than obtrude my opinions on men against the wishes of my country, and make them my enemies".

b. *The Dutch Cartesian Geometry : The Universal Mathesis*

Spinoza's second encounter with the mathematical method was with the Dutch mathematicians who translated Descartes's *La Géométrie* into Latin and developed the Cartesian *mathesis universalis,* and with Huygens who used Euclid's *Elements* as means of discovery concerning the nature of light and the rainbow. None of these works constructs demonstrations *in more geometrico* deriving consequences from postulate sets, and they combine analytic with synthetic, *a priori* with *a posteriori* demonstrations, in discovery and proof.

Frans van Schooten's *Treatise on the Production of Geometric Demonstrations from Algebraic Calculations* is in two parts, the first on Analysis or Resolution into a principle, the second on Synthesis or Composition from a principle established by resolution. The use of 'resolution' as a synonym of 'analysis' would carry an echo for a seventeenth-century reader of another tradition, in which analysis was not set in opposition to synthesis, but was distinguished into two kinds of analysis. Aristotle's *Prior* and *Posterior Analytics* were known in the Middle Ages as the *First* and the *Second Resolutoria,* the first being the analysis of the syllogism into valid modes, the second the analysis of the apodeictic syllogism which yields true and necessary conclusions. For van Schooten algebraic calculations are syntheses from which one may discover principles or derive consequences from established principles. In his Preface to the treatise, van Schooten's brother reiterates Descartes's conviction that the ancients used the analytic method but concealed it by using the synthetic method in their writings, whereas van Schooten tried to show that the analytic method is the most certain art of discovery and that the synthetic mode of demonstrating is contained in it. In his lectures on the 'Principles of Universal Mathesis or Introduction to the Method of Cartesian Geometry' van Schooten says that the only method of discovery is by composition and resolution, which recent mathematicians have reduced to certain laws of the 'Analytic Art'. Spinoza's library contained copies of van Schooten's translation of Descartes's *De Geometria,* of his *Principia Matheseos Universalia,* and of his *Exercitationes Mathematicae.*

Analysis and synthesis are different methods used on different subject matters in Descartes's *Meditations* and *Principles*. In his *Principles of Descartes's Philosophy*, Spinoza merged them in the geometric manner of deriving conclusions from principles. He merges analysis and synthesis without recourse to the geometric *manner*, but by recourse to the universal mathesis, in his *Treatise on the Rainbow* and his *Calculation of Chances*, both based on the work of Huygens. Huygens had transformed Descartes's theory of the rainbow by abandoning the apparently empirical tables of reflection and refraction of light passing through globes filled with liquids of different densities, and made new discoveries based only on the use of propositions from the first six books of Euclid's *Elements*. In like fashion, Huygens departed, in his treatise *De Ratiociniis in Aleae Ludo*, from the earlier tradition of works on probability in which mathematicians proposed problems and worked out solutions but did not examine or reveal their methods. Huygens stated the elements and explained the method he used in calculating probabilities. His treatise ends with five problems, without indication of the methods by which they might be solved. Spinoza's treatise is devoted to discovering and proving solutions for those problems. Many other mathematicians contributed to the early development of probability theory on the basis of solutions they devised to the same problems. I have discussed the background and methods of these two works of Spinoza in 'Spinoza on the Rainbow and on Probability'.[1]

c. *Spinoza's Use of the Geometric Method in Ethics, Politics and Religion*

Conclusions demonstrated in the geometric *manner*, in a work like the *Principles of Descartes's Philosophy*, may be true, false or dubious depending on the principles from which they are derived. Conclusions demonstrated in the geometric *order*, in a work like the *Ethics*, must be certain, necessary and true, for the geometric order combines analysis with synthesis to discover true principles and to derive true conclusions which follow necessarily from them; and it combines *a priori* with *a posteriori* proofs to relate rational principles with empirical data and affective desiderata; it combines subjective with objective principles to relate what is thought to what is thought about. The full title of the *Ethics* is a succinct sketch of the geometric order: *Ethics, Demonstrated in the Geometric Order and Distinguished into*

---

1   *Jubilee Volume for Harry Wolfson*, II, American Academy for Jewish Studies, Jerusalem 1965, pp. 533–559.

Five Parts in which the Treatment is I. Concerning God, II. Concerning the Nature and Origin of the Human Mind, III. Concerning the Origin and Nature of the Affects, IV. Concerning Human Bondage, or Concerning the Strengths of the Affects, V. Concerning the Power of the Intellect, or Concerning Human Freedom. The First Part presents the analytic discovery of the principle of all things in the demonstration of the existence of God as cause of himself and the synthetic derivation of infinite things, in infinite modes, and of the intellect and will, finite and infinite, from the necessity of God's nature. The inversions in the titles of the second and third and of the fourth and fifth books are indications of the turns of the geometric order. The nature of the mind must be understood in Part II before examining how it came to be, and the motions of things are treated in lemmas to propositions about the thinking of minds, for the mind is an idea of a body, and ideas which are true relative to things are shown to be adequate relative to ideas. In nature, mind is a mode of an attribute of God; it comes to be and its origin is intelligible because the order and connection of ideas is the same as the order and connection of things. On the other hand, the origin of the affects, of passions and actions, in the interactions of things, must be examined in Part III before the nature of the effects of such interactions in minds and bodies can be discovered. In Part IV the enslavement of man, his submission to alien forces, is traced and rendered intelligible by determining the relative strengths of affects in action and resistance, while Part V turns from schemata of interacting emotions to self-perfection in the single development of the power of the intellect which constitutes human freedom.

The geometric order of the *Ethics* is a method of discovery and of proof, of demonstration and of causation, and of subjective adequacy and certainty and of objective truth and conclusiveness. Tschirnhaus asks Spinoza in Letter LIX, "When are we to have your Method of rightly controlling the Reason in acquiring knowledge of unknown truths, as also your General Physics?" He says that he knows about the physics from the lemmas in Part II of the *Ethics* and about the method from conversations with Spinoza, and he testifies that he has made advances in mathematics by use of the method, which consists in seeking in the investigation of a thing or a concept or idea the cause of the idea and the cause of the cause until he reaches a cause for which he finds no other causes. He also asks Spinoza to communicate to him the true definition of an adequate, a true, a false, a fictitious and a doubtful idea. Spinoza begins his reply in Letter LX by saying that he recognizes no difference between a true and an adequate idea except that 'true' refers to the agreement of the idea with its ideatum, and 'adequate' refers to the nature of the idea itself. In order to know from which idea, out of many, all properties of an object may be deduced, all that is required is that the definition of the thing express its efficient cause. Thus, the properties of a circle cannot be deduced from the definition of a circle as composed of innumerable right angles, but they can be deduced from a definition expressing its efficient cause, i.e. that it is the space described by a line of which one point is fixed and the other movable. Similarly the properties of God cannot be deduced from the definition of God as "the supremely perfect Being", but they can from the definition of God as cause of himself. The relations between the sequence of causation and the sequence of proof is examined in detail in my essay, "Causation and the Geometric Method in the Philosophy of Spinoza".[2] Since truth depends on the correspondence of knowledge to things known and adequacy depends on the nature of the knower, the development of science and knowledge depends on what we are, that is, on adequate ideas, and not on what happens to us, that is, on experiences and inadequate ideas. The art required for the establishment and increase of knowledge, therefore, is not an analytic inductive or a synthetic deductive logic of propositions or judgements, but, as the subtitle of the *De Emendatione Intellectus* specifies, "a way (*via*) in which the understanding may be directed towards a true knowledge of things", that is, a way in which true ideas may be discovered by separating adequate from inadequate ideas and by purging the mind of inadequate ideas. The *De Emendatione Intellectus* provides the definitions of adequate, true, fictitious and false ideas which Tschirnhaus requested. Spinoza differentiated four modes of perception: by hearsay, from vague perception, by inference in which the essence of one thing is concluded from the essence of another and by perception of a thing through its essence alone or through its proximate cause. Of these the fourth mode alone comprehends the adequate essence of things without danger of error. The true method is not reasoning for the purpose of understanding the causes of things; "it is to understand what is a true idea by distinguishing it from other perceptions and investigating its nature, in order that we may thence have knowledge of our power, and so accustom our mind that it may understand by that one standard all things that are to be understood, setting out for ourselves as aids certain rules, and taking care that

---

[2]   *The Philosophical Review*, XXXIX, No. 2 (March 1930), pp. 178–179, and No. 3 (May 1930), pp. 275–296.

the mind is not overburdened by useless facts".[3] The first part of the method of directing the mind according to the standard of a given true idea is to distinguish and separate true ideas from other perceptions and to restrain the mind from confusing fictitious, false, and doubtful ideas with true ideas.[4] The heart of the second part of the method, designed to acquire clear and distinct ideas, that is, such as arise from the mind alone and not from fortuitous movements of the body, turns wholly on knowing the conditions of good definition and on the manner of discovering these definitions.

Tschirnhaus adopted and elaborated on this therapeutic method of discovering scientific truths. After Spinoza's death he published, anonymously in 1687, and under his own name in 1695, *Medicina Mentis sive Tentamen Genuinae Logicae in qua Disseritur de Methodo Detegendi Incognitas Veritates.* In it he reviews the arts of discovery proposed by philosophers, before presenting the analytic method of the mathematicians as the art of discovery. Tschirnhaus throws light on the nature of the principles Spinoza sought, as well as on his method of discovering them. Spinoza had remarked to him that most philosophers begin with creatures, that Descartes begins with the mind, and that he, Spinoza, begins with God.

The geometric method may produce scientific knowledge of good and evil in the *Ethics,* but human action and human freedom require other guides than reason alone. In the Appendix to Part I of the *Ethics* Spinoza applies the method of emending the understanding to remove misconceptions which might impede understanding of his propositions about God and the universe: misconceptions concerning good and evil, virtue and sin, praise and blame, order and confusion, beauty and ugliness, and other things of this kind. In the second scholium of Prop. XXXVII of Part IV he recalls that he had promised to explain praise and blame, merit and sin, and just and unjust. Praise and blame are opinions, rather than knowledge, of good and evil, and merit and sin are measures by which action may be guided by imagination and power in religion and society. Similarly, at the beginning of the *De Emendatione Intellectus* Spinoza remarks that three things are usually sought in place of the good : wealth, honour and pleasure ; and he adds that in addition to devising a way of curing and purging the understanding to enable it to understand things correctly, one needs to take into account the formation

[3] *De Emendatione Intellectus, Spinoza Opera,* ed. C. Gebhardt, II, Heidelberg 1925, p. 15.
[4] *Ibid.,* p. 19.

of a society, moral philosophy, the theory of educating children, medicine and mechanics.

Spinoza made a sharp separation of the problems and principles of ethics, religion and politics. The end of ethics is freedom, achieved by the control of the passions by the understanding; but not all men are capable of the freedom achieved by the intellectual love of God. Religion influences action by imagination, not by reason. The Bible leaves reason absolutely free. It does not teach philosophy, and all that it contains is adapted to the understanding and the established opinions of the multitude. Spinoza argues, against Maimonides, that theology is not bound to serve reason, nor reason theology, but each has its own domain. "The domain [*regnum*] of reason is, as we have said, truth and wisdom; the domain of theology is piety and obedience, for the power of reason does not extend so far as to determine that men may be blessed or happy through simple obedience without understanding of things" (*Tractatus Theologico-Politicus,* Chap. 15). The morality based on theology and Scripture does not admit of mathematical proof, yet "the method [*methodus*] of interpreting Scripture does not differ much from the method of interpreting nature, but rather agrees with it in detail. For the interpretation of nature consists primarily in putting together a history of nature, from which we conclude as from surely established data [*ex certis datis*] definitions of natural things. So also in interpreting Scripture it is necessary to get ready a sound history of it, and from the history as from surely established data and principles [*ex certis datis et principiis*] conclude the mind of the authors of Scripture as legitimate consequences" (*ibid.,* Chap. 7).

The foundation of society, on the other hand, is found not in the imagination and love, but in nature and the passions. Nature has a sovereign right to do anything she can. It is the sovereign right of every individual being or person to act according to its natural condition. The natural right of the individual man is therefore not determined by sound reason but by desire and power. These rights and powers are ceded in the compact by which society is formed. It is a law of human nature that no one ever neglects anything he judges to be good except with the hope of securing a greater good. The compact is made valid by its utility, for it is a means for living a secure and tranquil life. Spinoza argues in Chapter 16 of *Tractatus Theologico-Politicus* that democracy is the constitution which is at once most simple, most natural and best founded on reason. It is also the one that is most conducive to peace and freedom. Reason has its uses, not in determining political action, but in formulating a science of politics. In the first chapter of the *Tractatus Politicus* Spinoza states his intention to use reason in examining the natural bases of human associations in the passions:

> Therefore when I applied my mind to politics, my intention was to demonstrate by certain and undoubted reason [*certa et indubitata ratione*] or to deduce from the very condition of human nature, not something new and unheard of, but only such things as agree best with practice. And in order to investigate the things which concern this science with the same freedom of the mind as we are used to in mathematics, I have taken care sedulously not to mock, lament, or execrate, but to understand human actions; and to do this I have considered the human affects, such as love, hatred, anger, envy, ambition, pity and the other perturbations of the mind, not as vices, but as properties, of human nature, which pertain to it as heat, cold, storm, thunder, and the like pertain to the nature of the atmosphere, which, though inconvenient, are nonetheless necessary and have certain causes [*certas causas*] by means of which we endeavour to understand their nature, and the mind has just as much pleasure in their contemplation as in cognition of those things which please the senses (*Tractatus Politicus*, Chap. 1, 4).

"Men are necessarily liable to the passions... Religion... teaches every man to love his neighbour as himself, that is, to defend another's right just as much as his own," but "this persuasion has too little power over the passions.... Reason can indeed do much to restrain and moderate the passions," but "... the road of reason... is very steep," and "the multitude, or men distracted by politics" can never "be induced to live according to the bare dictate of reason" (*Tractatus Politicus*, Chap. 1, 5).

d. *Universal Mathematics Versus Universal Mechanics*

Spinoza's background brought him into contact with the universal mathematics of the Dutch Cartesians. In his long correspondence with Henry Oldenburg, Secretary of the Royal Society, he was brought into contact with the universal mechanics of Robert Boyle. In the universal mathematics the only method of discovery is by composition and resolution, which are combined in the laws of the Analytic Art. Mechanics is a part of mathematics. In the universal mechanics of Boyle and later of Newton principles are discovered by observation and experimentation, and mathematics is a part of mechanics. In Letter I, dated August 1661, when Spinoza was twenty-nine years

[43]

old and Oldenburg forty-six, Oldenburg recalls their conversations in Rhynsburg "about God, infinite Extension and Thought, about the difference and agreement of those attributes, about the nature of the union of the human soul with the body, also about the Principles of the Cartesian and Baconian Philosophy". He asks Spinoza two questions: what is the true distinction between Extension and Thought, and what are the defects of the philosophy of Descartes and of Bacon. He also announces that Boyle's *Certain Physiological Essays* are in press and undertakes to send Spinoza a copy. Spinoza replies in Letter II that it is not his custom to expose the errors of others, but to gratify Oldenburg he is willing to answer his question. "The first, then, and greatest error, is that they have strayed from the knowledge of the First Cause and of the origin of all things. The second is that they did not know the true nature of the human Mind. The third is that they never arrived at the true cause of Error".

In Letter VI Spinoza sets down detailed criticisms of Boyle's book *On Nitre, Fluidity and Firmness,* based on his conviction that —

> notions which are derived from popular usage, or which explain Nature not as it is in itself but as it appears to human sense, should by no means be numbered among the highest generic terms, nor should they be mixed up (not to say confounded) with notions which are pure and which explain Nature as it is in itself. Of this kind are motion, rest, and their laws; of the former kind are the terms visible and invisible, hot and cold and, to say it at once, fluid and firm, etc.

When Boyle sought confirmation by chemical experimentation, Spinoza comments: "One will never be able to prove this by chemical or other experiments, but only by reason and calculation." When Boyle undertakes to show that all tactile qualities depend only on motion, figure and other mechanical affections, Spinoza objects that "since they [the reasons] are not advanced by the Honorable Gentleman as mathematical, there is no need to examine whether they are directly conclusive. But meanwhile I do not understand why the Honorable Gentleman should try to collect this from his experiment, since it was demonstrated sufficiently and more than sufficiently first by Bacon and then by Descartes". In the same letter, in answer to Oldenburg's "new question, namely, how things began to be and by what cause they are bound to the first cause", Spinoza refers him to the *Short Treatise* and also the *De Emendatione Intellectus,* in which that question is treated. When the correspondence was resumed in 1675, after a long interruption, Spinoza devoted great effort to removing Oldenburg's misconceptions of the *Tractatus Theologico-Politicus,* which Oldenburg had at first thought was intended to harm true religion and sound philosophy (Letter LXI).

IV. MATTERS AND MEANS IN LIFE AND THOUGHT: POSSIBILITIES OF FREEDOM AND DETERMINATIONS OF NECESSITY

Freedom is a central concept in ethics, politics and religion. Part V of the *Ethics* is about the power of the intellect or human freedom, or the manner (*modus*) or way (*via*) which leads to freedom. Freedom of the mind is the synonym of happiness or blessedness (*beatitudo*). The manner and means by which the intellect must be perfected, and the art by which the body must be cured, however, are not functions of ethics but of logic and medicine. Freedom depends on the power of mind or reason, and in particular on the power of reason to moderate and control the emotions. The last proposition of the *Ethics* proves that happiness or blessedness is not the reward of virtue but virtue itself. The full title of the *Tractatus Theologico-Politicus* specifies that it is concerned with freedom of philosophizing — "containing some dissertations in which it is shown that freedom of philosophizing not only may be conceded without endangering piety and the peace of the republic, but also that it may not be taken away without taking the peace of the republic and piety away with it". The full title of the *Tractatus Politicus* continues : *in which it is demonstrated how a society in which monarchical dominion has a place, as well as one in which an elite rules, should be instituted so that it should not lapse into tyranny and so that the peace and freedom of its citizens may be preserved inviolate.* Spinoza is the first major philosopher to undertake to prove that democracy is the best form of constitution. Freedom is also central in the life of Spinoza. The works of his that have come to us are testimony to his exercise of freedom of philosophizing, but his freedom to publish the results of his philosophizing was seriously hampered. He enjoyed freedom of religion and belief in the Netherlands, and expressed his piety and his knowledge of Scripture and theology in his works, but he was excommunicated from his synagogue because of fear that the heresies produced by his philosophizing might lead to the repression of religious freedom. He saw democracy come to Holland and be transmuted into monarchy or tyranny under circumstances which made him fear for the fate of freedom. The conditions of freedom in the circumstances which formed the background of his life influenced his life and his philosophy. He had the intellectual freedom which constitutes moral happiness, but the philosophizing which resulted in the exercise of that freedom was thought by some to constitute a danger to established religion and the public peace. The works containing those philosophical reflections continue to have, three hundred years after his death, a relevance to the problems we face today in philosophy, ethics, politics and religion. Consideration of the influence of Spinoza's background on his thought and life may properly close by particularizing his observation at the end of the *Ethics*: the road he has shown is difficult and is seldom discovered, but all excellent things (*omnia praeclara*) are as difficult as they are rare.

E. LEVINAS

Paris

Réponse au Professeur McKeon

I

L'EXPOSÉ DU *background* de Spinoza par le Professeur McKeon m'a paru riche et instructif. C'est sur un seul point que je voudrais revenir : les relations de Spinoza avec la Communauté juive d'Amsterdam. Le rapporteur a montré le rôle que le souvenir de l'excommunication a joué dans l'identification spinoziste de la béatitude avec la liberté et de la liberté avec la liberté de penser. Il a aussi parlé de l'école juive d'Amsterdam et de la scolarité brillante de Spinoza et, notamment, de l'admiration que lui vouait à l'Ecole Rabbi Saül Morteira, professeur de Talmud. Pourtant, les travaux de Van Dias et Van der Tak, publiés en néerlandais au cours des dernières décennies, donnent une vision moins dramatique de l'excommunication de Spinoza : celle-ci ne serait restée définitive qu'à cause du désir probable de Spinoza de quitter le cadre d'une communauté confessionnelle. De plus, ces travaux permettent de mettre en doute bien des points de la biographie traditionnellement admise de Spinoza comme, par exemple, les études qu'il aurait poursuivies en vue du rabbinat ; en effet, Spinoza ne figure pas sur la liste des élèves de la Section Supérieure de l'Ecole Juive d'Amsterdam, consacrée aux études talmudiques et n'aurait pas été l'élève de Rabbi Morteira.[1]
La destruction de la légende ne compromet certes pas la réputation de Spinoza en tant que connaisseur de l'hébreu et compétent en Ecritures Saintes. Elle ne tendrait à mettre en question que l'étendue et

---

[1] Les travaux de Van Dias et Van der Tak sont fondés sur toute une documentation des archives communales et sur des ouvrages relatifs à l'Ecole, publiés à l'époque. Ils permettent de reconstituer les programmes et la structure administrative de cet établissement de la Communauté juive d'Amsterdam.

la profondeur de sa pratique du Talmud. Mais s'il faut prêter une certaine attention aux conclusions de ces recherches — dont la valeur dépend des hypothèses et des déductions qu'elles impliquent — c'est, peut-être, surtout à cause de certains aspects des écrits mêmes de Spinoza. En lisant le *Traité théologico-politique* — en le relisant encore assez récemment, à l'occasion du beau livre que lui consacrait mon ami Sylvain Zac — j'avais l'impression que, pour avoir connu parfaitement la philosophie juive médiévale et certains écrits cabbalistiques, Spinoza n'avait pas eu de contact direct avec l'oeuvre prémédiévale du Talmud. Il se peut, d'ailleurs, que ce contact ait déjà été rompu dans sa communauté natale elle-même où les idées, les coutumes et les préoccupations du marranisme étaient encore des souvenirs très vifs et où l'intérêt pour la Cabbale et l'attente eschatologique l'emportaient sur l'attrait que devaient exercer la haute dialectique du Talmud et la discussion rabbinique. Rien, dans les recherches historiques dont nous parlons, ne mesure le potentiel talmudique de la vie juive à Amsterdam à l'époque de Spinoza, et il serait inexact de penser que les communautés juives — et même leurs rabbins — sont, toujours et partout, les interprètes authentiques de la tradition talmudique ; celle-ci, très souvent, s'impose sous des aspects décadents, figés ou morts.

Il n'est donc nullement certain que, dans le domaine de la science talmudique, le *background* de Spinoza ait été favorisé. Ce point a plus qu'une importance biographique. En effet, l'exégèse rabbinique de l'Ecriture — dans la critique qu'en fait le *Traité théologico-politique* — est comme séparée de son âme qu'est le Talmud et, dès lors, apparaît comme une apologétique aveugle et dogmatique des 'pharisiens' attachés à la lettre (mais prompts à lui prêter un sens arbitraire) et comme une réconciliation forcée de textes, évidemment disparates. *"Rabini... plane delirant"* (ch. 9); *"rem plane fingunt"* (ch. 2). C'est là, plus que dans la compulsion de documents, que Spinoza peut être soupçonné d'ignorance — l'ignorance étant plus vraisemblable, dans le cas d'un Spinoza, qu'une quelconque méconnaissance ou incompréhension.

Ce n'est ni le moment ni le lieu de présenter le Talmud pour luimême. Je rappellerai seulement sa structure unique en son genre : il maintient les problèmes à l'état de discussions ; des thèses s'opposent en lui et restent cependant, les unes et les autres, "paroles du Dieu vivant", selon sa propre expression. Il accrédite l'idée d'un Esprit *Un,* malgré les contradictions de dialogues sans conclusion. Dialectique ouverte. Elle ne se sépare pas de l'étude vivante dont elle devient le thème ; cette étude répercute et amplifie le dynamisme affolant du texte. Il faut ici la parole du maître ; et tout dépend de la façon dont il 'talmudise', si l'on peut s'exprimer ainsi. *Loi orale* : c'est le nom et l'essence du Talmud, même si — du moins depuis la fin du sixième siècle — il est consigné par écrit. Spinoza a-t-il jamais entendu la bonne façon de 'talmudiser' ? Certes, personne n'est assez sot pour penser que les très grands esprits s'expliquent par ce qui les nourrit dans leurs études et leur entourage ; mais le *background* comporte sa causalité propre, sans quoi il n'aurait pas été utile d'écouter le si remarquable rapport de MacKeon.

II

Qu'il me suffise d'évoquer quelques possibilités de l'exégèse animée par le Talmud — cette exégèse qui se bornerait à violenter les textes, si l'on en croit la critique de Spinoza et la méthode philologique qu'il avance contre elle.

L'incessant retour des docteurs du Talmud sur les versets — dont Spinoza dit : *"verba scripturae extorquere conantur ut id quod plane non vult dicat"* (ch. 2) — aboutit en effet à des interprétations multiples s'éloignant en apparence du sens obvie. Mais ce qui est recherché par là — et souvent accompli — c'est une lecture grâce à laquelle le passage commenté éclaire le lecteur sur sa préoccupation actuelle (qu'elle lui soit propre ou commune à sa génération), et grâce à laquelle, réciproquement, le verset se renouvelle. C'est ce que j'appellerai l'essence homilétique du texte. L'homélie, avant d'être l'édification d'une Communauté, est bien d'abord cette relation intime avec le texte, ce renouvellement, cette réactualisation du sens. L'herméneutique que, dans sa préface à Bultmann, Ricoeur désigne comme "le déchiffrage même de la vie au miroir du texte" est, à sa façon, pratiquée et même instaurée ici.

Chez ceux que Spinoza désigne comme pharisiens se fixait peut-être, pour l'exégèse, un modèle que suivirent les religions issues de la Bible. L'Ecriture comme écriture comporte un appel à la postérité, et c'est grâce à l'exégèse qu'une époque pourrait avoir un sens pour une autre. Ainsi, l'histoire n'est pas ce qui rend relative la vérité du sens. La distance qui sépare le texte du lecteur est au contraire l'intervalle où se loge le devenir même de l'Esprit. Grâce à elle, le sens acquiert sa pleine signification et se renouvelle. Il est ainsi possible, à partir de l'exégèse, de parler de Révélation continue, comme on parle en théologie et en philosophie de Création continue. Selon un apologue talmudique (Traité *Menahoth,* 29b), ce qui s'enseigne à l'école de Rabbi Aquiba serait incompréhensible à Moïse, mais constituerait cependant l'enseignement même de Moïse. La Thora, selon un autre apologue (Traité *Baba Metsia*, 59b), n'est plus au Ciel, mais dans les discussions des hommes ; s'obstiner à quérir son sens original — son sens céleste — reviendrait, paradoxablement, à chercher à déraciner des arbres ou à renverser le courant des fleuves. L'exégèse — dépassement de la lettre — est aussi dépassement de l'intention psychologique de l'écrivain. Un pluralisme est ainsi admis dans l'interprétation du même verset, du même personnage biblique, du même "événement fondateur", par cette reconnaissance des divers niveaux, de diverses profondeurs du sens. *Polysémie du sens* : le Verbe est comme "le marteau qui frappe le rocher en faisant jaillir d'innombrables étincelles" ; les diverses époques et les diverses personnalités des exégètes constituent la modalité même sous laquelle cette polysémie existe. Il y aurait, bien au contraire, de l'irrévélé dans la Révélation, si à l'exégèse manquait une seule âme dans sa singularité. Que ces renouveaux puissent passer pour des altérations du texte n'est pas ignoré par les docteurs du Talmud. D'où l'ironie évidente d'exclamations telles que: "Aquiba, ne fausse plus les versets, retourne aux thèmes de l'Ecriture où tu excelles, à ceux qui concernent la pureté et l'impureté."

Mais ce va-et-vient du texte au lecteur et du lecteur au texte et ce renouvellement du sens sont peut-être le propre de tout écrit, de toute littérature, même quand elle ne se prétend pas Saintes-Ecritures. Le sens qui se dégage d'une authentique expression de l'humain excède le contenu psychologique de l'intention de l'écrivain, qu'il soit prophète, philosophe ou poète. En s'exprimant, l'intention traverse des courants de significations objectivement portés par le langage et l'expérience d'un peuple. Ces courants assurent au *dit* son équilibre, sa réussite et ses résonnances. Le dire fait vibrer ce qui en lui précède le pensé. L'interprétation le dégage. Elle n'est pas seulement perception, elle est constitution du sens. De ce point de vue, tout texte est inspiré: il contient plus qu'il ne contient explicitement. L'exégèse de toute littérature tient à la façon dont le sens obvie que la lettre suggère se situe déjà dans l'impensé. Les Ecritures Saintes ont certes un autre secret, une essence supplémentaire que, peut-être, les textes purement littéraires ont perdue ; mais elles n'en sont pas moins textes littéraires. Et c'est parce que toute littérature est inspirée que la révélation religieuse peut se faire texte et se montrer à l'herméneutique.

III

Le critique spinoziste ne fait aucun état de cette 'ontologie' du sens. Si Spinoza — le génial Spinoza — avait connu intimement la vie du Talmud, il n'aurait pu ni réduire cette ontologie à une mauvaise foi des pharisiens, ni l'expliquer par le fait qu' "à partir des paroles et d'images on peut combiner bien plus d'idées qu'à partir des seuls principes et notions sur lesquels se construit notre connaissance naturelle" (*nam ex verbis et imaginibus longe plures ideae componi possunt quam ex solis principiis et notionibus, quibus tota nostra naturalis cognitio superstruitur*) (ch. I).

Aucune autre dimension ne s'ajoute, chez Spinoza, aux règles de la philologie que préconise le *Traité théologico-politique* et qui désignent, sans conteste, le champ de la lecture moderne de textes. Or la lecture moderne ne s'en tient pas, pensons-nous, à ce champ. Pour Spinoza tout savoir qui résume une expérience temporelle tout ce qui revêt un style poétique porte la marque de l'imaginaire. La Bible, conditionnée par le temps, est en-dehors des idées adéquates; sa cohérence n'est faite que de *figmenta* des commentateurs. N'est réelle que sa réalité subjective, avec ses intentions subjectives. Retrouver la réalité des actes de la pensée et leurs intentions subjectives telles qu'elles sont consignées dans le texte — voilà tout ce qu'un savoir soucieux de réalité peut chercher dans l'Ecriture. *"Mentem authorum Scripturae concludere"* : l'intention subjective et ses causes et non point sa portée imaginaire ! Il s'agit donc d'établir la genèse du texte plutôt que d'en faire l'exégèse. Le sens est, certes, rapporté aux circonstances de sa formulation, mais il est déjà, dès le début, pleinement lui-même, réifié dans le texte et quasiment emboîté en lui, et ceci avant même tout développement historique, avant toute herméneutique : l'absolu est dit de l'origine, non pas du résultat. Mais, dès lors, Spinoza ne ramène pas seulement la Bible au rang de tout texte ; il assimile l'exploration de toute écriture à l'exploration de la Nature : *"Dico methodum interpretandi Scripturam haud differre a methodo interpretandi Naturam sed cum ea prorsus convenir"* (ch. 6).

Spinoza aura certainement affranchi la modernité de l'obsession des Ecritures en tant que source unique de divin. Est divin, pour lui, ce qui, en elles, concorde avec les conséquences pratiques de son Ethique. *"Quare scripturae divinitas ex hoc solo constare debet quod ipsa veram virtutem doceat"* (III, 173). Mais Spinoza n'aura conféré aucun rôle au lecteur dans la production du sens — si l'on peut s'exprimer ainsi — n'aura prêté à l'oreille aucune don de prophétie. Pour l'homme d'aujourd'hui, au contraire, l'attention au message — le moment religieux de toute lecture des livres et de toute jouissance poétique — est liée à l'avènement du sens à travers les signes donnés dans leur immédiateté, à son avènement grâce à une herméneutique. Ce qui, de plus, nous permet de comprendre en quoi il peut y avoir de nombreuses interprétations possibles du spinozisme, qui n'excluent pas, mais attestent sa vérité.

G. FUNKE

Mainz

Anonymous Presuppositions in Spinoza's Philosophy

PROFESSOR MCKEON has presented the historical background of Spinoza's philosophy in a comprehensive manner, marking out exactly all the individual points. The connections with both the history of philosophy and the contemporary historical events have thus been made eminently clear.

The possibility now exists of briefly identifying those presuppositions not actually expressed, the anonymous presuppositions which make up the 'implicit' philosophy of Spinoza. Such conditions are listed below :

1. Spinoza's proposition *omnis determinatio est negatio* (Letter LIX).
2. Spinoza's use of analogy : *comparatio proportione* (*Short Treatise*, dt. edition of Chr. Sigwart, 1869, Chap. 1, p. 9).
3. Spinoza's concept of being *quod in se est — quod in alio est* (*Ethics* I, Axiom I).
4. Spinoza's *causa sui* concept (*Ethics* I, Def. I).
5. Spinoza's spatial metaphor *in se / in alio esse* (*Ethics* I, Axiom I).
6. Spinoza's *hemiplegia gnoseologica* in the knowledge of the two attributes (*Ethics* I, Props. X–XI).
7. Spinoza's parallelism proposition: *ordo et connexio idearum idem est ac ordo et connexio rerum* (*Ethics* II, Prop. VII).
8. Spinoza's use of the *esse intentionale* (*Ethics* II, Prop. XLIX).
9. Spinoza's treatment of the 'will' as a *modus cogitandi* (*Ethics* I, Prop. XXXII).
10. Spinoza's conception of time: *duratio est indefinita existendi continuatio* (*Ethics* II, Def. V).
11. Spinoza's proposition *deus sive natura* (*Ethics* I, Defs. I, VI).
12. Spinoza's *modus* (*accidens*) : *id quod in alio est, per quod etiam concipitur* (*Ethics* I, Def. V).

[53]

13. Spinoza's adoption of *imaginatio, experientia vaga, ratiocinatio, cognitio* (*Ethics* II, Prop. XL, n. 2).

We are confronted with the underlying, presumedly self-evident positions in a threefold way: (1) We have to deal with preconditions which are logically implied, even when they are contested openly; implicitly they are acknowledged, explicitly, disputed. (2) We encounter presuppositions which have been adopted by tradition and are taken over without being discussed. (3) We have to take into consideration presumptions which are shared commonly for representing expressedly some specific popular thinking and which seem to be convincing for Spinoza.

1. Spinoza's proposition *omnis determinatio est negatio*[1] also has a longer form: *omnis determinatio est negatio — determinatio ad rem juxta suum esse non pertinet, sed e contra est eius non esse*, or: every determination is negation. A determination does not belong to a thing in regard to its being but rather in regard to its not-being.[2] This means that each determination is of a limiting type and therefore negative. It separates an X from a Y and explains that the thing thus being determined is not another.

Although the literature in the history of philosophy has willingly taken up this idea, the proposition is nevertheless only half true. Spinoza believes that out of the universal being in which everything of which we can possibly conceive is posited, we only determine a specific entity in so far as we deny everything else in it. This thought leads far beyond that of Spinoza's own time, beyond Campanella, who also knew the idea *determinatio est negatio*.[3] It belongs to the self-evident ideas of classic (Platonic) philosophy. In the *Sophist* Plato describes how every something is *not* something else. At the same time he says that every something thereby consists of its own being and innumerable non-beings.[4]

Systematically regarded, however, the thought is really the following. We think (determine) a being by delineating that which it is not. In this way we can think of as many others as we please as points for comparison, denying these others of the first something. But to wish to exclude the so-called other and to deny it contains, and has as its presupposition, the thought that the something which we wish to

---

1 Letter LIX.
2 Cf. Kuno Fischer, *Spinozas Leben, Werke und Lehre*, Heidelberg 1946, pp. 365 f.
3 T. Campanella, *Universalis Philosophiae seu metaphysicicarum rerum juxta propia dogmata*, Partes tres, II, Parisiis 1638, 13.
4 *Sophist* 238A (Schlechte II, 6).

determine already has its own nature. It must have its own nature before we can deny those things which do not belong to it. Thus the thing in its determination is *not primarily* negative, as it seems to be according to Spinoza, and was impossible in any case since Plato's *Sophist*. It is much more the case that *omnis determinatio est positio*, because the determination (definiteness) of every something is in the first instance completely positive (and not negative), since only the positive nature of the something regarded as point of departure could cause us to deny all the others which it is not.

The following example will make it clearer.[5] What is, for example, *coniunxit*? (= he has unified, combined, connected). It is a verb, and therefore not a noun, not an adjective, not a preposition. It is perfect tense, therefore not present, not future, not..., not... It is the third person, and therefore not the second, not the first. It is singular, therefore not plural. Thus the entire positive constitution must be given before the negation of the other can result. In brief, the positive does *not* consist of mere negations but rather provides the basis for all possible particular denials.

The distinctions which are involved in knowing also cannot characterize their origin and beginning point of consciousness. Only that can be distinguished which one already has in a preliminary manner. Furthermore, a ground must be given for the distinction. In order to distinguish something from something else, it is also necessary to have this other in hand as well and to find it as positively given. In brief, as opposed to the proposition *omnis determinatio est negatio*, the following must also be brought in. When we say that A is not B, then not only A but B as well must be given to us in some positive fashion, and we must be able to compare them with one another by the application of a point of view still to be introduced. This means that after the positing of A and B as possible points of comparison, we come to the negation as an additional third thing, as a possibility based upon the positive definiteness of A and B. However, this negation is not present as the primary thing.[6]

This agrees as well with what Spinoza explains in a different context, when he speaks of "affirming" (and "denying") and of positing (and counter-positing), namely, that all of this 'is' only in the representation, in so far as the representation merely 'is'. Here Spinoza is opposed to Spinoza. In Letter LIX he starts from negation. In the note to Prop. XLIX of the *Ethics* II he holds fast to the positive.

---

5   Gustav Teichmüller, *Die wirkliche und die scheinbare Welt*, Breslau 1882, p. 154.
6   *Ibid.*, p. 65.

The demonstration here says: *voluntas, et intellectus nihil praeter ipsas singulares volitiones, et ideas sunt.* They are something in themselves, not just through negation.

It must certainly be admitted that when Spinoza denies the special existence of the will over and against thought in this passage, he does so in the tradition of Descartes. His use of the term *cogitatio* (which includes doubt and insight, as well as affirmation, negation, willing, non-willing, sensation, representation, etc.)[7] leaves room only for that generally found in consciousness, but not for that which pertains particularly to the will. If Descartes later frees himself from such a limiting conception, Spinoza does not follow him in this regard. For Spinoza it is more a question of being able to show that everything is already accomplished with the *positing character.* Seen in this light, the *negatio* presents a *super additum,* and the positing remains the implicit presupposition — the only basis on which Spinoza's doctrine is at all tenable.

2. When Spinoza determines substance, he determines it through its attributes. The main question then is: how can it be consistent to assume infinitely many attributes in God[8] and at the same time to maintain that only two of these attributes can be known. This numerical restriction contains a problem. One might ask how it is possible for Spinoza to advance from the limited and bounded, which he knows, to the supposed infinity, which he does not know.

The *Tractatus brevis de Deo et Homine eiusque felicitate* suggests a quick answer. The infinite substance has not just two but rather infinitely many attributes because : nothing has no attributes, something has several, and the infinite infinitely many.[9] The formal procedure of analogy employed here is neither founded in itself, nor does it not prove what it should. In the first place, nothing follows from nothing; in the second, Spinoza does not show us any somethings with *several* attributes; thirdly, he knows only *one* reality in general, just the infinite substance with its numerically problematic attributes. The series nothing–something–infinite which was used for the application of the analogy procedure is immediately dropped. Something (with the so-called 'several' attributes) is just as nonsensical as nothing. In Spinoza's metaphysical construction this helping concept of the 'something with several attributes' also immediately disappears.

---

7 Descartes, *Meditations* II, 8.
8 *Ethics* I, Prop. II.
9 Halle 1852, dt. as *Kurzer Traktat von Gott, dem Menschen und dessen Glückseligkeit,* ed. Christoph Sigwart, Gotha 1869[2], p. 18.

In the *Short Treatise*[10] Spinoza takes refuge in a superficial attempt to explain the origin of our knowledge concerning the *infinite attributes* of the infinite: "From where else than from the infinite properties themselves, which tell us that they exist, without telling us what they are, since only of two do we know what they are".[11] The background here is not so much the Cartesian proof for the existence of God. Nor is it the procedure of analogy, once used so quickly in the inference from nothing to the something and then to the infinite. It is, much more, the ordinary although undetermined concept of God as the infinitely highest being. It is self-evident that infinitely many attributes can be ascribed to such a being, even if only two of these are accessible to the knowing man.[12] But how can this access be possible, if not through their being known by man? The procedure of analogy, adopted without question, demonstrates its power of producing conviction in the following manner : nothing does not have attributes ; a something has several ; the infinite is distinguished by its infinitely many attributes. The power of conviction in this connection is silently counted upon by Spinoza.

3. Spinoza has a 'naive' relation to the concept of being. Descartes, after his completion of the procedure of doubt (*Med.* I : *de iis, quae in dubium revocari possunt*, and *Med.* II : *de natura mentis humanae, quod ipsa sit notior quam corpus*, held firmly to the proposition *cogito, ergo sum*, which Spinoza wishes to allow in the form : *"cogito, ergo sum" unica est proposito, quae huic "Ego sum cogitans" aequivalet.*[13] In both cases the statement that, in any case, I, the doubter, *am*, is made as if both Descartes and Spinoza knew, in a self-evident manner, what 'being' meant, and that they could express it in *one* meaning without any further ado.

Descartes defends himself against a critique aimed in this direction when he explains : "I believe that no one has been so stupid as to have to learn what existence *is* before he could conclude and maintain that he existed." In the *Recherche de la vérité par la lumière naturelle*,[14] Descartes has Eudoxe ask the peasant Poliander whether it is not completely self-evident to him what being, doubt and thought

---

10 *Short Treatise*, Chap. 1, p. 9.
11 *Loc. cit.*
12 *Ethics* II, Axiom V.
13 Spinoza, *Renati Des Cartes Principiorum Philosophiae*, Pars I et II, *more geometrico demonstratae*, Heidelberg edition, ed. Gebhardt, *Opera* I, p. 144.
14 Ed. Adam–Tannery, X, pp. 523 ff. Cf. *Oeuvres de Descartes*, ed. A. Prevost, Paris 1855, p. 459.

are. And he uses these concepts simply in the sense in which they lie ready in the uncritically accepted 'natural consciousness'.

Spinoza, although he touches instead on ancient convictions, formulates his definition of substance in a similar manner, as if it were self-evident that substance is that which is in itself and is understood from itself.[15] The *ignoratio elenchi* is to be found in the fact that he proceeds in *Ethics* I, Def. III, without regard for 'what is in itself'. However, a preliminary definition and division of being, into being-in-itself and being-from-another, is still lacking, and where it is a question of final grounding, this must be dealt with. Thus, the conception taken over from the classical *notiones communes* merely replaces convictions based on dogmas of the in-itself in accordance with Christian revelation. At best, this replacement of one tradition by another does not render the inner connection of Spinoza's own teaching any more convincing.

4. Spinoza adopts the ontological argument in his teaching of the *causa sui*. He says: *Per causam sui intelligo id, cuius essentia involvit existentiam, sive id, cuius natura non potest concipi nisi existens.*[16] It is quite apparent that the ontological argument is contained in this first definition of Spinoza in the *Ethics*. It is expressed as follows: *ad naturam substantiae pertinet existere.* When Spinoza therefore says: by cause of itself I understand that whose definition includes existence, this (in the context of *Ethics* I, Defs. III–IV, VI) is the only actual substance, to whom existence necessarily belongs, and which must be understood as existing absolutely (as God).

As opposed to this traditional ontological train of thought, the discussion of the distinction between 'in-itselfness' and self causation appears to be new in Spinoza. The complete being-in-itself or being-through-itself of the mediaeval theological speculation expresses nothing more and nothing less than absolute self-reliance and independence, as referred to God. When something is designated as *a se*, this means negatively only '*non ab alio*'. Spinoza's concept of the *causa sui* must be compared with this.

If one wishes to argue that in order to cause itself an X must already exist before its actual existence (merely in order to bring itself about), that is nonsense.[17] Spinoza cannot mean by self causation (*causa sui*) that a being has produced itself at some point in time. Further,

---

[15] *Ethics* I, Def. III.

[16] *Ethics* I, Def. I.

[17] Cf. Walter Schulz, *Der Gott der neuzeitlichen Metaphysik*, Pfullingen 1957, p. 66.

Spinoza does not investigate time in any way, but stops with logical-ontological distinctions. He follows neither Augustine nor Descartes. *Causa sui* expresses the self-sufficiency of substance, which, as that which really is and which rests in itself, is only conceivable through itself. It is thus alone and unique in its kind, that which is only to be thought as the *ens absolute infinitum*,[18] that is, as God.[19] In Descartes, substance is designated as *res, quae ita existit, ut nulla alia re indigeat ad existendum.*[20] This thought provides the transition to Spinoza. Thus the first axiom in the *Ethics* says : everything which is is either in itself or in another. With this juxtaposition the problematic of being is not really dealt with at all. This train of thought connotes, rather, the following : that which is in itself is called substance, that which is in another is called mode. Everything which is is thereby either substance or mode. If there is only *one* substance, called God, then aside from God there is no other substance,[21] and outside of this substance there are no modes ; and aside from substance and modes, nothing at all.[22] Everything which is, in itself or in another, is, thereby, through God or in God (or *quidquid est, in Deo est, et nihil sine Deo esse neque concipi potest*). If it is in God, then all things (*modi*) thus follow necessarily from the essence of God. To this extent God is the cause and ground of things. This means that they follow from *him alone* and in no way at all *ab alio*. Correspondingly, God *is* through himself (the cause of himself) ; he knows no cause outside of himself and is thereby the first (absolute) cause.[23] God is *omnium rerum causa immanens, non vero transiens.* '*Transiens*' here does not denote something passing (as opposed to continual or eternal), but rather the *immanent* cause, the cause not directed 'outwards', not 'leading out beyond itself'.[24]

From this logical-ontological argumentation there is no 'resolution' to the world or to the creation of the world. The world exists with God, through God, in God. In this sense Spinoza explains : concerning God and nature I think in a completely different manner from those Christians of the new sort, because I hold God to be the inner cause of things, not the outer. It is just the traditional theory of external influence or of transient effect which is rejected by the con-

---

18 *Ethics* I, Def. VI.
19 Schulz (*op. cit.*, n. 17), p. 66.
20 Descartes, *Principia philosophiae* I, 51.
21 *Ethics* I, Theorem 14.
22 Cf. Fischer (*op. cit.*, n. 2), p. 359.
23 *Ethics* I, Prop. XVI, notes 1–3.
24 *Ethics* I, Prop. XVII, Letter LXXIII.

cept of the *causa sui*. For God is *the* one substance, and as substance he logically precedes the nature in God, that is, the world, as a particular type and manner of existence. This is expressed in the following manner : *substantia prior est natura suis affectionibus*.[25] In so far as substance is, in its essence, earlier (if you will, *a priori*) than its determinations, it remains, as *causa immanens* (and not *transiens*), fundamentally *causa sui*. The cosmological immanence is thus maintained over and against any other possible immanence, whether of consciousness, experience or knowledge. God is the active cause of both the existence and essence of things, due to his immanent nature.[26] Because, according to Spinoza, there is, apart from the one substance, God, and, apart from his essence, no further original ground of possible efficacy, power and essence are identical in God : *Dei potentia est ipsa ipsius essentia*.[27] The doctrine of creation in time — the same wherever one might seek it — shows itself here to be an anonymous opponent of Spinoza.

5. Spinoza belongs to those philosophers in modern philosophy who have defined the concept of substance. He says : by substance I understand that which is in itself and is understood from itself. That is to say that it is something whose concept can be formed without recourse to the concept of another thing.[28] Correspondingly, an accident must then be that which is in another, through which it is known or conceived.

The definition that substance is to be understood as that which is in itself refers directly to the metaphor of the accident being that which is in another. However, this image, taken from the spatial realm (as the eye in the head, the wine in the barrel), is distorted as soon as one passes from the attribute of extension (*extensio*) to that of thought.[29] In the latter the image in-itself / in-another turns into a relation of a completely different type — that between the particular and the universal (as, for example, in the sentence "the lion is a mammal").[30]

Spinoza's definition in regard to substance, and the distinction between being-in-itself and being-in-another, call for an explanation of the concept 'being'. For the spatial and the logical meanings of the term being refer in their differentiation to exactly that higher universal

---

25   *Ethics* I, Prop. I.
26   *Ethics* I, Props. XXIV–XXV.
27   *Ethics* I, Prop. XXXIV.
28   *Ethics* I, Def. I.
29   *Ethics* II, Theorems 1–2.
30   Example in Teichmüller (*op. cit.*, n. 5), p. 121.

under which being, in both these meanings, can be subsumed. Because Spinoza does not show how this can be done, the related concept of being itself vacillates. We encounter difficulties if we assume that, in the case of being-in-another, we are dealing with logical subordination. If, as in the above-mentioned example, the lion is brought under the concept 'mammal' by means of the species concept, and if he is 'contained' in this concept, one still cannot say, according to the logical metaphor, that the actual lion is 'in' the mammal. The use of these separate meanings of being prevents us from confronting the problem facing us. And the metaphor being-in-another continues to be employed as a spatial metaphor only because 'one' has grown accustomed to it in philosophy. This unexplained use of both the metaphysical and the logical meaning has an effect on the discussion of the problem of substance. Spinoza certainly regarded the objective entirely from the point of view of substance. The question about the substantiality of substance he has taken over from Descartes. This is the result of the assumption of an illumination which occurs through the 'natural light' of the intuitive knowledge of the pure subject. If it is true that Spinoza is completely opposed to anthropomorphism in knowledge (of theology and philosophy), then this opposition is lacking in the question of being, for it is most certainly employed in the popular sense.

6. Spinoza completely separates the attribute of extension, ascribed to the 'All-one', from the attribute of thought,[31] for each attribute is conceived from itself *without* the aid of another. This fundamental division does not prevent Spinoza from discussing the particular forms in which extension appears, although according to the distinction made in *Ethics* II, Prop. VI, these could not be brought to knowledge at all were there not something non-extensional (that is 'thought'). The proof of this is not difficult to state : we cannot separate or divide A (for example, thought) from B (extension) if we do not know B. Since, according to *Ethics* I, Props. X–XI, the two attributes cannot have an effect on one another, and since, also, knowing can be determined only through cognitions, when we speak of extension as something in addition to thinking and knowing, we can do so only in an inauthentic manner, or under the tacit presupposition of the fundamental intentionality of consciousness.

A similar argument must be employed when we wish to go far beyond the recognition of a *single* particular attribute in addition to thought (namely extension) — to the assumption of innumerable, in principle

---

[31] *Ethics* II, Props. I–II.

an infinite number of attributes. Since only two such attributes (thought and extension) can be reached by man, this means, in the context of the writing of an 'Ethic', that only two are 'attainable at all'. Finally, extension is reported on, not through extension, but through thought. Thus, what results is not merely the 'partial paralysis' (hemiplegia) of Spinoza's system described by Teichmüller, but rather a complete paralysis.[32]

If it is Spinoza's position that only substance (and its two attributes, thought and extension) can be considered as a principle, then, without having any further details we still have not answered the obvious traditional-idealistic objection — that the attribute of extension can in no way be taken to be a particular form of being, since something spatial (extension) can only be given in the *modus cogitandi* and must be transposed into ideal, cognitive being before it can be rendered 'understandable'. The scholastic concept of the mental in-existence or intentionality, which must be presupposed, remains unexplained and uncriticized. Correspondingly, extension, as a concrete attribute of God, remains, in Spinoza, something like a *caput mortuum.*

7. Spinoza discusses the possible types of knowledge in the following manner. In the *Short Treatise*,[33] understanding is a pure passion, that is, it is a becoming aware (*perceptio*) of the essence and existence of things... in such a way that *we* ourselves neither ascertain nor fail to ascertain something in regard to the thing. Instead, it is the thing itself which, from itself, either affirms or denies something in us.[34]

It is thereby obvious that, essentially everything encountered by the consciousness must be 'true'. For the proposition that knowledge is passive in character leaves no room for any possible explanation of error, and even excludes its possibility. In order to provide the necessary explanation of error, Spinoza takes recourse in the claim that it is not the entire object but only a part of it which comes to positive givenness (is affirmed) ; however, this part is obviously taken for the whole.[35]

In *On the Emendation of the Understanding,* this doctrine of the passivity of knowledge has already been dropped. The negative second part (*pars destruens*) already presupposes the active character of knowledge.[36] This occurs in the following way : Spinoza introduces a faculty of representation (*imaginatio*) which has its *own* role in

---

32 Teichmüller (*op. cit.,* n. 5), p. 102.
33 *Kurzer Traktat* (*op. cit.,* n. 9), p. 99.
34 *Ibid.,* p. 105.
35 *Ibid.,* p. 107.
36 Ed. Gebhardt (*op. cit.,* n. 13), I, p. 28.

[62]

addition to that of the understanding (*intellectus*). He goes on to explain that through imagination [37] one can understand what one wishes, as long as this imagination is distinguished from the understanding and brings the soul into a passive relationship (:*unde habeat anima rationem patientis*).[38] The understanding (*mens*) is thereby implicitly imputed to be active.

Spinoza develops this train of thought in the *Ethics*.[39] In Part II, Prop. X, he says that each attribute of a substance must be understood from itself. But the only way to comprehend the attribute of extension (which is not and cannot be the thinking, knowing conception of itself) consists in accepting the fact that thought, as an attribute of substance, is or must be given parallel to the attribute of extension. Were this not the case, there would be no possibility at all of comprehending extension, and thought would remain empty. The parallelism thesis arises from the fact that thought, if it is thought, presents the thought of a content. If *only* thought and extension are accessible to human beings, then they are only accessible in this parallel association. *God* goes on to think of the infinitely many attributes accessible to him ; man stops at the thought of thought and the thought of extension. In Spinoza's view, it must be a tautology to say that a concept is related to an object. For if I say 'concept', this already means the 'concept of an object': *Ordo et connexio idearum idem est ac ordo et connexio rerum.*[40]

8. In his anti-idealistic and anti-transcendental objectivism, Spinoza explains that one must always proceed from the object precisely because thought is always the thought of an object. Now, thought and the thought of extension are coordinates in human apprehension. In God, however, thought extends further. God thinks, and God is extended [41] — we understand it so far. However, in himself God thinks not only thought and extension but also his infinite capacities according to all his possible attributes. The acquaintance with and knowledge of the modes of extension is guaranteed by the fact that the modes of thought, corresponding to things, run parallel to them.[42] Representations and ideas are representations and ideas of represented or ideated things, in the sense of thoroughgoing intentionality.

For the nominalist Spinoza, there are only stones and not 'stone-

---

[37] Cf. Bernard Alexander, *Spinoza,* Munich 1923, p. 57.
[38] Ed. Gebhardt *(op. cit.,* n. 13), I, p. 29.
[39] *Ethics* I, Prop. X; II, Prop. XL, n. 2.
[40] *Ethics* II, Prop. VII.
[41] *Ethics* II, Props. I–II.
[42] *Ethics* I, Prop. II.

ness', only things and not thinghood, etc. Only the individual truly exists as mode. While universal concepts such as summaries are certainly important and necessary subjectively, they do not exist objectively. Traditionally, when a 'faculty' of affirmation and negation is mentioned, every such purported faculty is essentially identical with the representation itself.[43] The proposition : the soul affirms that the three angles of a triangle are equal to two right angles, says nothing more than that which is contained in the representation itself. It is not the case that we have the idea of a triangle and, in addition, affirm[44] *that* the three angles belonging to it make up two right angles. In Spinoza's conception every so-called 'willing' is only an ostensible one.

If there is no actual 'faculty of the will', then, according to Spinoza, there is no need to concern ourselves with the 'freedom' of this non-existent capacity.[45] This position, simply taken over from the nominalists, frees Spinoza from any further investigation here. From the parallelism of the attributes and the assumption of a possible knowledge of the attributes (which is performed by the *cogitatio*), it follows with necessity that there is something like the conception of the intentionality of consciousness. However, while such a capacity is neither introduced nor justified by Spinoza at this place or in this sense, it is nonetheless necessary as a condition for the possibility of his systematic position.

9. Spinoza takes the will to be a mere phenomenon of consciousness, a *modus cogitandi* : *voluntas certus tantum cogitandi modus est, sicuti intellectus.*[46] It is evident that in so doing he ignores the specifically 'wilful' character of the will. For a person who does not will something can have the representations accompanying an act of will just as easily as the person who actually does will it.[47] The will represents an accomplishment, which joins in as an act when a representation is given in consciousness. It does not do justice to willing to merely describe the processes of consciousness or thought. For that purpose one needs a whole arsenal of particular expressions which relate specifically to the will and which do not disappear into this or that aspect of consciousness. This becomes evident in forms such as *placet, iuvat, nolo, veto, bibamus, indigeamus,* etc.

Thus Spinoza is *not* in the tradition of Descartes. When Descartes

---

43 *Ethics* II, Prop. XLIX.
44 Cf. Alexander *(op. cit.,* n. 37), p. 113.
45 *Ethics* II, Prop. XLIX, Conclusion, note.
46 *Ethics* I, Prop. XXXII.
47 Teichmüller *(op. cit.,* n. 5), p. 102.

G. Funke

determines that the will (the *volonté*) is a representation (*pensée*), he must finally admit that something must be added to the mere cogitative element : *j'ajoute aussi quelque autre chose par cette action à l'idée.*[48] He thus again distinguishes between *cogitatio* and *volitio* and does not sublimate the will to a representation or a *modus cogitandi*. In the Ethics, Spinoza says : *Voluntas et intellectus nihil praeter ipsas singulares volitiones, et ideas sunt. At singularis volitio, et idea unum, et idem sunt, ergo voluntas, et intellectus unum, et idem sunt.*[49] As opposed to Spinoza, Descartes needs the will for his doctrine of error. This doctrine of error is added in Descartes but allowed to drop in Spinoza. Descartes defends the notion that the term activity of the will designates the will only, according to its essence, and that any accompanying representation should be considered completely separate, as it remains representation, that is, is not transformed in any way. This question of truth or error, still so important for Descartes,[50] is handled in Spinoza in that he explains error in the old manner : A partial representation is thought to be the *whole* (which is false). Error and falsehood are explained as resulting from the *lack* of something which should actually be given, that is, in the sense of a privation. An example of this type of 'deprivation' (*privatio*) would be a predicate that does not ascribe to the subject everything which actually belongs to its content and essence.

In such a logic of negation, Spinoza does not need the will for his doctrine of error. The privative exclusion and negation are understood on the model of the proposition *omnis determinatio est negatio.* Thus the retreat to the purely cognitive region, as well as the traditional anti-voluntaristic intellectualism, becomes clear.

10. Spinoza occupied himself at length with extension and what is extended. He dismissed time rather quickly. In the *Meditations*, Descartes holds that the certainty of being was given only in the moment of doubt itself and only for that moment: *quamdiu et quoties.*[51] In the first place, man has no guarantee of a temporal connection with temporal duration. In face of the hypothetically assumed *genius malignus*, it can only be said: *fallat quantum potest, nunquam tamen efficiet, ut nihil sin* quamdiu *me aliquid esse cogitabo. Adeo, ut omnibus satis superque pensitatis, denique statuendem sit hoc pronunciatum, Ego sum, ego existo,* quoties *a me profertur, vel mente*

48 *Oeuvres (op. cit., n.* 14), p. 127.
49 *Ethics* II, Prop. XLIX, Proof.
50 Descartes, *Meditations* IV, 5.
51 Descartes, *Meditations* II, 1.

[65]

concipitur, necessario esse verum.[52] "Always then, when..." is the certainty of existence given to consciousness. There can be no question of any connection with existence for a being whose existence is only affirmed at different points.

The connection can only be grasped in the isolated moment: *quoniam enim omne tempus vitae in partes innumeras dividi potest, quarum singulae a reliquis nullo modo dependent, ex eo quod paulo ante fuerim, non sequitur me nunc debere esse, nisi aliqua causa me quasi rursus creet ad hoc momentum, hoc est me conservet.*[53] This means that I do not necessarily exist now, even though I have existed shortly before, unless some new cause does not produce me once again, that is, does not sustain me. We are only assured of the "if..., so...", the *quamdiu et quoties.*

It is thus impossible to speak seriously of a self-sufficiency of sub-jectivity in Descartes and of the new beginning of philosophy under the viewpoint of the independence of subjective thought. But that is not what is important here. It is also obvious that there is a con-fusion between duration and time, when Descartes conceives of both as the sum of discrete parts.

On his part, Spinoza, from the very beginning, accords no importance to a critical investigation of time, space, etc. (in contrast to Leibniz), presupposing them to be that by which they are already known in their popular meaning. This procedure is most obvious when he defines: *duratio est indefinita existendi continuatio,*[54] where *duratio* (duration) is explained through *continuatio* (that is, through con-tinuing duration). However, to know the same through the same, in a self-evident manner, is mere tautology. Spinoza does not shrink from this.

11.   It is Spinoza's intention to counter the traditionally held *special position of man* (as opposed to nature) and of *subjectivity* (as op-posed to the objective).[55] Indeed, he does devote particular attention to the subjective as it comes to expression in man ; otherwise he would not have written an *Ethics*. But he does not single man out in order to detach him from the substantive unity of beings. That there is a *proper* position for man in nature does not imply that he holds a *special* place in it.

If the theme is the fundamental similarity of the human appearance to the usual appearances of nature, then man belongs, like all ac-

---

[52]   Adam–Tannery (*op. cit.,* n. 14), VII, p. 25.
[53]   *Ibid.,* VII, p. 48 f.
[54]   *Ethics* II, Def. V.
[55]   Cf. Schulz (*op. cit.,* n. 17), pp. 64 ff.

cidental things in general, to the *natura naturata*. Just like all other appearances of nature, he belongs to the temporary forms of the one being, to the representations of the one reality which, as accidents, depend upon substance. Thus: the being of substance does *not* belong to the essence of man, or : substance does *not* constitute the reality of man.[56] This means that the so-called truth of a thing always presents itself from one particular point of view, in one particular form of appearance. Expressed differently : substance is always represented in a particular context through a determined mode, whereby these forms of appearance pass away, and only substance alone remains.

Spinoza has given two names to his absolute substance :[57] God and nature. This means for him : by substance I understand that which is in itself and which is conceived through itself, that is, that whose concept does not require the concept of another thing in order for it to have to be formed. By God I understand the absolutely infinite being, that is, substance which consists of infinite attributes. By creative nature I understand that which is in itself and is conceived from itself..., that is, God, in so far as he is regarded as free cause. By created nature, however, I understand everything which follows from the necessity of the nature of God or any one of his divine attributes, that is, all modes of the attributes of God, in so far as they are regarded as things which are in God and which without God could neither be nor be conceived.[58]

The identification of the three expressions — substance, God and nature — is problematic. In the case of the concept of God, anthropomorphism makes its appearance due to human myth-building phantasies with subjective qualities. The concept of nature is ordinarily penetrated by the conception of an extrahuman reality, which stands in opposition to the world of consciousness, as something separate from it — a notion which cannot correspond to that of Spinoza. The teaching of the *one* substance enters only in the shadow of the *deus sive natura* doctrine.

12. Spinoza maintains that an accident, in contrast to substance, is that "whose concept requires the concept of another thing in order for it to be formed", and here the leap from the logical realm into that of reality becomes even more apparent.

With the use of the spatial metaphor "being-in-another", one can no longer understand what is meant by : the wine in the barrel is known

---

56 *Ethics* II, Axiom II.
57 Cf. Richard Falkenberg, *Geschichte des deutschen Idealismus*, I–II, Munich 1909, I, p. 122.
58 *Ethics* I, Defs. III, VI; Prop. XXIX, note.

through the barrel (or the nail by means of the wall to which it is fixed). With the use of the logical meaning, still other questions arise. The adoption of unacknowledged presuppositions is visible in the following :

The nature of the syllogism seems to confirm that each particular proposition (including those of mathematics) is understood through more universal propositions. But the correctness of this assumption disappears if we look at the apagogic proof. Since Aristotle, the *abductio* has proceeded from a valid major premise and from a minor premise which, although not certain, is at least as believable as the conclusion drawn from these two premises. As 'indirect proof', the apagogic procedure demonstrates the correctness of an assertion by proving the incorrectness of its opposite, in a *deductio ad absurdum*. Now, one can know exactly the universal propositions from which a particular proposition is supposedly derived without having any idea at all of the new particular truth of the conclusion, for this new piece of knowledge is only the result of the relation of the universal propositions to each other. However, the decisive relatedness here is not something universal, but just the particular, which supposedly can be understood only through the universal. It is something new, conceived *through itself* and thus not from another. Or, it is conceived when this *relation* is actually carried out in thought.[59]

It is justifiable to charge that here Spinoza has not directed himself to the origin and scope of the concepts he uses ; nor does he establish the legitimacy for their use. The terms substance and accident go back to Aristotle. However, the *terma* substance-attribute-mode cannot be employed schematically according to that model.

13. Spinoza presupposes the everyday, normal consciousness with its knowledge as fundamental to the fixing of the beginning of metaphysics. It is for him (as it was later for Hegel) the self-evident point of departure. Due to this presupposition, he proceeds in a pre-scientific way. To begin with an analysis of the normal consciousness, and to abstract from the given, step by step, as Spinoza does, is certainly legitimate. No speculative theory can bypass this procedure, which deduces anew, and makes more understandable, the contents of normal consciousness, diluted in the abstraction, from hypothetically or dogmatically posited principles.

In the *Ethics*, Spinoza begins by setting forth his governing points of view, which he terms definitions and axioms.[60] The process of ab-

---

[59] Teichmüller (*op. cit.*, n. 5), pp. 121–122.
[60] Not so in *Ethics*, Part III.

straction leads to the type of 'thinning out' in which one can no longer think anything at all using these principles; or, in concrete cases, one is secretly forced to remember the temporarily eliminated, self-evident presuppositions, namely the very facts of consciousness that provided the occasion for the formation of these speculative concepts. That this is so can be seen from the fact that a corresponding, common, normal consciousness is assumed whenever one person is supposed to understand someone else. This is also the case with Spinoza himself. He formulates the definitions and axioms according to the Aristotelean procedure of concept-proof-judgement-and-conclusion, which is self evident to him, and not to the exhibition procedure of Paul or Simon Magus, etc.

In this way, Spinoza's conceptions of the theory of knowledge succumb to change.

It is in the *Short* Treatise [61] that we find Spinoza's own theory of knowledge for the first time. Four types of knowledge are distinguished : that which we know from hearsay, from experience, in true belief, and through clear and distinct knowledge. The first two can deceive us; the latter two cannot. The theory is illustrated in the example of the rule *de tri,* in which three numbers are given and the problem is to find a fourth which is related to the third in the same way that the second is related to the first.

This example is found in *On the Emendation of Understanding,*[62] as well as in the *Short Treatise,*[63] and, finally, also in the *Ethics.*[64] The thought process is as follows : (1) Whoever hears the rule that the fourth number can be obtained if the second number is multiplied by the third and the result then divided by the first, can have this knowledge in a fourfold manner. Examples are provided by the series $1, 2, 3, 6$; $4, 8, 16, 32$; $5, 10, 15, 30$. One could then spout the results like a parrot who had memorized them mechanically. (2) Someone not content with hearsay could endeavour to give it a stronger basis by specific trial-and-error calculations, and then believe in the rule even though possible error is not thereby excluded — for experience with a few individual cases or examples shows that the step to universalization is not legitimate enough. (3) One might also seek the reason for the rule and thus discover the law of proportionality. This method would result in what Spinoza calls true belief.

---

[61] *Tractatus Theologico-Politicus,* Part II.

[62] *Sämtliche Werke aus dem Lateinischen von Berthold Auerbarch,* I, Stuttgart 1881, p. 530.

[63] *Tractatus Theologico-Politicus,* Part II, Chap. 1.

[64] *Ethics* II, Prop. XL, n. 2.

(4) One could go beyond hearsay, experience and the procedure of proof, and grasp the proportion in an immediately clear intuition. In the *Short Treatise,* that which is called illusion (referring to the first two types of knowledge), and then belief (at the third level) and knowledge (at the fourth level), is presented in *On the Emendation of Understanding* on four levels : *imaginatio, experientia vaga, ratiocinatio* and *cognitio.*

In the *Ethics,* universal concepts come from sensibility or from signs through which we recall imagined things by association.[65] This is knowledge from uncertain experience or knowledge of the first grade (opinion). When knowledge through reason is brought in to this, we have *notiones communes, termini transcendentales* and *notiones universales.* Knowledge is adequate (rational). The third grade of knowledge, characterized by the adequate knowledge of the essence of things, is intuitive *(scientia intuitiva).* This discerning of the different grades of knowledge offers Spinoza the opportunity to separate true from false 'knowledge' and thus to develop a kind of doctrine of the idols. If Spinoza immediately allows this matter to drop, this is understandable on the basis of his ethical interests. For from what are called mere opinions in the epistemological sphere emerge those passions that contradict reason. From rational reflections arise good desires. And true and real love are based on the complete insight of the *scientia intuitiva.*

As a whole, Spinoza's epistemological approach is close to the Platonic doctrine of knowledge,[66] with its allegory of the cave and of the divided line, passed on in innumerable variations — with the appearance of truth, belief in the senses, insight of the understanding, and science.

Applying immanent criticisms to a given position like Spinoza's, we are obliged to continuously encounter the most fundamental and even transcendent problems of particular relevance in philosophy, and we avoid specific kinds of ulterior hermeneutical deviations, comparisons or modernizations not rooted in outside dialectics.

---

[65] *Loc. cit.*
[66] *Statesman* VII, 533 D.

YIRMIYAHU YOVEL

Jerusalem

Substance without Spirit
On Hegel's Critique of Spinoza

I. BACKGROUND AND METHOD

"EITHER SPINOZISM or no philosophy", says Hegel in one of several aphorisms of similar strength. And, indeed, among the many forerunners whom Hegel absorbed as moments into the synthesis of his own system, Spinoza enjoys a privileged position comparable only to that of Aristotle and Kant. In the unfolding of the *Logic*, Spinoza's system, modified and criticized, corresponds to the climax of the 'Objective Logic', leading to the 'Subjective Logic' and to Hegel's own theory of the 'Concept'. (This passage is mediated by Kant's discovery that the structure of the object and the structure of the subject are one.) Spinoza serves Hegel as a basis for presenting his own thinking in the *Phenomenology* as well, when he speaks of the absolute as a result, and of viewing truth in terms of a subject and not only of substance.

Hegel's critique of Spinoza may also serve as a paradigm for what he takes to be a proper dialectical refutation of a philosophical system. Indeed, it is with respect to Spinoza that Hegel restates most clearly his methodological principle:

> In Rücksicht auf die Widerlegung eines philosophischen Systems ist anderwärts gleichfalls die allgemeine Bemerkung gemacht worden, dass daraus die schiefe Vorstellung zu verbannen ist, als ob das System als durchaus *falsch* dargestellt werden solle, und als ob das *wahre* System dagegen dem falschen *nur entgegengesetzt sei*... Das Substantialitätsverhältnis erzeugte sich durch die Natur des *Wesens*; dies Verhältnis, so wie seine zu einem Ganzen erweiterte Darstellung in einem Systeme ist daher ein *notwendiger Standpunkt,* auf welchen das Absolute sich stellt. Ein solcher Stand-

[71]

punkt ist daher nicht als eine Meinung, . . . eines Individuums, als eine Verirrung der Spekulation anzusehen. . . . Aber es ist *nicht der höchste Standpunkt.* Allein insofern kann das System nicht als *falsch,* als der *Widerlegung* bedürftig und fähig angesehen werden ; sondern nur dies daran ist als das *Falsche* zu betrachten, dass es der höchste Standpunkt sei. Das *wahre* System kann daher auch nicht das Verhältnis zu ihm haben, ihm nur *entgegengesetzt* zu sein ; denn so wäre dies Entgegengesetzte selbst ein Einseitiges. Vielmehr als das Höhere muss es das Untergeordnete in sich enthalten.[1]

Going on to stress the need for an *immanent* refutation, and dismissing an external critique as useless, Hegel concludes :

Die einzige Widerlegung des Spinozismus kann daher nur darin bestehen, dass sein Standpunkt zuerst als wesentlich und notwendig anerkannt werde, dass aber zweitens dieser Standpunkt *aus sich selbst* auf den höhern gehoben werde. Das Substantialitätsverhältnis, ganz nur *an und für sich selbst* betrachtet, führt sich zu seinem Gegenteil, dem *Begriffe,* über. Die im letzten Buch enthaltene Exposition der Substanz, welche zum *Begriffe* überführt, ist daher die einzige und wahrhafte Widerlegung des Spinozismus.[2]

There are indeed two forms for a proper dialectical refutation of a historical system, depending on whether we consider the process diachronically (in historical order) or synchronically (systematically). From the viewpoint of their historical sequence, systems of philosophy are properly refuted in that one accepts the element of partial truth contained in them while developing their logical implications to the point where their inconsistencies — due to the partiality and one-sidedness of their governing principle — are brought to light. This calls for transcending the system towards a more satisfactory one that preserves the basic ideas of the former in a more coherent form. This process continues as long as the final system of philosophy — the synoptic synthesis of 'absolute knowledge' — is not attained. However, when the final system emerges, we gain a new and better viewpoint for refuting former philosophical theories. Now the great systems of the past, duly criticized and transformed, figure *synchronically* as moments within the absolute system of knowledge. In this capacity, the critique of a system — say, Spinoza's — consists, as our

---

1   Hegel, *Wissenschaft der Logik,* II, ed. G. Lasson, Hamburg 1963, p. 217.
2   *Ibid.,* p. 218.

quotation has it, in the exposition of the category of 'substance' and the notion of the 'absolute' as they emerge systematically within the *Logic* and in the dialectical passage to the higher category of the 'Concept'.

This dual aspect shows itself in Hegel's actual critique of Spinoza. We have two ways of reconstructing his critique, one implicit and one explicit. The implicit way (which is the more revealing) consists in examining the concluding part of the 'Objective Logic' (the chapter on 'Actuality', with special attention to the sections of the 'Absolute' and the 'Absolute Relation') and its passage to the 'Subjective Logic', in order to see—following Hegel's own advice—how the major Spinozistic ideas, such as the Substance or the Absolute, are integrated, developed and *aufgehoben* in the systematic unfolding of the *Logic*. The other way is to use Hegel's direct references to Spinoza, such as his section on Spinoza in the *History of Philosophy* or his specific Note on Spinoza at the end of the section on the 'Absolute Relation' in the *Logic*. In this paper I shall use both methods, giving some preference to the systematic approach.

II. MAIN POINTS OF CRITICISM

Generally speaking, Hegel understands his critique of Spinoza as an attempt to specify the *coherence conditions* for maintaining Spinoza's own principles, above all his principle of pantheism or immanent totality. It is because Hegel accepts and wishes to maintain Spinoza's pantheistic totality that he demands, for coherence's sake, to remove those other ingredients of Spinoza's thought that make the coherent explication of his main idea impossible.

In particular, Hegel criticizes Spinoza for his one-sided view of negation; his non-dialectical (and therefore incoherent) construal of the concept of totality; and, as a consequence, his view of the totality as an inert thing, a substance, and not an organic and conscious subject. Most of Hegel's detailed criticisms are such that even non-Hegelians might (and often did) voice them. But Hegel tries to *systematize* the various difficulties found in Spinoza by attributing them to a common root : his 'one-sided' view of negation, or his non-dialectical concept of totality. The main flaws are :

1. Substance *qua* substance is only pure being and simple identity, excluding all negation.
2. In that, the absolute also excludes all inner differences and particularization.

3. For this reason, Spinoza cannot show the necessity of there being particular things at all; the finite aspect of the universe remains inexplicable and at best contingent.

4. Even as contingent, Spinoza cannot attribute reality to the finite modes. Although declared to be real, they must be considered the fruit of an 'external reflection' — or the *imaginatio.*

5. Similarly, the so-called attributes cannot count as self-specifications of the substance, but only as external and subjective projections of our minds.

6. The absolute is there as a beginning, not as a result; the modes depend upon the substance unilaterally and do not condition, in their turn, the possibility of the substance itself. The substance is *causa sui* in itself, prior to and independently of its being the cause of the particular modes. (This is the single most important expression of a non-dialectical, non-reciprocal system.)

7. The former points add up to a fundamental break between both aspects of the universe: the infinite and the finite, *natura naturans* and *natura naturata.*

8. Because the totality as such has no inner negativity, it also lacks movement, development and life. (There is movement among the particular modes, but not movement as a constituent of their principle of unity; the totality *qua* this unity remains inert and static.)

9. Finally (and partly as a result of the former), the absolute is perceived as a mere thing (*res*), an unconscious object, devoid of subjectivity, personality and spirit.

Points 1–7 sum up *the lack of dialectical logic in Spinoza.* Point 9 indicates the *lack of subjectivity,* and Point 8 serves as a link between them. Accordingly, Hegel would demand two dialectical corrections in order to overcome Spinoza's shortcomings:

a. The totality must be governed by the negation of negation (or dialectical reciprocity); in other words, the absolute must be conceived as a *result.*

b. The totality must also be conceived as subject.

The first dialectical correction takes place *still on the level of substance* (or 'Objective Logic'); the second correction completes the *Aufhebung* of substance in the 'Subjective Logic' (Kant → Fichte → Hegel).

III. "THE HISTORY OF PHILOSOPHY"

Before elaborating the above points, most of which are reconstructed from the *Logic,* let me examine the section on Spinoza in *The History of Philosophy.* Hegel considers Spinoza here from three different angles : his 'acosmism' ; his improper use of method ; and, as in the *Logic,* his failure to ascribe negativity and subjectivity to the absolute.

1. *Atheism, 'Acosmism' and Pantheism*

Spinoza was traditionally charged with atheism. Hegel reverses the charge, claiming that, on the contrary, the trouble with Spinoza is that "with him there is too much God". In other words, it is not God the infinite, but the finite and particular modes, that are denied actual reality; and this makes Spinoza's system a form not of atheism but, in Hegel's polemical coinage, of 'acosmism' (denial of the reality of the world of finite things).

This critique is based upon the systematic implications of Spinoza's doctrine, not on his official position. Having started with absolute unity and identity, and lacking a dialectical logic, Spinoza is unable to maintain the actuality of particular and finite things. His totality becomes an overpowering principle in which all differences are obliterated and which allows of no real distinctions in the universe — only of modal variations of the same; and whatever does appear as distinct and specific is such by virtue of the imagination, or, in Hegel's language : of an "external reflection" and not by virtue of its objective ontological status. Only the substance, existing *in se* and conceivable *per se,* is an actual individual; whereas the finite modes are but passing and fluctuating *affections* of this single substance. This inability to do justice to the realm of the finite is what Hegel means by having "too much God".

At the same time, and on the same point, Hegel praises Spinoza's achievement in grasping the structure of reality in terms of a single totality in which the dualism of God and world, the transcendent and the immanent, is overcome. This 'pantheism' will serve as the foundation of Hegel's own system ; but in Hegel it will be given a processual and a spiritual dimension. The absolute totality does not exist beforehand and eternally as in Spinoza, but *produces itself as absolute* in the process of history ; and rather than being conceived as an inert or reified substance, the totality of God and world is viewed as a free subject.

Hegel's modified version of Spinoza's pantheism is not less, but more 'scandalous' in terms of conventional theology. With all his daring ideas, Spinoza still adhered to the traditional view that God was eternal and subject to no becoming or change. In Hegel God is not only deprived of his position of absolute transcendence, but is

[75]

even made *the product of a process in time,* namely, of the self-actualization of spirit through human history. Rather than being absolute and eternal from the outset, God, the absolute unity of the immanent and the transcendent, emerges in Hegel as the *outcome* of a process of self-constitution and self-mediation. This view of the 'becoming God' should have earned Hegel — from the viewpoint of traditional theology — an even greater crown of thorns than the one placed on Spinoza's head.

2. The Deductive Method — and Method in General

Hegel's second criticism concerns Spinoza's use of the geometrical method. But Hegel fails to observe that whatever Spinoza does in the *Ethics,* at least in his *Tractatus de Intellectus Emendatione (DIE),* Spinoza provides a rare anticipation of Hegel's own position that any *a priori* method is improper in philosophy.

i. The formal-deductive method is rejected from philosophy because the latter must reflect the 'inner movement' of its own subject matter. Kant distinguished the 'mathematical' from the 'philosophical' method. In philosophy (thus Kant), reason has only itself to build upon, working its way from the less clear and articulate to the more clear and articulate. Clarity and distinctness can be expected in philosophy only at the end, not, as in a deductive system, at the very beginning; and accordingly, the method of philosophy is the *gradual self-explication of reason.* In the 'mathematical' method, on the contrary, we have full clarity and conclusive certainty *at any stage* of the deduction; we do not move, as in philosophy, from lesser to greater clarity of a whole context, but proceed on the level of absolute clarity from one particular item to the next. Hegel's additional reasons: (a) Verification in philosophy depends on the complete systematic context and cannot be obtained prior to its full unfolding ("the true is the whole"). (b) The logical genesis of an idea in philosophy is an integral part of its meaning and truth; it cannot be communicated as a single 'conclusion' and yet retain its meaning or truth-value; and in the same way, the 'proof' is not an external ladder that can be disposed of once the ensuing 'proposition' is reached. In the deductive (or formal) method, however, the process of demonstration is external to the ensuing conclusion, which has a truth-value and a meaning in itself. The logical equipment of 'proofs', 'propositions', etc., indicates an external relation between process and consequent, and is proper, therefore, only in the formal and the empirical sciences (as well as in daily argumentation), but not in philosophy. (c) Philosophy is based on *Vernunft*, not on *Verstand* ; its subject matter is actual reality, which can be expressed only in a logical form that has the characteristics of its content, namely, of organic totality rather than a series of single propositions. (d) More broadly speaking, in philosophy one cannot separate form from content, method from subject matter ; the philosopher is supposed to follow the immanent movement of *die Sache selbst*, as it evolves through contradictions and their partial resolutions ; and the 'method' of philosophy is nothing but the structure of the completed process as it comes to light in *retrospect*. Thus, philosophy has no *a priori* method at all ; it lets its subject matter *structure itself* — and the ensuing shape is called its 'method'.

ii. On the latter point, however, Hegel did not recognize that Spinoza (at least in *DIE*), was his most important forerunner. From Bacon and Galileo, through Descartes to Locke and Kant, modern philosophers have given logical priority to the study of method — or, put more broadly, of epistemology — over the substantive sciences. In order to know, one was first supposed to learn what knowledge was and how it could be correctly obtained.

Spinoza, in the fashion of the day, set out to write in *DIE* his own "essay on method" prior to writing his substantive system ; but what happened to him was not dissimilar — in reverse — to the fate of the biblical Balaam, who came to curse and ended up blessing. Starting with the programme of investigating method prior to having substantive knowledge, Spinoza reverses his original position : method, as the form of true knowledge, can be known only in retrospect, by reflecting upon the structure and properties of some true knowledge that we *already possess*. Method is an 'idea of an idea' (i.e., reflective knowledge) ; but, in order to have this reflection, we must first have the basic true idea. Method is better understood — and the capacity to obtain true knowledge is strengthened — the more substantive knowledge we obtain in fact.

Spinoza may not have been faithful to this doctrine, or he might have had in mind the general idea of epistemology (not method in the narrow sense). Perhaps he violated his own theory, and perhaps he used 'method' to denote the knowledge of knowledge in general, stressing that such a meta-science is possible only by regressing from a given true science and examining its nature and conditions (in which case Spinoza had anticipated a Kantian idea). Be this as it may, the literal text of *DIE*, at least, comes as close to Hegel's rejection of an *a priori* method in philosophy as any important predecessor has ever come.

3. *The Absolute as Simple Identity and Spiritless Substance*

The third criticism in *The History of Philosophy* already overlaps with the fuller discussion in the *Logic,* and so I shall combine them.

In rejecting the formal-deductive method Hegel undoubtedly also rejects the non-dialectical view of negation implied in this method. This is the link between the flaws of method and the flaws of content that Hegel finds in Spinoza's metaphysics :

> Because negation was thus conceived by Spinoza in one-sided fashion merely, there is, in the third place, in his system an utter blotting out of the principle of subjectivity, individuality, personality, the moment of self-consciousness in Being.[3]

This is the most important criticism voiced by Hegel, and it includes many of the points mentioned above. In particular, we see that for Hegel *the lack of a dialectical logic is also responsible for the lack of subjectivity in the absolute.* The 'one-sided' view of negation seems to stand at the root of all of Spinoza's important problems, and therefore it is worthwhile to begin with it.

a. Spinoza conceives of the absolute substance in terms of pure being and simple identity. Its agreement with itself is not based upon a primordial self-differentiating ; it is not construed, as in a dialectical system, as a *return* to self, or as a process of self-*identification* on the basis of previous self-separation ; but the identity of the substance is given beforehand, simply and immediately, in a way that makes any further differentiation logically *impossible.*

This situation is due primarily to the fact that Spinoza defined the absolute, God, as pure being that *"involves no negation"* (*Ethics,* Part I, Def. VI, Expl.). The totality is absolute affirmation, with no inherent principle of negativity. But this, Hegel claims, will make it impossible for it to have inner differences, to particularize itself, to give rise to finite modes or to any other form of limitation — or to movement, change and life. In other words, the exclusion of negativity from the substance *qua* substance must lead to a Parmenidean type of unity, obliterating all distinctions and making all finite entities, all change and dynamism, ontologically impossible.

Hegel understands this criticism to be immanent, based upon Spinoza's own principle that *"determinatio negatio est"*, and on the traditional logic of particularization, as established ever since the Pre-Socratics, according to which all differentiation and movement in the 'one'

---

3   *History of Philosophy,* translation by E.S. Haldane and F.H. Simson, London 1955, p. 287.

presuppose the work of a negative principle in being (Parmenides' "that which is not").

b. If the negation is external to the substance, no finite things can have ontological reality, but must — again in the fashion of Parmenides — be considered the products of a lesser degree of knowledge, the *imaginatio,* or, as Hegel says, an "external reflection". This is, at least in part, admitted by Spinoza himself when he claims that no real distinction exists in the universe, either between the substance and its attributes or modes, or between any two modes. In other words, there are *no real individuals in* the world, except the world as one totality; and all differences must be dismissed as superficial fluctuations or passing states of the same entity. (In claiming that modes are unreal, Hegel does not represent Spinoza's official doctrine, but takes sides in a well-known interpretative debate.)

c. Even assuming, for the sake of the argument, that the modes can be explained as real, they are still merely contingent in the sense that there is no necessity for the substance to produce them. In fact, Spinoza is unable to show the necessity of there being particular things at all, and the finite aspect of reality (his *natura naturata*) remains inexplicable and, at best, contingent. Not only is every particular mode contingent in itself — namely, there is nothing inconceivable in its not having been — but the very existence of a *natura naturata* must be considered contingent, for, given the lack of negativity in the absolute, it is perfectly conceivable that there would be no finite things at all. Thus, contrary to Hegel's dialectical conception of a totality (in which the contingent aspect of being is itself logically necessary), in Spinoza there is no logical necessity in there being contingent entities at all ("contingency itself is contingent"). This criticism could be made also by a non-Hegelian, when closely examining one of the most crucial propositions in the *Ethics* (Part I, Prop. XVI). This proposition introduces, for the first time, the plurality of modes that are supposed to flow "necessarily" from the substance. Yet Prop. XVI itself has a somewhat contingent (or arbitrary) status, for it is not deduced from the foregoing propositions or axioms, but is rather defended in isolation, as if it represented a new First Principle.

In Hegelian terms this problem is only *formal*; to Hegel the whole deductive chain is but a stylistic cover for a system whose real organization lies on a deeper and covert level. But at least he could find here a seemingly isolated difficulty which, although it might also be noticed by other critics, Hegel could interpret more systematically by grounding it, too, in the same basic flaw in Spinoza.

[79]

d. The so-called 'attributes', as well, cannot be construed as inner specifications of the one substance; we must therefore dismiss them as products of our subjective minds, which we *project* upon the structure of the substance. In this criticism Hegel again gives a more fundamental interpretation to a well-known Spinozistic problem. Spinoza defines an attribute as "that *which the intellect perceives* as constituting the essence of substance" (*Ethics,* Part I, Def. IV). Hegel reads this as if the attribute is only subjective, explaining this, too, by the lack of inner negativity in the absolute, which deprives it of objective self-differentiation. Hegel thus takes sides in a well-known interpretative controversy over the nature of the attributes; and, although he might even have started this debate, his reading of Spinoza does not necessarily presuppose a specific Hegelian outlook, and was in fact shared by others. Yet, while other readers would ground the subjectivity of the attributes only on textual evidence such as the above-quoted definition, Hegel further supports his reading by his deeper systematic criticism: It is *because* the substance is conceived as a simple and not as a dialectical identity that the attributes must be merely subjective and empirical, expressing the limitations of our minds rather than objective differences within the absolute.

e. All the former points indicate a non-dialectical construal of totality. In fact, ever since the Milesian school, the problem of totality — the relation of the One and the Many within a single system — has not been solved satisfactorily. Either the One was put forth as predominant, in which case, as in Parmenides, even in Plato, and (Hegel thinks) certainly Spinoza, the Many could not be done justice to; or, the Many were predominant, in which case the One would be sacrificed and a form of nominalism or empiricism would ensue. Nor was dualism the answer, at least not for an avowed monist like Spinoza. The only coherent construal of a totality, Hegel argues, is by way of a dialectical logic; any other construal would break down into a new dualism, or sacrifice one side for the sake of the other. The very concept of a totality implies a contradiction: a system that is at once One and Many, Universal and Particular, Being and Becoming, etc. Indeed, in the dialectical construal of the concept of totality, all the old Platonic opposites are considered as mediating each other in a single process; the universal becomes such only by way of its self-particularization, from which it is reconstituted as a 'concrete' universal; the One becomes what it is only by way of the Many which evolve from it and, in their regained unity, *constitute* the One; the identity of the system is constituted by way of a process of self-differentiation and as a movement of 'return to self' from this differentiation; identity is not immediately and simply given, but is the result of a process of *reidentification*, etc. A dialectical construal of the totality would require, first, the understanding that the absolute involves negation in its inner constitution, and, consequently, that it is the *result* of a process of self-particularization by which it regains (or, constitutes) its dialectical unity and its very status as absolute. For this reason, the major flaw that Hegel finds in Spinoza's theory of substance is that the modes depend upon the substance *unilaterally* : the substance is considered first as *causa sui*, independently of the modes, and, then, it is also supposed to be the cause of the modes as a distinct and secondary act.

IV. THE "LOGIC": THE FIRST DIALECTICAL CORRECTION

Most of Hegel's chapter on the 'Absolute' in the *Logic* is given to refuting this view and presenting his first dialectical correction to Spinoza's outlook — a correction that, as we have seen, already takes place on the level of substance and 'Objective Logic' — namely, that the absolute is the result of its own process of self-constitution, a process that takes place through the mediation of the finite modes. Certainly, the substance is cause of itself, but what is the 'itself' of which it is the cause? Is it a tautological identity, or is it its own 'self' in the form of an 'other'? Only the latter would satisfy both the dialectical concept of totality and the coherence conditions for maintaining such a concept at all. The substance is cause of itself in that it is the cause of the infinity of modes which is nothing but itself in the form of its opposite; or : the infinite, eternal, unitarian aspect of the universe is cause of itself in that it is the cause of the finite, temporal, pluralistic aspect of the universe; both being opposite moments of the *same* system, of the same dialectical unity. The world as *natura naturans* and the world as *natura naturata* are one, Spinoza says; let him then construe them in such a way that *natura naturans* will be *causa sui*, not directly and in itself, but in that it is the cause of the *natura naturata* — which is nothing but itself in the form of 'otherness'. In a word, the concept of *causa sui* is realized in that the one substance particularizes itself into the modes and becomes cause of itself *through being the cause of the modes*. Only then, as the *result* of this mediation, can the absolute totality emerge and be constituted as such.

[81]

V. THE SECOND DIALECTICAL CORRECTION: THE ABSOLUTE AS SUBJECT

By introducing negativity into the absolute as such and viewing it as a result, we have reinterpreted the substance as an *organic* totality. A dialectical totality is organic in that its unity is the result of the inter-relation of the many particulars — which also are not primordial, but emerge from their unifying principle while at the same time reconstituting it. An organic totality, however, is a *subject-like* totality. The concept of 'subject' denotes, in Hegel, not only a conscious being, but, in a more primitive sense, any organized totality whose governing logic is the same as that governing the activity of the 'ego'. The unity of a subject in the sense of 'ego' or self-consciousness is such — as Kant has already shown — that his identity is not given beforehand, but is a *result* of a process of self-identification: only by ascribing to himself, as his own particularizations, his many thoughts, can he also constitute and recognize his own identity as self. Here the main difference between Kant and Hegel is that, for Kant, the manifold of cogitations is given externally, while Hegel speaks of this manifold as self-particularizations of the subject. However, they both agree on the other point, that the identity is constituted and is not given immediately. In this way, *the structure of the subject as 'Ego' is a model of the structure of any dialectical totality* (it is, Hegel says, "the concept of the Concept").

And, since we have already found a dialectical (or organic) totality on the level of substance, this means that we have discovered there a subject-like structure, or that we have discovered, implicitly, our own structure as subjects within the structure of what seemed to be a merely 'objective' and 'reified' substance. In this way, the first dialectical correction leads to the second — to the *Aufhebung* of the whole sphere of the substance and of 'Objective Logic' — and to the revolutionary discovery, made explicit with Kant, that *the structure of the object and that of the subject is basically the same.*

By introducing a dialectical logic into the Spinozistic totality we have not only brought the 'Objective Logic' to its climax, but negated the purely objectivist approach to the world. With Spinoza's totality made organic, we discover our own subjective image in what we have all along considered as something purely external, which only *confronted* us. By contemplating the external world in terms of a totality, and in trying to make the Spinozistic view more coherent, our thinking has been driven back to itself, finding its own shape and mark in what seemed to be an inert substance. It is not to itself as mere

subject confronting an object which is merely external that our thinking was pushed back, but to itself as a principle of the objective
world, too; it is the principle of idealism — the basic unity of the
structure of the object and the structure of the subject — that has
now come to the fore.*

VI. CRITICAL COMMENTS

Hegel's main criticism does apply to Spinoza. The break between
the finite and the infinite aspects of reality is indeed an inevitable
systematic consequence in Spinoza — and a rather averse one from
his own monistic viewpoint. Moreover, I think one can defend the
claim that the dialectical conception of totality is the only coherent
construal of this concept, and that only such a dialectical conception
could have remedied the dualistic impasse in Plato, the early Pre-
Socratics, or any other form of dualism or of unsuccessful monism
as well. However, the question is why should we conceive the world
as a totality at all, or, more specifically, as a global unification of
finite particulars. It may be that — as Hegel tries to show systematically and as others have claimed rather dogmatically — this is 'in
the nature' of human rationality : we look for unity, plurality and
totality in the world. Supposing that we do, I think that Spinoza
has not given a fully coherent answer, and that Hegel's is superior.
But even if, as rational creatures, we demand to have systematic
explanations of the world as a totality, perhaps there is no legitimate
answer at all, neither that of Spinoza nor its logical improvement in
Hegel's system? Perhaps, as Kant claims, any such metaphysics will

---

*   This subjectivation of the absolute also does justice, of course, to the
religious metaphor of God as a person, a singular mind, as against the
picture of God as a mere thing or an inert nature.

But subject and spirit are not synonyms; there is still a way to go from
the first subjectivation of the absolute to the realization of Spirit in its
full sense. The latter will not be attained in the field of philosophy or
contemplation alone, as a sphere closed upon itself, but will require the
mediation of human practice in history as a precondition for the emergence
of absolute philosophical knowledge. Indeed, the higher sense of the absolute being a 'subject' — or better, of its being Spirit — implies its inevitable historization. And it is also the lack of a historical dimension in
Spinoza's system — his failure to ascribe dynamism to being and to view
the absolute spirit as the result of its own self-constitution, as well as his
attempt to reduce all reality to a rigid mechanistic or 'mathematical'
model — that calls forth Hegel's supreme objection.

be 'dogmatic' in that it transcends the limits of human reason and commits the flaw of constructing a speculative answer to questions we cannot renounce. Coherence is not the ultimate virtue; observing the limits of human rationality is more important, I think, than consummating its speculative potential.

Y. BELAVAL

Paris

Réponse au Professeur Yovel

IL EST DIFFICILE d'être clair sur des auteurs aussi difficiles que Spinoza, Hegel, et vous l'avez été. Que pourrais-je donc vous répondre ? Le plus sage serait de vous féliciter et de me taire. Condamné à parler, je ne puis que vous démarquer en déplaçant vos points de vue.

Le sujet que vous avez choisi, "Substance without Spirit", est tellement central que c'est à lui, je crois, qu'il faut penser, pour comprendre la fameuse proclamation de la *Geschichte der Philosophie* (*Jubilee*, éd. Glockner, XV, p. 374) : "*Spinoza ist Hauptpunkt der modernen Philosophie : entweder Spinozismus oder keine Philosophie.*" Et, plus loin (p. 376) : "*Wenn man anfangt zu philosophieren, so muss zuerst spinozist seyn.*" Sujet central, non seulement pour la critique de Spinoza par Hegel, mais pour toute la philosophie hégélienne.

Quelle lecture Hegel a-t-il fait de Spinoza ? Quelle lecture faites-vous vous-même de Hegel?

Hegel, il nous le dit, a travaillé sur l'édition Paulus (1802–1803) à laquelle il a collaboré en s'aidant (p. 371) d'une traduction française ; il a lu les articles de Brucker (démarqués par Diderot dans l'*Encyclopédie*), et il a eu aussi recours à la *Geschichte der neueren Philosophie* de Bukle (p. 397). Il ne cite pas l'article de Bayle. Que retient-il de ces lectures ? Avant tout, ce qui intéresse la *Substance* et le *mos geometricum* dans l'*Ethique*. Curieusement, ce n'est pas dans l'*Ethique*, mais dans la Lettre L à Jarig Jelles qu'il va chercher la formule-clef de sa critique : *Omnis determinatio est negatio*, illustré par l'exemple du cercle, comme si cet objet d'entendement, figé dans l'étendue inerte, dénonçait par lui-même l'insuffisance de la réflexion externe, nous invitait à rendre à *determinatio* son double sens, actif et passif, de *déterminant/déterminé* et, du coup, à *negatio*, son double sens. Hegel n'a pas lu que l'*Ethique*. Il ne s'attarde pas au *De intellectus emendatione* qui, pourtant, vous en avez fait la

[85]

remarque, semble anticiper la critique hégélienne : la méthode *a priori* est impropre à la philosophie. Hegel ne cite pas toujours ses sources. Dans la *Phénoménologie de l'Esprit*, Section VI, il parle des Grecs, de l'*Aufklärung*, etc., mais, écrit le P. Dominique Dubarle, "la vraie référence, la référence concrète et concrètement vécue, c'est Spinoza et le *Tractatus theologico-politicus*, bien plus que Sophocle et Antigone, si remarquable que soit ce que Hegel en dit au début de la Section 'Esprit'..." ; et, plus loin (p. 273), à propos du *Gottesdienst*, "la philosophie hégélienne se fait en tout ceci fort proche de celle du *Tractatus theologico-politicus*" où la théologie et l'éthique, d'un mot la dimension spécifiquement intellectuelle de la religion passe à la philosophie ("De la Foi au Savoir dans la Phénoménologie de l'Esprit", *Revue des Sciences Philosophiques et Théologiques*, LIX[1975], pp. 3–37, 243–277, 399–425).

A quoi tendent ces remarques préliminaires ? A se demander dans quelle mesure on ne risque pas de commettre une "mauvaise abstraction" — comme l'entend Hegel — en extrayant d'un tout systématique certains textes plutôt que d'autres. On répliquera que cela est inévitable. Bien sûr ! Mais il n'est pas inévitable d'éviter la question, surtout quand elle est "trop connue", *zu bekannt*.

En ce qui vous concerne, Monsieur, vous avez retenu l'article *Spinoza* dans l'*Histoire de la philosophie* et la Section sur la *Wirklichkeit*, au Livre II de la *Wissenschaft der Logik*, plus précisément le chapitre sur l'Absolu, avec son *Anmerkung*, et le chapitre sur le rapport absolu. Ce choix s'imposait même si, Hegel n'ayant pas répété toujours les mêmes choses sur Spinoza, on devait indiquer parfois des variantes. En fait, c'est l'*Histoire de la philosophie* qui vous requiert le plus : 13 pages de votre Résumé sur 17. On s'en étonne un peu. Car enfin, cet article sur Spinoza est un Cours dont de nombreuses pages sont à peine rédigées, tandis que la Section III, Livre II, de la *Logique* est d'une rédaction serrée, et la place qu'y occupe Spinoza d'une particulière signification. Mais n'importe !

Ce qui importe davantage est le risque de "mauvaise abstraction" auquel, encore une fois, on s'expose en séparant un auteur de ses conditions historiques. En vous en tenant à vos textes, vous mettez en dialogue Hegel et Spinoza. Cela présuppose qu'ils s'expriment dans la même langue et que nous-mêmes nous les comprenons — dans quelle langue? Je crois que nous avons besoin d'un interprète entre Spinoza et Hegel. Je m'en suis convaincu expérimentalement lorsque j'ai voulu mettre en dialogue Hegel et Leibniz sur le problème de l'essence, ce qui m'a entraîné au Commentaire presque littéral du Livre II de la *Logique* (voir mes *Etudes leibniziennes*, éd. Gallimard,

Paris 1976). Mon interprète a été Kant. J'ai commencé à y voir clair en découvrant — et, je l'espère, en démontrant — que ce Livre II suivait le plan et les idées, les *Reflexionsbegriffe,* de *l'Amphibologie* à la fin de cette *Analytique* qu'on pourrait appeler le *Traité de l'Entendement* du philosophe de Koenigsberg : par l'intermédiaire de ce Manifeste anti-leibnizien Hegel pouvait entrer en dialogue avec Leibniz. Qu'il y ait eu en Philosophie une révolution copernicienne signifie que rien n'est plus *après* comme *avant* et que les mêmes mots ne gardent plus le même sens. Le post-cartésien Spinoza et le post-kantien Hegel ne parlent plus la même langue. Pour en rester à votre propos, et à quelques exemples, on ne traduira pas *Substantia* (*Res aut Substantia,* dit Descartes) par *Substanz* (Sujet), *Cogito* (constatatif) par *Ich denke* (constitutif), *Realitas* (ou même *Actualitas*) par *Wirklichkeit,* l'*in se* de l'intuition intellectuelle — *per Substantiam intelligo id, quod in se est, et per se concipitur,* dèf. 3 — par *in sich, a priori* causal par *a priori* conditionnant (ou déterminant), etc. etc. C'est à la lumière de ces différences que je voudrais reprendre, pour les éclairer autrement, quelques idées essentielles à votre Communication.

Je m'en tiendrai à la *Substance.*

Où Hegel en parle-t-il ? Dans l'article de la *Geschichte* ce ne peut être qu'au début, puisqu'il y commente, dans l'ordre, l'*Ethique* : que ce soit au début ne signifie rien d'autre. Au contraire, la place qu'occupe, dans la *Wissenschaft der Logik,* la critique de la substance spinoziste est importante par sa signification dialectique. Elle se situe à la fin de la *Logique objective* (= de l'objet), ce qui nous apprend tout de suite : (1) que ce qui est critiqué, c'est la substance-objet; (2) et que cette substance-objet doit être "dépassée", car nous avons encore à lire la *Logique subjective* et, on le sait, *die Bewegung des Wesens ist überhaupt das Werden zum Begriffe* (II, 153).

D'une manière plus précise, comme la *Wissenschaft der Logik* se modèle sur les catégories kantiennes qu'elle dialectise et transpose de la topique psychologique *(Sinnlichkeit–Verstand–Vernunft)* à la topique de la logique dialectique *(Sein–Schein–Begriff),* la critique de la substance spinoziste se situe au niveau de la *Modalité* dont elle emprunte — aux Postulats de la pensée empirique — le titre, *die Wirklichkeit,* et les notions modales de *bestimmbar / Bestimmung* exploitées dans l'*Amphibologie.* Toute l'Analytique de la *Critique de la raison pure* s'est appliquée à la constitution de l'*objet du physicien* — Newton, par exemple — qu'on appelle le *Monde.* Il s'agit du seul monde des phénomènes. La substance qui figure dans la Catégorie de la Relation n'est donc pas celle du métaphysicien, mais *substantia phenomenôn*. Ce n'est plus une chose en soi, un *Ding an sich*, mais seulement une chose par nous et pour nous.

Il en résulte, chez Hegel qui interprète Spinoza à travers Kant — et Fichte — que la substance-objet, en tant qu'elle nous apparaît — c'est-à-dire *scheint*, est conçue par son essence, et *erscheint*, se phénoménise (la deuxième Section du Livre II est passée du *Schein* à l'*Existenz* et à l'*Erscheinung*) — cette substance ne peut plus être entendue comme *id, quod in se est*. L'un des deux attributs divins qu'invoque Spinoza, l'étendue, se *désubstantialise* et, du même coup, le monde, dont il est le support, retombe au rang des "apparences". Hegel — peu importe l'inspiration accidentelle qu'il a pu ici recevoir de Jacobi et du *Pantheismus-streit* — se croit donc en droit de conclure à l'*akosmismus* (*Gesch.* pp. 373, 390) et de sauver ainsi Spinoza de l'athéisme.

Le second attribut divin que nous connaissons, la Pensée, n'est qu'en partie une "apparence". Il est "apparence" comme *gedacht*, mais "être" comme *Denken*. Le *Ich denke* kantien *fait* les phénomènes en unifiant les données de la sensibilité sous les formes des Catégories et par l'intermédiaire du schématisme : mais lui-même il n'apparaît pas, il ne peut être phénomène. Fichte corrige Kant en détachant de l'entendement les Catégories pour les attacher à l'imagination, et supprime l'idée de noumène, ce qui revient à rompre avec le *Ding an sich* et, par conséquent, avec la substance-objet. En outre, à propos du *Ich denke*, il accuse la différence entre *connaissant* et *connu*. Tout est prêt pour la critique idéaliste de la substance spinoziste. Rompant avec la topique psychologique de Kant (*Sinnlichkeit-Verstand-Vernunft*), dépassant la topique de la *Phénoménologie de l'Esprit* qui traite de la Conscience (*Bewusstsein–Selbstbewusstsein–Vernunft*), établissant son onto-logique sur la topique *Sein–Schein–Begriff*, Hegel consomme la rupture avec le noumène kantien en faisant du *Ich denke* le concept des concepts, le déterminant des déterminants, sous la régulation suprême de l'Idée.

Et il reprend de Fichte l'opposition du connaissant et du connu. On dira que l'opposition est banale. Oui. Mais elle ne peut avoir le même sens après Descartes et après Kant. A la lumière du *Cogito* cartésien, le *connaître* est assimilé au regard : il ne produit pas l'idée innée, il la découvre, il la reçoit. L'*activité* de la pensée s'applique à la *passivité* de l'entendement. Spinoza, certes, n'adopte pas cette conséquence du dualisme : la troisième définition du Livre II de l'*Ethique*, suivie de son Explication, distingue *concept* et *perception* : *Dico potius conceptum quam perceptionem, quia perceptionis nomen indicare videtur, Mentem ab objecto pati ; at conceptus actionem Mentis exprimere videtur.* Mais cette *Explicatio* maintient la dualité du sujet et de l'objet sans introduire entre eux leur propre différence et, donc, leur mouvement réciproque, leur *Bewegung* dialectique. De même, dans le couple cause/effet, l'activité reste du côté de la cause, et la passivité est attribuée à l'effet. Suffit-il de passer *à l'infini* pour parvenir à l'*unité* de la cause et de l'effet ? On le croirait d'abord. Hegel salue dans la *Causa sui* spinoziste un vrai concept spéculatif, car s'y affirme l'unité de la cause et de l'effet, de l'essence et de l'existence. Malheureusement cette affirmation est *unmittelbar*, abstraite en vocabulaire hégélien. D'où la condamnation en fin de paragraphe : *"Hätte Spinoza näher entwickelt, was in der Causa sui liegt, so wäre seine Substanz nicht das Starre"* (*Gesch.*, p. 379). Cette substance demeure figée, pétrifiée: une *Res*. On comprend que Condillac se soit récrié: "Que penser d'un langage qui mène à dire qu'une substance s'est produite elle-même ?" (*Traité des Systèmes*, dans *Oeuvres*, Livre I, éd. Leroy, Paris 1947–1948, p. 189). Et, en effet, ce langage peut paraître absurde tant qu'il s'agit d'une substance-objet. Qu'a-t-il manqué à Spinoza ?

Sans doute — mais pour cela il fallait être post-kantien et non post-cartésien — de traduire *Causa sui* en *Reflexion*. Le *Ich denke* ne se fait apparaître (*der Schein*) comme *Moi* (*Mich*) que par le retour à *soi*, sans lequel il ne saurait pas qu'il se produit : il ne s'objective qu'en s'intériorisant. C'est le retour en soi réflexif qui fait défaut à la substance spinoziste. Dès lors, ses déterminations sont abstraites, elles s'arrêtent à des négations de logique formelle ; l'absence de retour en soi empêche de les dépasser, de les nier dialectiquement par la négation interne de la négation extérieure. Ainsi, la totalité ne peut plus être obtenue comme accomplissement de la réflexion spéculative. L'absolu se fige en objet. Il n'est pas l'abîme où, d'abord, la réflexion se perd, l'*Abgrund* où toutes les déterminations vont par le fond (*zugrunde gehen*) et qui pourtant en est aussi le *Grund* (*W. d. L.*, Livre II, p. 159). Tandis, donc, que des deux attributs divins connaissables, l'étendue ne s'accorde qu'avec l'apparence du monde et ne soutient qu'un acosmisme, la pensée, parce qu'elle n'est pas intériorisée (*erinnerte*) par la réflexion, ne remonte pas jusqu'au Sujet absolu dont elle émane.

Hegel, avais-je noté au début, a surtout retenu de l'*Ethique* ce qui intéresse la *Substance* et le *mos geometricum*. Nous comprenons pourquoi. C'est que la dialectique serait incompatible avec la substance-objet, elle ne peut être la logique de l'infini qu'avec la substance-sujet ; c'est aussi qu'après le passage de la logique formelle à la logique transcendentale qu'elle parachève, elle est incompatible avec la réflexion extérieure du *mos geometricum*. Quand Marx prétendra remettre sur ses pieds la philosophie hégélienne, tout en en conservant la dialectique, il n'en reviendra pas pour autant à la substance-objet, mais il substituera à la substance-sujet, dont l'Esprit interdit le matérialisme, ce qu'on peut appeler la substance-action et son activité permet le mouvement dialectique.

WERNER MARX

Freiburg

Reply to Professor Yovel

PROFESSOR YOVEL has given an accurate, most lucid and excellently organized account of Hegel's own arguments as stated in the *Logic* and the *History of Philosophy*. Hegel's arguments are meant, first of all, to criticize Spinoza's position by pointing out what is lacking in Spinoza's system, and, secondly, to demonstrate and show how Spinoza's position served as the foundation of Hegel's own system. I have no quarrel with Yovel's rendering of Hegel, except that I might have placed Spinoza's *causa sui* in the centre, as Hegel considered it a "fundamental term of everything speculative". Hegel writes: "If Spinoza would have more closely developed what is inherent in the *causa sui*, then his substance would not have remained something rigid." [1]

Yovel has added one note of his own to his account by entitling his contribution "Substance without Spirit". He took his clue from the famous dictum in the Preface to the *Phenomenology of Spirit*, according to which that which is true should be comprehended not only as substance but also as subject. [2]

The *Phenomenology of Spirit* [3] is the science which demonstrates the pathway of Spirit in shapes of phenomenal knowledge (*erscheinendes Wissen*) and actions which follow each other necessarily — resulting in the last shape, where Spirit as absolute knowledge is able to

---

1   G.W.F. Hegel, *Sämtliche Werke — Jubiläumsausgabe*, Stuttgart 1969, p. 379.
2   G. W. F. Hegel, *Phänomenologie des Geistes*, Hamburg 1952, p. 19. See also p. 41 of the full text of Yovel's paper as printed in the collection of papers submitted to me prior to the Entretiens in Jerusalem (quoted here as *Collection*).
3   Cf. regarding the following: W. Marx, *Hegel's Phenomenology of Spirit, Its Point and Purpose — A Commentary on the Preface and Introduction*, New York–Evanston–San Francisco 1975, pp. 7 ff.

demonstrate the absolute in the form of the science of logic. Yovel obviously has only the pathway of the *Phenomenology* of 1807 in mind when he attempts to establish the specific difference between Hegel and Spinoza by pointing out that both the special pathway and its result are lacking in the Spinozistic system.

It is of great importance for Yovel's understanding of the Hegelian absolute that he consider this pathway of phenomenal knowledge and actions — which at the same time is the self-actualization of Spirit and return of absolute Spirit to itself[4] — solely as human history, which he in turn qualifies as one of "human practice". Yovel states : "... the realization of Spirit in its full sense... will not be attained in the sphere of contemplation, or on mere philosophy, but would require human practice in history."[5]

It is history so conceived which serves Yovel as the basis for his differentiation between Hegel and Spinoza.[6]

Yovel declares furthermore that the absolute itself is historized. I quote Yovel : "It is, in the last analysis, the lack of a historical dimension in Spinoza's thought that constitutes Hegel's supreme objection, and it is the *historization* of the absolute that constitutes the higher sense of its being a subject..."[7]

As my first point of criticism, I would like to take issue with this

---

4   *Ibid.,* pp. 54 ff.
5   *Collection,* p. 65.
6   The full text of the paragraph changed reads:

This subjectivization of the absolute also does justice, of course, to the religious metaphor of God as a person, a singular mind — as against the picture of God as a mere thing or an inert nature. But subject and spirit are not synonyms ; there is still a way to go from the first subjectivization of the absolute to the realization of Spirit in its full sense — the latter will not be attained in the sphere of contemplation, or mere philosophy alone but would require human practice in history. Hence the last and perhaps most important aspect of Hegel's criticism of Spinoza we have mentioned in passing which must come explicitly to the foreground at the end : the totality of God and world, of the immanent and the transcendent — in that it is a result and not an absolute beginning, in that it constitutes itself as absolute by way of a process of self-differentiation, in that it actualizes the principle of pantheism in a more coherent (i.e., subjective and developmental) sense — must therefore be conceived at *historical.* It is, in the last analysis, the lack of a historical dimension in Spinoza's thought that constitutes Hegel's supreme objection, and it is the *historization* of the absolute that constitutes the higher sense of its being a 'subject' — or rather, as we may call it in this context — of its being *Spirit.*

7   *Ibid.,* p. 66.

thesis of Yovel's paper. It obviously involves Hegel scholarship, and I admit at the outset in fairness to Prof. Yovel that there can be many different readings of Hegel. However, to speak of a "historization" of the absolute seems in itself to be a *contradictio in adjecto*. A view according to which history has such a power over the absolute is obviously a relativistic one, and in my view could never be Hegel's. Prof. Yovel seems to have arrived at this unfortunate expression because he did not clearly define the role which history has in the self-production of Spirit and in the Hegelian system as a whole. No doubt, in the *Phenomenology of the Spirit* history, i.e. time, is the element within which Spirit becomes increasingly manifest to itself. This is, however, only the external element of Spirit itself.[8] Spirit in its adequate form, in its truth, that is absolute Spirit, is not historical, if to be "historical" means to be a "product of time". It would be more appropriate to say that time, history, and man's activity are products of absolute Spirit which has "reduced" itself by itself to a state of mere "appearance".[9] The *Phenomenology* is, in this sense, *eine erscheinende Wissenschaft*.[10] True, the *Phenomenology* is a *Bildungsgeschichte*, a history where the subject *qua* phenomenal knowledge recognizes more and more that, and in which way, it is Spirit and has been Spirit all along, until it rises to the point of view of Science. This *Bildungsgeschichte* is, however, nothing but the medium where Spirit attains the consciousness of itself, conceives of itself, i.e. returns to itself.

In reading the *Phenomenology* one must never lose sight of the movement of Spirit.[11] The philosopher who accompanies phenomenal knowledge and actions on their way knows all along that the timeless categories which in the *Phenomenology* are embodied in shapes of consciousness have been steering this history from its beginning and have organized it.[12] Yovel does not recognize this fact, nor does he see that once "phenomenal" knowledge has become absolute knowledge, and that is knowledge of the absolute, history as *Bildungsge-*

---

8   *Phänomenologie des Geistes,* pp. 31 ff.

9   N. Rotenstreich, *From Substance to Subject,* The Hague 1974, pp. 57 ff.

10 Cf. *Phänomenologie des Geistes (op. cit.,* n. 2), p. 66. W. Marx *(op. cit.,* n. 3), pp. 24 f., 87.

11 *Phänomenologie des Geistes (op. cit.,* n. 2), pp. 32 f. ; cf. W. Marx *(op. cit.,* n. 3), p. 87.

12 Cf. in W. Marx *(op. cit.,* n. 3), the chapter "The Role of the Phenomenologist and the Genesis of the Concept of Science", specifically pp. 85 ff., and idem, "Die Dialektik und die Rolle des Phänomenologen", *Hegel-Jahrbuch* 1974, Köln 1975, pp. 381–387 (X. Internationaler Hegel-Kongress, Moskau 1974).

schichte ceases; the goal of the *Phenomenology* is reached: consciousness has risen to the point of view of Science, which is tantamount to Spirit knowing itself as Spirit. History no longer has any function. For Yovel history seems to go on, it seems to proceed in the manner of a bad infinity, while for Hegel the timeless genesis of the System begins.[13] This is the development of "concept in itself" (*Begriff an sich*), which in its most concrete form in the *objective Logic* is the relationship of *substance* to *Begriff für sich* ("concept for itself"), in the *subjective Logic*, and that means to *subject*. This timeless genesis in the *Science of Logic*, and not "history", is the authentic element which demonstrates why "that which is true should be comprehended not only as substance but as subject", and which establishes the relationship of the absolute and the infinite to the finite, which constitutes the problem of "pantheism". The dictum quoted is contained in the preface to the *Phenomenology*, which Hegel also meant as a preface to the *Science of Logic*.

Since I cannot share Prof. Yovel's conception of the role of history in Hegel, I cannot agree with the thesis of his paper, that it is the lack of a historical dimension in Spinoza's thought that constitutes Hegel's supreme objection, and I certainly do not agree with his reading of Hegel, that it is "the *historization* of the absolute that constitutes the higher sense of its being a 'subject' ".[14] This concludes my first point of criticism. I now proceed to the second.

Yovel has, in my view, quite correctly explained the power of the subjectivity or negativity which, working as it were within the totality, produces the logical genesis. This is actually the movement of identity. At the end of his paper Prof. Yovel has characterized this movement in a language which prompts me to ask for a clarification. When describing "totality" as "subject-like", he characterizes it as one "whose governing logic is the same as the one governing the activity of the ego".[15] In doing so, Yovel correctly refers to Kant, however, without specifically mentioning his conception of the "transcendental apperception". What irritates me is that he proceeds to explain — I quote — that "the structure of the subject as Ego is a model of the structure of any dialectical totality." [16]

---

13   I note that Yovel has now accepted at least some important points of my view regarding the relationship of history and the Absolute set forth in the following, in stating that "the mediation of human practice in history" is only a "precondition of absolute philosophical knowledge" (*Collection*, p. 64).

14   *Ibid.*, p. 66.

15   *Ibid.*, p. 63.

16   *Ibid.*, p. 66.

He also declares: "With Spinoza's totality made organic, we discover our own subjective image in what we have all along considered as something purely external, that only confronted us."[17] "Our thinking was driven back to itself" — Prof. Yovel states in another passage[18] — "finding its own shape and mark in what seemed to be an inert substance". I am not quite sure whether in so characterizing "subject" Yovel does not covertly assume two totalities, one of the ego and another one of the sphere of the non-ego. Fichte had seen reality in this way; Schelling also still treated the two spheres by way of two systems, the system of the philosophy of nature, and the system of transcendental idealism. Hegel's new step, already at a time when he was still Schelling's closest friend, i.e. in the *Differenzschrift* of 1801, is to be seen in his insight that both spheres are one because identity is "identity of non-identity and identity". In his essays in the *Journalschriften* Hegel has explicitly shown this relationship within identity to be the principle constituting all reality. He demonstrated why "transcendental apperception" as the unity of thinking and being must be understood not statically but as the movement of a negating self-relation, i.e. self-differentiation and self-determination. In his later writings Hegel made it very clear that this principle posits difference as the sphere of the other; but because this sphere of the other is the "otherness of itself" (*das Andere seiner selbst*), it is also self-relating negation and, therefore, identity by way of negation. Thus, it returns to the original self-negating unity of identity. This process of the principle produces as its result a totality of interrelated differences and determinations, a totality which Rotenstreich, in his important book *From Substance to Subject*, has called an "organic totality". Precisely because for Hegel this one principle is the principle of all that is, it seems to be somewhat misleading when Yovel speaks of the objective side as being fashioned according to the model, image, mark or shape of the subjective side.

I wish to mention as a third point of criticism the fact that Prof. Yovel does not deal with the possibility of a meta-critique of Hegel in his paper. It is surprising that he has failed to do so when one considers the entire point of departure of his paper. He calls it "Substance without Spirit", a title which clearly refers to Spinoza's conception of substance, and not to Hegel's. As to Hegel's conception of substance, Hegel depicted it in the *Science of Logic*[19] as that of a totality

---

17 *Ibid.*, p. 64.
18 *Loc. cit.*
19 G. W. F. Hegel, *Wissenschaft der Logik*, II, ed. G. Lasson, Hamburg 1963, pp. 170, 184, 186.

developed from negatively relational categories, specifically from actuality — the power which "manifests itself or shines" in its own sphere of otherness, in its own sphere of accidents or modes and their totality, world. This particular conception of actuality and of substance is possible because, in the *Science of Logic*, right from the start, the concept in itself, the absolute, the *causa sui*, had duality, difference, negativity in itself, and must, therefore, in its own logical element differentiate and determine itself until it reveals itself to be concept for itself : subject. The Hegelian "substance" is so construed that it *cannot possibly be one "without" subject,* or, expressed in terms of the *Phenomenology* and of *Realphilosophy,* "without Spirit". But what about *Spinoza's* substance ; was his substance not so construed from the outset that it should never be subject or Spirit ? What about a substance which has, in so many words, been defined to be one which precludes all negations, all determinations and limitations ; to be a substance and as such a *causa sui* which precisely does not have negativity, duality, difference in itself, and which therefore can not be self-developing and self-determining ? Must one not therefore raise the question whether Spinoza called substance "unique" (in the Correlarium 1b, Prop. XIV, Part I, *Ethics*) because it should never suffer determination, and has he not conceived of the attributes in such a way that they can never be dialectically developed from substance as Hegel demanded ? To develop these questions a little further : What precisely was the status of the attributes in Spinoza ? I admit this is a very controversial issue. Were they, however, ever meant to be "determinations" of absolute substance ? Were they not rather conceived of as infinites in themselves, and if so how could they possible be negatives, as they are with Hegel? They are — according to Def. 4 of *Ethics* I, *"that* which the intellect" — be it finite or infinite — "perceives of substance", and the intellect is only a modification of one attribute of substance, and is, in its highest mode, actualized by the philosopher's "intuitive knowledge". Could Spinoza then ever have ascribed to "finite intellect" the power to demonstrate through speculative logic the eternal essence of God, a power which Hegel in the preface to the *Science of Logic* ascribed to a philosophical thought-actualizing concept?

Furthermore, Hegel gave primacy to thought over extension, understanding extension as the abstract relation of an externalization to be sublated into thought. Must Spinoza's conception of God's "materiality" in the sense that he is a *res extensa,* according to Prop. II of *Ethics* II, not have meant something entirely different from God's externalization into an abstract relation which is to be sublated into thought? How could Spinoza have insisted on the independence of the two attributes from each other and on their equal status if the one were to be sublated into the other? Finally, could Spinoza ever have demanded, as Hegel did, that the attributes be deduced from substance, since they were meant to be "constitutive" of substance according to Def. 6, *Ethics* I? These are only a few questions which might point to the possibility that Spinoza intended to conceive of substance without subject or Spirit, and that Hegel has read into Spinoza's total conception something alien to it. This view would, of course, leave us with the question how to explain the logical inconsistencies in Spinoza. But did Spinoza aspire to such total consistency?

Professor Yovel himself has remarked in his brief "Critical Comments"[20] that "coherence is not the ultimate criterion". Why did he then not raise the question whether Spinoza himself might not have had a total conception, and specifically one of a *Deus sive natura*, which he — Spinoza — knews perfectly well would not meet the standard of coherence in every respect?

True enough, Hegel's System is able to provide for the necessity and reality of finite modes and for a *principium individuationis* — which Spinoza was not able to provide — not only by virtue of the fact that the mode for Hegel is the negation *as* negation, but also by developing actuality in the way mentioned, i.e. as a manifestation or as a shining by itself in its own otherness, in its own finite modes and their totality, the world.

It is on the basis of such a shining of the absolute within the finite that the finite, the cosmos, and its real distinctions enjoy a reality of their own and, yet, necessarily belong to the absolute. Thus, in Hegel pantheism does indeed not obliterate the modes; it is not the "acosmism" as which Hegel had diagnosed Spinoza's pantheism.

It might be of interest to add, as a footnote to these observations, that another proponent of idealism, Schelling,[21] tried to guarantee necessity, reality and diversity of the finite modes, of the finite creation, through God's own contraction reminiscent of the cabbalistic *zimzum*. The living God in his freedom "contracts" himself and thereby creates a "ground" for all finite entities. This ground is neither God nor the world; it is as such independent from God. And yet, God, the absolute, remains in the ground as a shining light, a *Licht-*

---

[20] *Collection*, p. 67.
[21] Cf. for the following: W. Marx, *Schelling — Geschichte, System, Freiheit*, Freiburg im Breisgau 1977.

blick. Thus — similar to Hegel's conception — finite creation enjoys reality because of such a shining of the absolute within it.

Furthermore, God is for Schelling not a God of the dead but of the living, He manifests himself only in entities which are similar to himself. The representatives of divinity are living, i.e. self-reliant personalities only because God is such a self-reliant personality himself. Modes thus derive an absoluteness of their own from the absolute, from God. Schelling thus tried to solve the problem of pantheism in a twofold manner, i.e. through the notion of contraction and through the notion of a "derived absoluteness". He also did this by transforming Spinoza's basic conceptions.

YIRMIYAHU YOVEL

Jerusalem

Reply to Professor Marx

HEGEL'S CRITIQUE of Spinoza starts with ontology and leads into history. My paper was written, as invited, on Hegel's critique of Spinoza's *ontology*. It deals with such concepts as negation and being, the finite and the infinite, totality and its particularization. However, since I believe that Hegel's critique only attains its climax in the field of history, I included a short remark to this effect at the end of my text. But this remark is not, as Prof. Marx twice refers to it, "the thesis" of my paper. It is neither analysed nor spelled out ; rather than summing up a discussion that preceded it, it serves to indicate what is still lacking in my current paper (and, perhaps, calls for another paper).

Prof. Marx's concentration in his comments on my alleged views of Hegel's theory of history is unwarranted, since the present paper supplies him with very imperfect information on this aspect. This lack of information has sometimes led him to attribute to me views which happen to be the exact opposite of those I hold. For instance, Prof. Marx writes that I see history in Hegel as never-ending, when my interpretation assumes that Hegel is logically committed to the idea of 'the end of history'. He also attributes to me the claim that Hegel holds practice to be higher than theory, when I have variously stressed the opposite (most recently, in the Epilogue of my *Kant and the Philosophy of History,* Princeton 1980). Hegel makes practice a *necessary condition* for the actualization of the Spirit, which is, however, consummated in "absolute knowledge". Either side of this dual condition may be stressed according to context. In my paper, speaking of realizing the Spirit in its full sense, I say "it will not be attained in the sphere of contemplation, or mere philosophy *alone,* but would require human practice in history" (italics added). Professor Marx quotes this sentence, but omits the word "alone".

I think that his misunderstanding was induced by my use of the word "historization", which the two of us understand in different senses. I do not use this word to mean the relativization of the absolute, but rather its submission to the sphere of time and empirical externality, *as a necessary condition for its becoming an absolute.* The absolute is not such all along; it is not ready-made, but constitutes itself *qua* absolute by its historization and by the sublation of its own historicality in the "end of history".

Here, however, a real difference exists between Prof. Marx and myself. I do not agree that "Spirit in its adequate form, is its truth", to quote his phrase, exists in Hegel *prior* to its historical manifestation and independently of it. This would be much too close to the traditional theologies of creation and of emanation (and also to Spinoza, from which Hegel's dialectic radically departs). But this interesting debate may find its proper place when we deal explicitly with Hegel and History.

To Prof. Marx's two other, and shorter, comments I reply : (a) I see in Hegel not two but one single totality, in which neither the subjective nor the objective has the upper hand. (b) Spinoza certainly did not intend to construe his absolute as Spirit; he did pursue coherence and thought he had attained it.

A. Z. BAR-ON

Jerusalem

The Ontological Proof — Spinoza's Version
In Comparison with Those of St. Anselm and Descartes

I

MY CHIEF CONCERN in this paper is the question : in what way, if at all, did Spinoza incorporate the Ontological Proof of the Existence of God (OP) into his philosophical system? It may be proper, however, to first consider another question : what kind of proof of the existence of God is it appropriate to call 'ontological' ? This cannot be gathered from Spinoza's writings for the simple reason that the term was coined more than a century after his death. It was done by Kant in his Transcendental Dialectic within his classification of the traditional arguments for the existence of God, each class to be refuted in its turn.[1]

There is enough textual evidence to show that in the refutation of the OP Kant was taking issue with an argument found in Descartes's texts, first and foremost in his Fifth Meditation. Once christened 'ontological', however, arguments of this pattern have been traced by post-Kantian scholars to works of philosophers both preceding and succeeding Descartes. The search for the origin led eventually to St. Anselm's *Proslogion,* which has been recognized as containing the classical version of the OP. Still, Descartes's rendition remained a milestone in the history of the OP, both in view of Descartes's impact upon the whole course of modern philosophy and of the importance of the OP in the Cartesian system. This is particularly relevant to our context in view of the considerable impact of Descartes upon Spinoza's philosophy.

Under the circumstances a comparative analysis of St. Anselm's,

---

[1] See *Immanuel Kant's Critique of Pure Reason,* translated by Norman Kemp Smith, New York 1961, pp. 500 ff.

Descartes's and Spinoza's versions of the OP will prepare the ground for dealing with my main question. In adopting this strategy I follow Harry Wolfson.[2] In my view, however, Wolfson's implementation of this method resulted in a highly objectionable conception of the OP. Let us examine Wolfson's argument to see what I have in mind.

II

Wolfson's analysis is based on the assumption that Spinoza indeed employed the OP in his system, the specific feature of his version being the way in which he combined two different considerations, one semantic and the other epistemological.[3] The first involves a classification of ideas by the so-called 'criterion of reality', i.e. of their referring or not referring to extra-mental objects. As against the "real" ideas which do refer to existant, extra-mental objects, Spinoza specifies three kinds of "unreal" ideas : (1) the fictitious (e.g. a mermaid) ; (2) the rational (like genera and species) ; and (3) the merely verbal, which refer neither to mental nor to extra-mental objects (e.g. a square circle).

The epistemological consideration seeks to point out the methods by which we in fact apply the main semantic division, i.e. how we tell real from unreal ideas. This again involves a classification, this time of sources and/or kinds of cognition. Not unlike Descartes and his predecessors, Spinoza distinguishes between immediate and mediated cognition, the main class of the latter being deduction. Immediate cognition is again divided into the classes of sense-perception and unperceptional intuition. All three types of cognition are being used, but only two of them are reliable enough to serve for acquiring scientific knowledge : deduction and unperceptual intuition. Spinoza finds intuitive knowledge even more reliable than deduction, presumably because he assumes the latter to be dependent upon the former, but not *vice versa*.

Now, Spinoza's intention in propounding his version of the OP was, according to Wolfson, nothing else but disclosure of the following two facts : (a) that the idea of God is neither fictitious, nor rational, nor verbal, but definitely real, having an extra-mental object corresponding to it ; and (b) that the reality of this idea is ascertained

---

2   See H. A. Wolfson, *The Philosophy of Spinoza*, I, New York 1958, pp. 158 ff.
3   *Ibid.*, p. 161.

[102]

by means of immediate intuitive knowledge. In other words, Spinoza's OP is paradoxically supposed to show us that the proposition of God's existence *is not* a conclusion of an argument; it is rather the content of an act of immediate experience, namely the act of intuiting the idea of God as real.

Moreover, in his OP Spinoza has not, according to Wolfson, strayed from the path followed by his predecessors, St. Anselm and Descartes. Neither of them meant *to prove* in this particular framework the existence of God or the necessity of his existence; neither of them intended to present the statement "God exists" or "God exists necessarily" as a conclusion of a syllogism in the ordinary Aristotelian sense of this term — the sense of producing science, of arriving at something in the conclusion which was not contained in the major premiss.

Thus far the three versions are identical. They differ from each other in their ways of rendering the idea of God, the aspect of this idea on which their authors' intuition was focussed. According to Wolfson, St. Anselm spoke of the greatest being, and Descartes of the most perfect being, while Spinoza called it the being that is *causa sui*. Still, all of them assumed that the knowledge of his existence is *contained* in this idea, and the OP merely states this simple but crucial fact.

Wolfson summarizes his analysis as follows:

> ... none of the ontological proofs in their various forms as given by its three main exponents, Anselm, Descartes, and Spinoza, prove directly that God exists. What they prove is that the existence of God is known to us by a certain kind of immediate knowledge. Their various proofs can be reduced to the following syllogism:
>
> If we have an idea of God as the greatest, the most perfect, or a self-caused being, then God is immediately perceived by us to exist.
>
> But we have an idea of God as the greatest, or as the most perfect, or as a self-caused being.
>
> Therefore, God is immediately perceived by us to exist.[4]

It appears that this conception of Wolfson has to some extent determined the way in which Spinoza (and perhaps also St. Anselm and Descartes) are being interpreted today and taught. It does not, however, find much support in the relevant texts. As I read these texts, the clear

---

4   *Ibid.*, p. 174.

intention of the three authors was (a) to prove that *God exists* (and is not merely perceived by us as existing) ; and (b) *to prove* that he exists, i.e. to present an argument in which the statement of God's existence is the conclusion, in the strict sense of this term.

III

How did St. Anselm attempt to do this ? [5]
Let us first of all observe that the key concept in his reasoning is not "the greatest being", as Wolfson puts it, but that-than-which-nothing-greater-can-be-thought. The argument that is supposed to show that such a being does exist has the form of a *reductio ad absurdum* : Suppose that that-than-which-nothing-greater-can-be-thought exists in thought only. Now, if it exists in thought, it can at least be thought of as existing in reality. But existence in reality is greater than existence in thought only. It follows that that-than-which-nothing-greater-can-be-thought is something-than-which-something-greater-can-be-thought — itself, as existing in reality. We are thus caught in a contradiction. Hence, the premise of the *reductio* is false ; its negation is true, and we have proved that that-than-which-nothing-greater-can-be-thought exists not only in thought but also in reality.
As a matter of fact, this is only the first stage of St. Anselm's OP, or, alternatively, the first of his ontological proofs. In an argument of a similar structure he attempts to prove that that-than-which-nothing-greater-can-be-thought not only exists, but also that it exists necessarily.[6] The proof runs as follows : suppose that the existence of that-than-which-nothing-greater-can-be-thought is not necessary, i.e. that that being can be thought not to exist. Such an assumption will involve us in the very same contradiction as the previous one, if we add to it the following two — unexceptionable in St. Anselm's view — propositions : (1) if that-than-which-nothing-greater-can-be-thought can be thought not to exist, then it can also be thought as that which cannot be thought not to exist ; and (2) what cannot be thought not to exist is greater than what can be thought not to exist. To escape the contradiction we must agree that God, as that-than-which-nothing-

---

5 See *St. Anselm's Proslogion with A Reply on Behalf of the Fool by Gaunilo and the Author's Reply to Gaunilo*, translated with an introduction and philosophical commentary by M. J. Charlesworth, Oxford 1965, p. 117.
6 *Ibid.,* p. 119.

greater-can-be-thought, cannot be thought of as not existing, i.e. that
he exists necessarily.

Wolfson seems to have ignored these two arguments with their distinct inferential steps. Not so, however, St. Anselm, in answer to his
first known objector, Gaunilon, the monk from Marmoutier. It was
here that Wolfson sought support for his interpretation. Having
quoted from St. Anselm's appeal to the monk's "faith and conscience"
to attest that his objection was false, Wolfson comments :

> Is it not possible that in appealing to faith and conscience Anselm
> is really invoking the argument from revelation as attested by
> tradition by which the existence of God is established as a fact
> of immediate personal experience? Such an argument from
> revelation is common in Jewish philosophy, and it may be con-
> sidered as partly psychological, in so far as the proof from
> revelation derives its validity from the fact that it is an im-
> mediate experience, and partly historical and social, in so far
> as the truth of the fact of revelation is attested by an unbroken
> chain of tradition universally accredited within a certain group.[7]

This, however, won't hold water. In none of the relevant texts is there
a trace of an argument from revelation ; we do not find it in St.
Anselm and certainly not in Descartes ; it would be ridiculous to
expect it in Spinoza. Wolfson's impression that this type of argument
has been used is probably caused by careless reading. What do we
actually find in St. Anselm's reply to Gaunilon ? St. Anselm points
out at the beginning that the monk had advanced two propositions
against him. The first one says that it is not true that that-than-which-
nothing-greater-can-be-thought does exist, even in thought. The second
one says that even if it did exist in thought, it would be by no means
possible to derive logically from this fact the statement about its
existence in reality.[8] I see it as perfectly clear that St. Anselm appeals
to the faith and conscience of his antagonist to refute only the first
of these propositions. He is asking the monk to examine his consciousness and see whether after such an examination he could possibly
deny the meaningfulness of the concept of that-than-which-nothing-
greater-can-be-thought. There is no need to call on conscience and
faith in order to disprove the monk's second proposition. For that
St. Anselm has arguments which are supposed to speak to his reason.

---

7   Wolfson (*op. cit.*, n. 2), p. 171.
8   See Charlesworth (*op. cit.*, n. 5), p. 169.

Let us now compare St. Anselm's OP with that contained in the Fifth Meditation of Descartes. In what concerns the applicability of deduction, this comparison will leave us in no doubt as to the parallelism of the two arguments. Descartes says :

> It is certain that I no less find the idea of God, that is to say, the idea of a supremely perfect Being, in me, than that of any figure or number whatever it is; and I do not know any less clearly and distinctly that an actual and eternal existence pertains to this nature than I know all that which I am able to demonstrate of some figure or number truly pertains to the nature of this figure or number....[9]

Here Descartes draws a clear analogy between the procedure of acquiring knowledge and certainty within the framework of a deductive system, and the procedure of the OP, "...all that which I am able to demonstrate of some figure... truly pertains to that figure...." This feature of Cartesian meta-theory, which clearly supports my thesis and to which Wolfson turned a blind eye, is even more strongly expressed in the following part of Descartes's reasoning :

> ...when I think of it with more attention, I clearly see that existence can no more be separated from the essence of God than can its having its three angles equal to two right angles be separated from the essence of the rectilinear triangle, or the idea of a mountain from the idea of a valley; and so there is not any less repugnance to our conceiving a God (that is, a Being supremely perfect) to whom existence is lacking (that is to say, a certain perfection is lacking), than to conceive of a mountain which has no valley.[10]

I must admit that while the example of the triangle illuminates Descartes's conception, the one of the valley and mountain rather obscures it. (This last example could be taken as justifying the psychologistic conception of the Proof, which is advocated by Wolfson.) The factor of conceptual mediation, however, can hardly be missed from the next passage :

> ...although it is not necessary that I should at any time en-

[9]   The *Philosophical Works of Descartes,* translated by E. S. Haldane and G. R. T. Ross, I, New York 1955, pp. 180 ff.
[10] *Ibid.,* p. 181.

tertain the notion of God, nevertheless whenever it happens that I think of a first and sovereign Being, and, so to speak, derive the idea of him from the storehouse of my mind, it is necessary that I should attribute to him every sort of perfection, although I do not get so far as to enumerate them all, or to apply my mind to each one in particular. And this necessity suffices to make me conclude (*after having recognized that existence is a perfection*) that this first and sovereign Being really exists; just as though it is not necessary for me to imagine any triangle, yet, whenever I wish to consider a rectilinear figure composed only of three angles, it is absolutely essential that I should attribute to it all those properties which serve to bring about the conclusion that its three angles are not greater than two right angles, even though I may not then be considering this point in particular.[11]

The contradiction (or repugnance) spoken of in the previous quotation as necessitating our admission of God's existence, or — which is the same — our acknowledgement that God's essence implies his existence, would not emerge unless an independent premiss were added to the argument, this premiss stating that existence is a perfection. Once more, the psychologistic rendering of the OP as an act of immediate experience is discredited.

When considered in this respect, does Descartes's argument differ essentially from that of St. Anselm? Hardly. The only change we have to make in the Cartesian OP in order to assimilate it to the Anselmian pattern is the replacement of the "supremely perfect Being" by "that-than-which-nothing-more-perfect-can-be-thought". With this as the key concept, we shall get exactly the same result as that reached in Chapters 2 and 3 of the *Proslogion*; moreover, "the more perfect" may be taken as an interpretation of "the greater", which even St. Anselm would have accepted.[12]

V

Having satisfied ourselves with regard to the affinity between St. Anselm's and Descartes's arguments, let us consider Spinoza's conception. As in Descartes's case, there are several passages in Spinoza's works which have been identified as versions of the OP. The most

11 *Ibid.*, p. 182. (Italics added.)
12 See *The Author's Reply to Gaunilo* in Charlesworth (*op. cit.*, n. 5), p. 187. Cf. Charlesworth's comment on this point, *ibid.*, pp. 60 ff.

fully elaborated of them, however, is the one contained in the *Ethics*, Part I (EI). We shall concentrate on this version and begin the reconstruction of what is known as Spinoza's OP with Proposition XI of the EI, which reads : "God, or substance, consisting of infinite attributes, of which each expresses eternal and infinite essentiality, necessarily exists".[13]

This is only the conclusion of the argument, the end of the thread, which we shall have to follow all the way back through the premises, distinctions and definitions to arrive at the starting point.

There are four proofs to Proposition XI. As Wolfson rightly observed, only to the first one of them can we unreservedly attribute the required structure. The remaining proofs differ in various degrees from the familiar pattern. We shall therefore restrict ourselves to an analysis of the first proof.

Like St. Anselm's Proof, it is presented explicitly as a *reductio ad absurdum*. (Wolfson took note of this, but seemed not to have recognized the consequences of it, which certainly contradict his interpretation of the OP). The first proof runs as follows :

> If this be denied [that God, as infinite substance, exists necessarily], conceive, if possible that God does not exist. Then (by Axiom VII) his essence does not involve existence. But this (by Prop. VII) is absurd. Therefore God necessarily exists. Q.E.D.[14]

The proof of Proposition XI is supposed then to derive directly from Axiom VII and Proposition VII of the EI. Now, Axiom VII says that "if a thing can be conceived as non-existing, its essence does not involve existence". But, as it becomes clear from Proposition VII, Spinoza had already proved, or so he assumed, that it is impossible to conceive of substance as non-existent. How he did this can be learned from the proof of this same Proposition VII :

> Substance cannot be produced by anything external (Corollary, Prop. VI), it must, therefore, be its own cause — that is (according to Def. I) its essence necessarily involves existence, or existence belongs to its nature.

We have followed our thread diligently and, lo and behold, it leads to the very heart of Spinoza's metaphysics : the synthesis of the concept of substance with the concept of cause, which produces the main tool to be used in a rationalistic explanation of everything there is.

---

[13] See *Chief Works of Benedict Spinoza,* translated with an introduction by R. H. M. Elwes, II, New York 1951, p. 51.

[14] *Ibid.* (Text in square brackets added.)

We can see now that what was taken to be Spinoza's version of the OP is much more complex than the previous versions. In fact, it is a fragment of his whole system as presented *ordine geometrico,* and in the demonstration of its conclusion all the elements prior to Proposition XI of the EI (axioms, propositions, corollaries, etc.) are involved in one way or another. Can it be doubted that this piece of reasoning was presented by its author as a proof in the strict sense of the term and not as an act of direct cognition? We shall recognize it then as a proof. But is this proof ontological?

The answer to this question cannot be an unqualified "yes", since Kant's criterion for defining a proof as ontological (the existence of God has to be demonstrated without assuming the existence of any other object whatsoever) does not appear to be fulfilled in the case under consideration. Although among the axioms of Spinoza's system there is no explicit assumption of the existence of any particular being, these axioms make sense only when they are understood to presuppose — meta-theoretically, if you wish — that *something* exists. This is clearly implied by Axiom I of the EI : "Everything which exists, exists either in itself or in something else". If this interpretation is correct, the argument which has been repeatedly labelled as Spinoza's version of the OP can be reduced to the following syllogism : if anything exists, then God, as infinite substance, exists necessarily. But it is absurd to assume that nothing exists. Therefore, God, as infinite substance, exists necessarily.

In this form the argument is clearly ineligible for the OP category. If, however, my application of Kant's criterion to this case was incorrect, that is if Spinoza's system of EI does not presuppose existence in the sense forbidden for an OP, I have no other objection against giving Spinoza's argument the status of OP proper. How well the title does fit will be seen if we consider Definitions II and VI of the EI. The concept of a finite being is defined there (Def. II) as that than which a greater being *of its kind* can be thought. From here we arrive at a restricted concept of an infinite being as that than which nothing greater *of its kind* can be thought. Such a being, however, is still surpassable in thought : "a substance consisting of infinite attributes, of which each expresses eternal and infinite essentiality" (Def. VI) will be greater. Since, in the specified context of the EI, "having an attribute" and "being of a kind" are taken to be synonymous, we have finally re-established St. Anselm's key concept of that-than-which-nothing-greater-can-be-thought, and the way is open to an assimilation of Spinoza's argument to the original version of the OP.

R. BARCAN-MARCUS

New Haven

Bar-On on Spinoza's Ontological Proof

BAR-ON proposes to show how the ontological proof is incorporated, if at all, into Spinoza's philosophical system. Preliminary to that he wants, following Wolfson's strategy, to consider the nature of the ontological proof. Preliminary to that, in turn, he wants to show that Wolfson's claims about the ontological proofs in Anselm, Descartes, and Spinoza are "highly objectionable".

I should like in my comments to begin by defending Wolfson. It seems to me that his claims are not "highly objectionable". They are in fact well focussed and more consistent with Bar-On's analysis than he believes them to be. Consider the quoted passage from Wolfson : [1]

> ... none of the ontological proofs in their various forms as given by its three main exponents, Anselm, Descartes and Spinoza prove directly that God exists. What they prove is that the *existence of God is known to us by a certain kind of immediate knowledge*. Their various proofs can be reduced to the following syllogism : if we have an idea of God as the greatest, the most perfect, or a self caused being, then God is immediately perceived by us to exist.
> But we have an idea of God as the greatest or as the most perfect or as a self caused being.
> Therefore God is immediately perceived by us to exist.

What Wolfson says in the quoted passage is that the ontological proof is not a direct proof of God's existence. What he can be understood to be saying is that it is an indirect proof, but indirect proofs cannot be excluded as genuine. *Reductio ad absurdum,* which is the device of Anselm's version of the ontological proof is often called

---

[1]   H. A. Wolfson, *The Philosophy of Spinoza*, I, New York 1958, p. 176. Italics added.

'indirect proof'. However, I am not suggesting that it is this logical mode of indirection which is the basis of Wolfson's claim. It is rather, for want of some standard locution, what I will call an epistemological mode of indirection. In the quoted passage, Wolfson tells us that what is proved directly is that the existence of God is known to us by a certain kind of immediate knowledge. Suppose Wolfson's claim is correct; that what is proved directly is, in part, the proposition

It is known to us that God exists.

Now a plausible analysis of statements like

It is known that P

or

x knows that P

is that a necessary condition for their being true is that P be true. It is incoherent for P to be known and P to be false. There are some attempted analyses which challenge the claim that the truth of 'It is known that P' entails the truth of 'P'. Malcolm perhaps or Wittgenstein. Nevertheless the more generally accepted analysis is persuasive, and it does take

P is known and P is false

as inconsistent.

If therefore we can prove directly that

It is known that God exists

as Wolfson is claiming in the quoted passage then it requires one further step to arrive at

God exists.

The validity of that further step is not peculiar to the theological content. It is one step from

It is known that the sum of the angles of a triangle is equal to two right angles

to

The sum of the angles of a triangle is equal to two right angles.

Now we do not usually demonstrate propositions by first demonstrating that they are known and then showing that as a consequence of their being known they are true. But it is interesting to examine why, for it illuminates Wolfson's claims. What would a demonstration of, for example

It is known that the sum of the angles of a triangle consists of two right angles

consist in ?

Well, one obvious way is for some epistemological subject to produce a proof. On the common analysis of 'It is known that P' it is not merely a necessary condition that P be true but the knower, the epistemological subject, must be able to *justify* his claim. In mathematics that usually and perhaps always consists in providing a proof. I say usually because some mathematical realists sometimes claim mathematical knowledge intuitively and that such intuitions count as justifications. The claim is abetted by some of Godel's results, for one can interpret those results as having the consequence that there are mathematical truths for which there never will be a proper proof, which are undecidable, but for which intuitive knowledge might be claimed. It has even been suggested that intuitively accepted conjectures like Goldbach's, which has eluded proof for centuries, is such a mathematically undecidable proposition. But, setting those considerations aside for the moment, let us suppose that for mathematical propositions demonstrating that P is known consists in showing directly that someone has in fact produced a proof of P. But for that we would, in effect, have to display the proof. And displaying a proof is simultaneously a proof of P as well as of

It is known that P.

If our interest is in proving P and not in my knowing it, then the further step of asserting that I know it is otiose.

Now what counts as a mathematical proof can be made explicit by setting out canons or rules. There are of course in contemporary foundations of mathematics disagreements about appropriate canons, constructivist *vs.* nonconstructivist canons, for example. Still, whatever one's position on rules of proof, it is agreed that they must be wholly explicit so that a proof can be checked against them. There can therefore be a mechanical check against the canons, and there is a sense in which we can say of a mathematical demonstration that it is possible that it not merely be provable, but be proved, yet not known. A machine can be programmed to prove simple and even moderately complex theorems, some of which may be genuinely in doubt. If no epistemological subject examines those proofs and print-outs are discarded, P remains proved but not known. I deny, which I will not defend here, that the machine capable of generating those proofs can also be claimed to know that P.

Mathematical demonstrations, like most demonstrations, are not routed through an epistemological step of showing first that they are known. The cosmological arguments, the arguments from first cause for the existence of God, are such for which validity is claimed independent of any step about what is conceived or known. The insight of Wolfson is that what distinguishes the ontological argument is the indispensability of the epistemological subject in arriving, finally, at the conclusion that God exists. In this respect, the ontological argument is like the *cogito*. The conceiving, understanding, knowing subject is indispensable to the demonstration. In the ontological argument, what is established directly is that something is known to us, i.e. the existence of God. As noted above, it is a trivial step from

It is known that God exists

to

God exists.

What makes the ontological proof indirect is that it is routed through epistemological claims about what we conceive, understand and know.

That Bar-On may have failed to appreciate this gloss of Wolfson is manifest in the way he re-presents Wolfson's summary statement. Now it is clear from the given quotation of Wolfson's summary statement that "known to us" and "perceived by us" are being used synonymously. Yet Bar-On says, *contra* Wolfson,

> As I read these texts (Descartes, Anselm, Spinoza) the clear intention of the three authors was (a) to prove that *God exists* (and is not merely perceived by us as existing) and (b) *to prove* that he exists, i.e. to present an argument in which the statement of God's existence is the conclusion, in the strict sense of this term.

But the conclusion of the very syllogism which Bar-On quotes from Wolfson is that

God is immediately perceived by us *to* exist.

or

God is known by us (by a certain kind of immediate knowledge) *to* exist.

The force of Wolfson's "known by us *to* exist" or "perceived by us *to* exist" is quite different from Bar-On's re-presentation as "perceived by us *as* existing". Although Wolfson is not always very clear about what was or was not intended in the ontological argument, it is quite consistent with Wolfson's view that the ultimate intention of at least some of the philosophers cited was to prove that God exists and to present an argument in which the statement of God's existence is the conclusion in the strictest sense of the term.

Indeed, Wolfson[2] says as much in a passage immediately preceding the one which Bar-On quoted. In that passage "God exists" is finally

2   *Ibid.*, p. 176.

in the conclusion. Wolfson says

> Truly speaking, if the ontological proof were to be put into a syllogistic formula in such a way as to bring out its entire force, it would have to be as follows
>> Everything which is immediately perceived by us to exist exists.
>> God is immediately perceived by us to exist.
>> Therefore God exists.

The second premise, "God is immediately perceived by us to exist", is the conclusion of Wolfson's first quoted syllogism. The above is simply that very move from its being known or perceived that God exists to the conclusion that he does. The two syllogisms taken together form a sorites in which 'God exists' is finally a conclusion in the strictest sense of the term. But it is the first-quoted syllogism, the movement from having an idea or concept of God, to knowing that the *ideatum* to which it is adequate exists, which marks the peculiarity of the ontological argument.

Having defended Wolfson so far, I should like to go on to discuss a deficiency in his characterization, for I am in agreement with Bar-On that the account is not wholly adequate. But it is not at the same time "highly objectionable" or "belied by the texts" as Bar-On claims. It is rather, insufficient. Unless Wolfson tells us more explicitly what the special features of the "certain kind of immediate knowledge" are, too many arguments will count as ontological. Now the syllogism of Wolfson which Bar-On quotes and which Wolfson says displays the structure of the ontological argument is a hypothetical syllogism of which the conditional premise is

> If we have an idea of God as the greatest, the most perfect, or a self caused being, then God is immediately perceived by us to exist.

The premise for the antecedent is generally taken as non-controversial. It just says that we have the concept, i.e.

> We have an idea of God as the greatest, or as the most perfect or as a self caused being

from which it follows by *modus ponens* that

> God is immediately perceived by us or known by us to exist.

The deficiency in Wolfson's characterization is of course in failing to say more about the conditional premise which must be true if the conclusion is to follow. He does in his antecedent remarks say that the immediate perception, the immediate knowledge, is of "a certain kind", but he seems not to distinguish *that* kind from other claims to immediate knowledge such as that of the mystic or other psychological claims of immediacy. Bar-On is correct in suggesting that Wolfson's comments on Anselm's reply to Gaunilon indicate that he may have failed to make that distinction. He does not seem to have sorted out the "certain kind" of immediate knowledge of the ontological proof from other kinds of "immediate knowledge".

The insufficiency of Wolfson's characterization is then in his failing to say more about the conditional premise. It allows that it might be established by revelation or by claims of psychological immediacy. In any case, an argument of the form of Wolfson's syllogism, in which the conditional premise is unsupported by further rhetoric of a logical or rational sort, is not to be included among the ontological arguments. The assertion of the mystic, who insists without further explanation that to have the concept of God is to know that he exists *simpliciter,* is not in the spirit of those arguments of Anselm and Descartes which have been singled out as ontological. In stopping where he does, in failing to try to take the sorites back still another step, Wolfson does seem to classify among the ontological proofs those in which further support of a logical kind need not be given for the conditional premise. But what is crucial in Descartes's and Anselm's arguments and what marks them as ontological is that they do attempt to give rational support to the conditional premise. They try to show that a rational intelligence cannot deny that premise without incoherence. A rational intelligence cannot have the concept of the greatest or most perfect being and yet fail to know that God exists, for such a conjunction, they claim, leads to contradiction or perhaps to what Moore has called a pragmatic contradiction. A fool of course, devoid of some powers of reasoning, may fail to appreciate the incoherence and therefore, in the absence of faith and revelation, may say sincerely in his heart that there is no God.

If Wolfson is suggesting, and he seems to be, that in the conditional premise which goes from the idea of God to immediate knowledge of God's existence is the same kind of certain knowledge which the mystic claims, then, as Bar-On has correctly pointed out, there would be no accounting from some of the texts which purport to give an ontological argument. For they do attempt to give support for the conditional premise of a rational kind.

When Anselm appeals to Gaunilon's faith and conscience, it is surely an appeal to the faith and conscience of a man guided by reason. Gaunilon is no fool.

My disagreement with Bar-On is therefore on where to locate Wolfson's failure. It is the rational support for the conditional premise which Wolfson has failed to see as the special feature of an ontological argument. That rational support is manifestly clear in the quotations from Descartes which Bar-On presented. In the first quotation, Descartes simply says that he *finds the idea of God in himself and he knows from that idea clearly and distinctly that an actual and eternal existence pertains to this nature and that he knows that no less clearly and distinctly than that some property he is able to demonstrate about a figure or a number pertains to the nature of that figure or number.* Now Descartes is claiming an immediacy for that connection which Bar-On, in criticizing Wolfson for placing a premium on immediacy, has failed to appreciate. There is, in the quoted passage, not even a *reductio* argument. What Descartes is saying is that, without further demonstration, and from the idea of God, he knows that God exists with at least the clarity and distinctness that he knows a demonstrated mathematical truth. He is claiming that the knowledge, albeit immediate, is rational.

Again in the second quotation from Descartes, although there is the hint of a *reductio,* the immediacy of the move from concept to knowledge of existence is highlighted. We cannot, says Descartes, have the idea of a mountain without at the same time having the idea of a valley. Similarly, he says, it is repugnant, which I read as 'repugnant to reason', to conceive of a God to whom existence is lacking. A reasonable man cannot have the concept of God and yet fail to know immediately that God exists, and that is, after all, Wolfson's conditional premise.

What I have claimed in the foregoing is that Bar-On is correct in faulting Wolfson for being untrue to the texts. But it is not because Wolfson claims that the conclusion of the ontological argument is that God is known to us by a certain kind of immediate knowledge. It is rather Wolfson's failure to say something more about the conditional premise — his failure to distinguish the "immediacy" of the knowledge claimed in the ontological argument from that claimed for revelation or for kinds of psychological immediacy. The "certain kind of immediate knowledge" by which a knowledge of God is claimed in the ontological arguments should have been singled out as rational intuition. It is seeing with clarity and distinctness that having the idea, grasping the essence of God, leads us to know, again with clarity and distinctness, that he exists. Given that the conditional premise asserts immediacy between antecedent and consequent we cannot press the sorites back further in an obvious way. There is no further well laid out argument. That is after all what immediacy entails. But we can bolster the claim. We can get a rational man to see it for himself, akin to Socrates' efforts in the *Meno.*

We can claim an analogy with mathematical demonstration or with concepts which entail one another such as mountains and valleys. There are *reductio* supports; we can try to show that denying the conditional leads to incoherence.

Having said all that, the question remains, and Bar-On raises it, whether there is in Spinoza's writings an ontological proof. Let us even suppose that Spinoza has succeeded in showing that God and substance are one and the same; is there an ontological proof of substance? Is there an argument which goes from the idea of substance? And a claim that from that idea it is known that substance exists, to ultimately the existence of substance? Is there supporting rhetoric for the conditional premise such as analogies, *reductions* and the like?

Now it is quite likely that from Spinoza's complete text one might be able to cull such an argument. Perhaps Wolfson has succeeded in doing so. But, as Bar-On has indicated, there is one segment of the *Ethics* which has been singled out by Wolfson and others as constituting an ontological argument. Broadly understood, it is all of Part I, terminating in Proposition XI, which says that God or substance exists necessarily. Bar-On correctly questions whether it does constitute an ontological argument and answers that one cannot say "yes" unqualifiedly if one is to employ Kant's criterion. That criterion counts as ontological an argument which proceeds without assuming anything exists. For, says Bar-On, again correctly, the *Ethics* supposes from the outset that there are existent things. But I would make the claim stronger. If there is even the remotest intended analogy between Euclid's methods and Spinoza's, then the *Ethics* begins with the presumption of the existence of things, substance, attributes, modes, God and relations between them, including the relation of identity. The *Ethics* is largely an unpacking and elaboration of those relationships.

The definitions with which Spinoza begins are like Euclid's, 'real' definitions. It is not merely 'ideas' which are being defined, which must then be shown to correspond to their *ideata*. Euclid's definitions were understood as telling us what objects geometry is about and they define some of their essential properties. Spinoza's eight definitions are about things, finite and infinite, substance, attributes, modes, God, free things, compelled things and so on. It supposes simultaneously that we have ideas of those things which are true to them. That those ideas have *ideata* to which they are adequate is never in question. Some of those presumptions are spelled out in the axioms. Axiom I already tells us that everything is either in itself or in another. Given the definitions, existence of examples of each kind are presupposed. For example, Definition VII supposes that there are things which exist from the necessity of their own nature. They are called free things. Compelled things are those which are determined to existence by another. Now, the demonstration of Proposition VII,

It pertains to the nature of substance to exist,

is not a proof of the existence of substance. That is already supposed. It purports to show that the existence of substance, unlike other existences, follows from its own nature. Indeed, Spinoza wonders whether a demonstration of Proposition VII is even required. He says in the second Scholium of Proposition VIII

If men would attend to the nature of substance they could not entertain a single doubt of the truth of Proposition VII. Indeed, this proposition would be considered by all to be axiomatic and reckoned among common notions.

As for Proposition XI,

God or substance consisting of infinite attributes . . . , necessarily exists,

it is a direct consequence, an instance of Proposition VII. One cannot locate in Part I of the *Ethics* any *demonstration* that from the *idea* of God it follows that he is known to exist or that he exists. What is asserted in Proposition XI is that he exists in a certain way, necessarily. His existence, *simpliciter,* is never in question.

The demonstrations that substance and God exist in a certain way, i.e. necessarily, may misleadingly suggest the form of an ontological argument to those who do not trace it from the definitions. The Scholium of Proposition VII does say that "if men would attend to the nature of substance they could not entertain a single doubt that the existence of substance follows from its nature". Proposition XI does ask us to conceive if we can that God does not exist. But those urgings are used not to show that he exists or that he is known to exist but to show that we would be forced to deny that his essence involves his existence, which is one of the defining properties of God or substance. To argue that the existence of substance or God follows from its *nature* is quite a different matter from arguing that the existence of substance or God follows from our *concept* of it. That our idea of God has an *ideatum* (as all ideas do for Spinoza) and is furthermore adequate to its *ideatum* is, at least in the *Ethics,* taken as true at the outset. Wolfson was therefore correct but incomplete in his characterization of an ontological argument, but he was *wrong* in claiming that such an argument could be found in the *Ethics.* The appropriate place for an ontological argument in the *Ethics* would have been in support of some of the axioms and definitions.

I should like in conclusion to say something about the uses of modal logic in our understanding of proofs which have been classified as ontological. Some and perhaps much of the recent revival of interest in such proofs stems from the revived interest in modal logic and the belief that ontological arguments can be translated into modal arguments. I do not propose to go into those various efforts with respect to Anselm's and Descartes's versions, although the extent to which those efforts succeed, fail or are misapplied is itself illuminating. I should like just to mention in passing one such attempt with respect to Spinoza. In a paper "Spinoza's Ontological Argument" Charles Jarett [3] argues that if we interpret the first part of the *Ethics* as claiming that

(1) It is possible that God exists

(2) Necessarily (If God exists then he exists necessarily)

it follows in one of the strong modal systems (with some constraints on what is known as the Barcan formula) that

(3) Necessarily God exists.

I do not propose to discuss whether such an argument can be culled from the *Ethics*. A strong case has been made for it. As it and many such attempts stand, it is not an ontological argument which is being presented. It does not have the requisite epistemological features. There is no conditional which takes us from what is conceived to what is known or to what exists. There is no argument to warrant the identification of conceivable with possible. Indeed, if the modal operators are taken as operators for logical, or what Kripke has lately called metaphysical possibility and necessity, then modal arguments like Jarett's, if valid, would remain valid in the absence of an epistemological subject or an idea of God altogether. Still, modal logic is not without its uses in sorting out some of the confusions which stem from the interplay of modal and epistemic notions and in clarifying such relationships as they occur in rationalist arguments like the *cogito* and the ontological proofs.

---

[3] C. J. Jarett, "Spinoza's Ontological Argument", *Canadian Journal of Philosophy*, VI (1976), pp. 685–691.

P.F. STRAWSON

Oxford

Liberty and Necessity

A FIRST reading of the *Ethics* may leave the reader with a sense of strain or paradox. This is not because Spinoza both denies freedom of decision and celebrates freedom of mind. Even though all things follow with absolute necessity from the nature of God, there is nothing immediately paradoxical in distinguishing some of the conditions that thus follow with the honorific name of 'freedom'. What creates a first sense of strain is the fact that Spinoza recommends, urges, the following of a path — which he describes as a difficult path — to the achievement of such a condition, while assuring us that we have no choice in the matter, but only the illusion of choice. The strain can be accommodated. Spinoza understands that the illusion is inescapable. This knowledge, and perhaps his own subjection to the illusion, causes him to set out what can rationally be seen only as description in a form which will tend to promote in his fellows, or in some few of them, a state of affairs he himself values highly, desires to see more generally realized. Now a further effort of accommodation is required. Spinoza evaluates human propensities and conditions with some confidence. Yet he maintains that to a mind wholly free, a mind that truly comprehended the nature of things, all distinctions of value would lack application; they would not even be intelligible. We are to believe *both* that nothing is truly good or truly evil *and* that the supreme good is to approximate as nearly as possible that condition in which it would be understood that this is so. Again the accommodation can be made. We can reconstrue, reinterpret, the evaluations as descriptions of the causes and effects of certain human dispositions; note the effect such a description may itself have on some minds; note also the naturalness of the employment of a terminology which, by hypothesis, reflects the limitations of our own (and the author's) understanding; and *feel* the effect ourselves.

[120]

So the exercise is, in its way, superbly managed. The combination of total naturalism with a unique elevation of tone is, rather against the probabilities, splendidly brought off. Yet questions remain, both about the freedom which is declared to be illusion and about the freedom which is equated with blessedness and said to increase proportionately with increase of understanding. Spinoza attributes the illusion of freedom to our consciousness of our actions, decisions and desires and our ignorance of their causes. Here are two theses: first, that the sense of freedom is illusory, because it entails a belief which is incompatible with the universal reign of natural causality; second, that the sense of freedom is caused in a certain way. Both theses are questionable. That we have a sense of freedom, that we necessarily act, as Kant says, under the *idea* of freedom, is generally allowed. That this sense entails a belief incompatible with the universal reign of natural causality is frequently denied; by Kant for dubiously intelligible reasons; by others for more pedestrian reasons. The pedestrian compatibilist will maintain, not that free actions are free from all causality, but that they are free from certain kinds of causality — the causality, he will say, of constraint; and he will be ready enough to illustrate what he means by this with examples of physical force or intrusive psychological compulsion.

One who, on this ground, questions the first thesis is under an obligation of consistency to question also the second — the thesis about the causal source of the sense of freedom. He can scarcely allow that knowledge of causes would make those causes constraining which were not so before; and he would surely be hardly more willing to allow that such knowledge would cause an authentic sense of freedom to be displaced by an illusion of constraint. So, it seems, he must deny that the sense of freedom is caused by ignorance of causes. And then, in all intellectual decency, he may feel obliged to give another account of the source of that sense.

Can these requirements be met? At one level at least, they can. Men are not generally ignorant of the immediate causes of their actions: they often enough know what combinations of desire, preference, belief and perception prompt them to act as they do. Not all their reasons are rationalizations. As for the remoter causes of their actions, i.e. the causes of their own desires, dispositions and preferences, they will often enough have a reasonably accurate notion of the sources of these as well, acknowledging both the general determining power of education, training, environment and heredity and the specific influence of this or that element of these determining forces. Blank ignorance of causes does not exist; so the sense of freedom cannot be attributed to such ignorance. Whence, then, does this sense arise ? Or, better perhaps, what does it consist in ?

Here one can only sketch an answer. First, we should consider that our desires and preferences are not, in general, something we just note in ourselves as alien presences. To a large extent they *are* we. The point gains force from the very fact of exceptions to it : i.e. from the presence in some subjects, sometimes, of dispositions and desires which they do experience as intrusive compulsions. In respect of them, there is no sense of freedom, but its absence is not attributable to knowledge of their causes ; on the contrary, the sufferers from such compulsions may suffer also from just such ignorance of their causes as Spinoza would declare to be the source of the sense of freedom.

Second, we should consider the experience of deliberation and relate this experience to the point that our desires and preferences are not, in general, something we just note in ourselves as alien presences. A corollary of this point is that, in the experience of deliberation, we are not mere spectators of a scene in which — setting aside the element of reckoning, of calculation — contending desires struggle for mastery with ourselves as prize. This image may sometimes be appropriate, but it is not the image appropriate to the standard experience of deliberation. That experience heightens our sense of self ; [1] in the higher-order desire which determines what we call our choice we identify ourselves the more completely ; and this is why we call it our choice.

Finally, we should consider the experience of agency. When a basic action of ours issues by a normal causal route from a specific intention of so acting, which itself issues from a combination of relevant belief and desire, then we have immediate knowledge, not only that our action has been such as we intended to perform, but also that it has been performed intentionally. As has been pointed out by recent writers in the theory of action, it can sometimes happen that someone acts as he intended to act yet does not perform that action intentionally. The action may issue causally from the appropriate combination of desire and belief, but the causal route from desire and belief to action may be of the wrong kind. The anticipatory thought of action may, for example, so disturb or unnerve us that we find ourselves *unintentionally* making just such a bodily movement as we *intended* to make — as letting go the rope which holds

---

[1]   For my appreciation of the connection between the two, I am indebted to some unpublished work on self-determination by J. G. Strawson.

up the fellow mountaineer, in a famous example of Professor David-
son. In such cases the experience of agency is lacking. The cases
are worth mentioning in order to emphasize the fact that the experience is normally present, and to remind us of what it is like.

Here, then, is a part at least of the phenomenology of the sense of
freedom. The fact that we find ourselves in our desires and preferences
and do not, in general, find them as alien presences within ourselves;
the experience of deliberation which heightens and strengthens our
sense of self; and the constantly repeated experience of agency — all
these contribute to, perhaps constitute, the sense of freedom. Experiencing it ourselves, we attribute it also to others.

Suppose it is acknowledged that the sense of freedom, so regarded,
experienced in ourselves and attributed to others, is a natural fact;
not, in general, causally threatened by knowledge of particular causes,
nor logically threatened by a general belief in the reign of universal
causality; not logically threatened because not a belief and hence
not a belief incompatible with that general belief. Yet the sense
of freedom, this natural fact, is closely linked with other attitudes
to ourselves and others, with other feelings towards ourselves and
others and with other concepts which we apply to ourselves and
others; and it is often argued that the justification of some of these
attitudes and feelings, and of the application of some of these concepts, requires, and is seen by us to require, the truth of beliefs which
are incompatible with the general belief in the universal reign of
causality. Spinoza speaks of the notions of sin and merit, praise and
blame and of allied emotions. In general, we may say, what are at
issue are the notions, attitudes and feelings associated with moral
judgement, with the idea of moral desert. Now it certainly is generally
held — it is a thesis, one might say, of the common moral consciousness — that the appropriateness of these attitudes and feelings, the
applicability of these notions, requires, in respect of any occasion on
which these attitudes and notions are in question, that the agent
could have acted otherwise than he did act on that occasion. But —
so the argument runs — if the thesis of determinism is true, then it
is not true of any agent on any occasion that that agent could have
acted otherwise than he did act on that occasion. Hence, if the thesis
of determinism is true, the attitudes and notions in question are
never appropriate.

Is the thesis of the common moral consciousness correctly interpreted
in this line of reasoning? Is it, in any case, a line of reasoning which
Spinoza accepts, or could consistently accept, as it stands? The
reasoning depends heavily on the notions of 'appropriateness' or 'jus-

tification' of attitudes; and these notions, being alien to the profoundly naturalistic and descriptive style of Spinoza's thought, must at least be re-interpreted in terms of causes and effects. To put it crudely: the thesis that a certain attitude is justified only if a certain belief is true amounts, in its Spinozistic reconstrual, to the thesis that a certain attitude is causally dependent on a certain belief. Re-interpreting the reasoning in these terms, we must ask whether our proneness to the attitudes and feelings, and to the application of the concepts associated with moral judgement, is in fact dependent on beliefs incompatible with the truth of determinism.

The question returns us, with a difference, to the common moral consciousness. When, in a context of moral appraisal, the common moral consciousnescs delivers the judgement "He could have acted otherwise" (have φ-d, say, instead of ψ-ing, as he did), is this judgement really equivalent to "There was no sufficient natural impediment or bar, *of any kind whatsoever, however complex,* to his acting otherwise" (to his φ-ing, say, instead of ψ-ing) ? I find it difficult, as others have found it difficult, to accept this equivalence. The common judgement of this form amounts rather to the denial of any sufficient natural impediment *of certain specific kinds or ranges of kinds*. For example, "He could (easily) have helped them (instead of withholding help)" may amount to the denial of any lack on his part of adequate muscular power or financial means. Will the response, "It simply wasn't in his nature to do so" lead to a withdrawal of moral judgement in such a case? I hardly think so; rather to its reinforcement.

There is another reason, equally familiar, for questioning the proposed equivalence. Acceptance of the equivalence commits one to the view that the practice of moral appraisal is either rationally grounded on, or causally dependent on, the conscious or tacit rejection of the thesis of determinism. But when those who accept the equivalence are invited to enlarge on the question, how a belief in the absence of determining causes explains or justifies the practices and attitudes in question, their answers are singularly insufficient. It is hard to see how randomness, or a belief in randomness, could either explain or justify any such thing; and attempts to formulate the appropriate belief in other terms have never resulted in anything but either highflown nonsense or psychological descriptions which are in no way inconsistent with the thesis of determinism. No one has ever been able to state intelligibly what that state of affairs, that condition of freedom, which has been supposed to be necessary to ground our moral attitudes and judgements, would actually consist in. The question, "If we believe in such a condition, what exactly are we believing?", remains unanswered and, I think, unanswerable.

Some who have faced this fact, but also have felt, or thought they felt, an irreconcilable tension between the reign of causality and the holding of moral attitudes, have concluded that there is something inherently confused about moral attitudes. This conclusion echoes Spinoza.

Nevertheless it is the wrong conclusion to draw; or, at least, drawn in this way and for this reason, it is wrongly drawn. Our proneness to moral attitudes and feelings is a natural fact, just as the sense of freedom is a natural fact. I have remarked that they are linked, and it is time to say more about the link. In speaking of the sense of freedom, I connected it closely with the sense of self. Our desires, decisions, actions are not in general felt as alien, as things that simply happen in, or to, us, like a pain or a blow. They are we. Our awareness of them is awareness of ourselves. I remarked that we attribute to others this same sense of freedom and this same sense of self. We see others as other selves, and are aware that they so see each other. But this is not a matter of a conclusion drawn by analogical reasoning. In a variety of ways, inextricably bound up with the facts of mutual human involvement and interaction, we *feel* towards each other as to other selves ; and this variety is just the variety of moral and personal reactive attitudes and emotions which we experience towards others and which have their correlates in attitudes and emotions directed towards ourselves.[2] Of all, or most, of these emotions or attitudes, whether self-directed or other-directed, Spinoza himself treats in the *Ethics*. He treats of them as natural facts, bringing unparalleled psychological insight to bear on the detailed analysis of their causes and effects. For this analysis one can have nothing but admiration. What I have been concerned to dispute is the thesis that these emotions and attitudes, together with the associated sense of freedom, of self and of other selves, rest upon a belief, or beliefs, incompatible with the doctrine of the universal reign of natural causality.

But we must again distinguish. There is the thesis that these emotions and attitudes, together with the sense of freedom, rest upon *false belief*. And there is the thesis that this cluster of associated feelings rests upon *ignorance* : upon ignorance of the actual causes of desires, dispositions and actions. Clearly the two theses are logically inde-

---

[2] I have written at greater length of these attitudes in "Freedom and Resentment", included in *Freedom and Resentment,* London 1974.

pendent. The second could be true even if the first were false. Earlier I summarily rejected the second thesis, as far as the sense of freedom was concerned, as well as the first. At least I rejected it in its full generality, arguing that we could have a reasonably accurate notion of the causal sources of our desires and dispositions and those of others — as well as of our actions, and theirs — without being in the least disposed, as a result of this knowledge, to lose our sense of these desires, dispositions and actions as truly ours (or theirs), to lose our sense of our (or their) selves and our (or their) freedom in respect of them; whereas, on the other hand, we could sometimes experience as alien compulsions, in respect of which we had no sense of freedom, certain desires and dispositions of the causes of which we were truly ignorant, which we were quite at a loss to account for.

Yet further consideration of the second thesis is called for. I have spoken of a kind of non-specialist knowledge which we have of the sources of human dispositions, desires and actions. We explain ourselves and others to ourselves and others in terms which we might call human and social terms. We refer to inherited traits, to social influences, to the effect of education, training and experience, to the particular circumstances in which people find themselves. We speak of character and personality and the influences which form and modify them. We can develop considerable subtlety and expertise in this kind of knowledge. But it remains a relatively vague and inexact kind of knowledge; and there must be few who suppose that it will ever be anything else.

But we are also, and increasingly, able to view ourselves in a quite different kind of light — that of the physical and biological sciences; to see ourselves, in that light, as genetically programmed mechanisms of immense complexity, mechanisms constantly modified by their own history and responding, in constantly modified ways, to sensory inputs with behavioural outputs. The scope for the development of these sciences is no less immense than the complexity of the mechanisms which we must take ourselves to be; and we are only at the threshold of this development. Nevertheless the knowledge which these sciences deliver and promise differs in a fundamental respect from that knowledge of the causation of human behaviour which I have just spoken of; for it is, as far as it goes, *exact* knowledge. Let us suppose, then, that we were able to give complete causal explanations of human behaviour, including our own, in terms belonging to these exact sciences. Suppose, in a spirit entirely Spinozistic, that we were able to identify every thought, feeling, original impulse to action, with — or as the 'mental' aspect or correlate of — some

[126]

complex physical state of which we could, in turn, determine the sufficient physical causes, tracing the latter as far back as we needed or wished to. Might we not then be said to have replaced our present, inexact, inadequate knowledge and understanding of the causes of our desires, dispositions and actions with adequate knowledge and understanding? And might not such adequate knowledge remove the basis of the sense of freedom and the sense of self and hence of the associated moral and personal attitudes and emotions — thus vindicating the thesis that these last did indeed rest, if not on absolute ignorance, then at least on inadequate knowledge, of causes?

The suggestion involves obvious minor complications, inasmuch as such mental items as the sense of agency, say, or the sense of guilt, must themselves be supposed to have physical correlates and physical causes; so that it would at least be necessary to suppose substantial modifications in the mechanism itself to result from knowledge of its workings. But it is pointless to dwell on these complications. For the question which contains the suggestion is unanswerable. It is unanswerable because the supposition which gives rise to it could not conceivably be fulfilled. *X*, let us say, notices that *Y*'s last remark has caused embarrassment to *Z* and, wishing to spare *Z*'s feelings, *X* himself makes a remark intended to change the direction of the conversation. Can we seriously contemplate the possibility of being able to give, in terms belonging exclusively to the exact physical sciences, a complete causal account of the origin of precisely *this* complex of thought, feeling and action on *X*'s part? And of every other piece of human behaviour of even such modest complexity as this? The idea is absurd; and not because there would not be world enough and time to work out the solutions to such particular problems, as there is not world enough and time to work out the particular causal conditions of every movement of a leaf on the surface of a stream. It is more fundamentally absurd because there is no practical possibility of establishing the general principles on which any such calculation would have to be based. This does not mean that we must absolutely deny the existence of underlying psycho-physical correlations even in such cases as these. It does mean that the idea of such correlations, in such cases, must remain merely an idea — something without effect, quite empty in a practical point of view. So for the explanation of *X*'s behaviour, we must have recourse to the inexactitudes of: "That is the sort of man he is — and he has a tenderness for *Z* — and he is that sort of man partly because he was brought up in *that* society — and *Z* appeals to him because...."; and so on.

There is, of course, more to be said about the scope of physical explanations of human behaviour. In particular, two points must be made. First, if the fine connections, envisaged above, between the language of the exact sciences on the one hand and the language of mind and behaviour on the other, are unattainable, grosser connections *are* attainable. Many general kinds of dependence of the mental and behavioural on the physical are well enough known. We can modify perception, stimulate memory, reduce or enhance aggression, depression or sexual drive, say, by chemical or electrical means. A great extension of this kind of knowledge is to be foreseen ; and knowledge of such dependences, and of the availability of techniques for exploiting them, may surely, *in certain cases,* contribute to inhibiting those personal and moral attitudes and reactions whose basis is at issue, or at least to lessening their force. So why, it may be asked, should *this* inhibiting effect not be generalized ? *All* the general traits which manifest themselves in particular episodes of human behaviour, however *nuancé* may be the descriptions we are inclined to give of those episodes, must, we suppose, have a physical base. So why should the inhibiting effect of such knowledge be confined to certain cases ? I think the answer — or the beginnings of the answer — is to be found in first noting the fact that these are also the cases which we are favourably disposed to regarding as 'cases for treatment'. They are the cases in which the traits in question are displayed in a form which, of itself, tends to inhibit ordinary interpersonal attitudes in favour of 'objective' attitudes. That is why I said, of such knowledge of causal dependence, only that it *contributes,* in some cases, to inhibiting personal and moral reactions and attitudes. The matter deserves much fuller treatment ; but I have not space for it here.[3]

The second point to be made is this. I gave above a particular example of human behaviour and described it in the ordinary human terms of intention and motive. I dismissed the idea of being able, even in principle, to give adequate causal explanations of such episodes, so described, in the terms of the exact sciences. But suppose we were content to abandon the practice of describing behaviour in terms of intentional action in favour of describing it solely in terms of bodily movements. The general principles of exact and adequate causal explanation of behaviour, so understood, would no longer seem beyond our grasp ; for the mechanisms of bodily movement show no discontinuity with the finer electro-chemical mechanisms

3   See again "Freedom and Resentment" (*op. cit.,* n. 2).

of the human frame. The difficulties of explanation in particular cases would not be different in kind, though doubtless different in degree, from those of explaining the movements of the leaf on the stream.

I make this point only for the sake of completeness. What we were to contest was the thesis that knowledge of the causes of behaviour would undermine a certain range of attitudes and feelings. I pointed out that such general knowledge of causes as we actually possess has not in fact produced this effect. To the hypothetical question whether exact or 'adequate' knowledge would not produce it I respond with a distinction. So long as what we understand by 'human behaviour' is intentional action, such knowledge is unattainable. If we were to exclude from the description of human behaviour all reference to belief, desire and intention, if we were to see it as consisting simply in bodily movement, then such knowledge might indeed be in principle attainable. But this truth is simply irrelevant to the issue before us. To see human behaviour as consisting simply of physical movement would, *of itself,* exclude the attitudes and feelings in question ; for it is only in relation to behaviour understood, or experienced, as intentional action that these attitudes and feelings ever arise.

I have left myself little space to discuss Spinoza's positive conception of freedom of mind. The picture he draws of the free and rational man, in all his detachment, magnanimity and moderation, is, by and large, both coherent and impressive. It is, by and large, a recognizable picture. Yet there is one central thesis which leaves an insistent doubt. Spinoza equates increase of freedom with increase of understanding ; and the understanding he means is understanding of the nature of God, i.e. of the workings of Nature, including, pre-eminently, our own workings. The advances that have been made during the last three hundred years in this kind of understanding — in the natural sciences — are quite spectacularly great. It will hardly be thought that they have been matched by comparable advances towards deliverance from the bondage of human passions. The free and rational man, as so impressively, so coherently pictured by Spinoza, must indeed have a certain large vision of the world and a certain broad and sympathetic understanding of human nature. He must by no means be a fool. But it is not at all clear that he has to be a natural scientist.

CH. PERELMAN

Brussels

Métaphysique, éthique et langage chez Spinoza

J'AI ÉCOUTÉ avec grand intérêt l'exposé du Professeur Strawson, et je sympathise avec ses analyses et ses critiques. Mais je me demande quelles seraient les réactions de Spinoza à ce que nous venons d'entendre, et spécialement aux objections qui lui ont été présentées dans la perspective d'une phénoménologie de la délibération ou de l'analyse de l'acte moral ou de notre sens de la liberté.

Sa première réaction aurait sans doute été de récuser des descriptions fondées sur des notions confuses et une connaissance inadéquate de ce qui constitue tant notre moi que notre action et notre liberté. Car, pour les apprécier, il ne faut pas partir de ce que le sens commun et l'opinion commune nous enseignent, mais de ce qui est objectivement valable ; pour en juger, il faut d'abord être convaincu de la vérité de sa philosophie, et ensuite redéfinir toutes les notions conformément à ce que celle-ci exige et récuser comme illusoires ou imaginaires toutes les notions qui ne sont pas susceptibles d'une telle réduction.

Citons, à ce propos quelques passages de l'*Ethique* (ed. Pléiade, *Oeuvres Complètes,* Paris 1954) qui éclairent et justifient mon interprétation.

L'explication qu'il nous donne à la fin de la 3ème partie, après la définition de l'indignation (déf. XX) est la suivante : "Je sais que ces noms (des sentiments) ont, dans l'usage commun, une autre signification. Aussi bien mon dessein est-il d'expliquer, non la signification des mots, mais la nature des choses, et de désigner celles-ci par des termes dont la signification usuelle ne s'éloigne pas absolument de celle avec laquelle je veux les employer..." (pp. 475–476).

C'est ainsi que, sans se préoccuper de l'usage commun et de ce que pourrait nous apprendre une analyse linguistique, il nous dira que "cause" et "raison" sont synonymes (Préface de la 4ème partie, p. 488), que "par bon, j'entendrai ce que nous savons avec certitude nous être utile" (déf. p. 490), que "par fin, pour laquelle nous faisons quelque chose, j'entends l'appétit" (déf. VII, p. 491), "par vertu et puissance, j'entends la même chose..." (déf. VII, p. 491).

Il dira que "nous sommes actifs lorsque, en nous ou hors de nous, il se produit quelque chose dont nous sommes la cause adéquate, c'est-à-dire... que l'on peut comprendre clairement et distinctement par notre seule nature" (4ème partie, déf. II, p. 413) ; "...les hommes se croient libres par la seule raison qu'ils sont conscients de leurs actions et ignorants des causes par lesquelles ils sont déterminés..." (3ème partie, prop. II, scolie, p. 418). Il en résulte que c'est seulement par l'entendement que nous sommes dits actifs (5ème partie, prop. XL, corollaire, p. 593). Est libre celui qui est conduit par la Raison seule (4ème partie, prop. LXVIII, p. 548).

Il en résulte que non seulement toute délibération est l'expression de la confusion de nos idées, mais que croire à une décision libre, qui devrait en résulter, c'est "rêver les yeux ouverts" (3ème partie, prop. II, scolie, p. 419).

Pour lui, la liberté n'est que conformité à la raison, de sorte que "ce que la raison conseille à un homme, elle le conseille à tous les hommes" (4ème partie, LXXII, p. 551). Toutes les décisions libres sont donc impersonnelles, et conformes à la vérité.

Tout ce qui s'écarte de ces vues, et qui est relatif au bien et au mal, au mérite et à la faute, à la louange et au blâme, à l'ordre et à la confusion, à la beauté et à la laideur (Appendice, p. 347), ce ne sont que des préjugés fondés sur l'illusion. Toute valeur qui n'est pas réductible à une tendance naturelle, à l'accroissement de la puissance, n'est qu'un produit de notre imagination. C'est ainsi qu'il identifie la perfection à la réalité (2ème partie, déf. VI), que le bien et le beau ne sont que ce qui est utile, que le juste et l'injuste sont des notions extrinsèques, et non des attributs qui expliquent la nature de l'esprit (4ème partie, prop. XXXVII, scolie, p. 523).

Si l'on veut s'opposer à Spinoza, il ne suffit pas d'opposer à ses thèses les analyses conformes à l'opinion commune, mais il faut prendre position à l'égard de sa philosophie du langage. Peut-on vraiment prendre le modèle mathématique comme unique modèle de la connaissance adéquate, peut-on réduire la liberté à la conduite conforme à la vérité et à la raison, peut-on concevoir l'univers comme un système dont tous les éléments sont entièrement déterminés, peut-on négliger tout aspect du langage qui ne consiste pas en notions communes ? Nous sommes tentés de prendre le parti de Strawson plutôt que celui de Spinoza parce que, sur toutes ces questions, nous avons tendance à répondre négativement, alors que Spinoza fournit une réponse positive ; mais aussi parce que l'idéal de Spinoza — la création d'une société universelle fondée sur la connaissance de la vérité — nous semble une illusion dont nous ne pouvons nous contenter.

STUART HAMPSHIRE

Oxford

The Political and Social Philosophy of Spinoza
Freedom of the Individual and Freedom of the Citizen

MY QUESTION IS : what is the relation between Spinoza's ideal of freedom of mind, the ultimate goal which amounts to salvation for the individual, and the relatively liberal ideals of good government which he advocates in his two political works ? I believe that there is a rather closer connection than is sometimes suggested, and a connection that is interesting and worth considering and criticizing now.

I begin with his argument for religious toleration, and for freedom of belief within the limits set by the security of the State, as explicitly set out in the two political works.

I

In Chapter 20 of the *Tractatus Theologicus-Politicus* Spinoza argues that respect for liberal values is a necessary pre-requisite for good and stable government. The liberal values involved are freedom of thought and of belief in all issues of religion and *Weltanschaung*, and, within wide and definite limits, freedom of speech and of expression as well. The necessity of freedom of thought is characteristically inferred from a proposition in the philosophy of mind or in *a priori* psychology : that one cannot be compelled, by force, or by threats or legal sanctions, to believe a proposition, or to believe a set of propositions.

I shall not try to determine what kind of impossibility this was intended to be. That no one can be compelled to believe by governmental and state action, or by legislation, follows from the theory of belief which Spinoza defended against Descartes's theory of belief.

Neither to believe something, nor to come to believe it, are acts of will. We do not assent to a proposition, or withhold belief from it in our thought as an act of will. Belief, like desire, is a mode of thinking, and thinking proceeds by its own laws, just as physical processes proceed by their own laws. I do not conform my propositional attitudes to these laws by mental acts of will; I follow the laws in my thinking. Legislation prescribing particular beliefs is therefore necessarily ineffective, according to Spinoza. Legislation in this sphere can only be effective if it prescribes, not what men are to believe, but what beliefs they may publicly profess and advocate.

That a man cannot effectively be commanded by law, or otherwise commanded or forbidden, to believe certain propositions seems to me to be, with some qualifications, true, even though the arguments that I should choose from the literature to support this conclusion are not the same as Spinoza's.

Spinoza adds another argument : even if it were possible to prescribe, it would be undesirable, because such prescriptions would not lead to peace and social harmony, but to conflict; and peace and social harmony, together with freedom of mind, are the proper ends of any state and political association. They are the proper ends of the state and of governments, because these are the ends that men in fact pursue when they are thinking clearly and are not confused.

Therefore the law and governments, when they are reasonable, will be concerned only with expressions of belief and not with belief itself, with the advocacy of religious and moral doctrines and not with mere silent adherence to the doctrines. At this point in the argument Spinoza claims that the promotion and protection of freedom of mind, which is the natural end of human effort, rightly directed, requires as much freedom of expression as is compatible with public harmony and social order. The government of any state has the natural right to protect itself against seditious opinions, publicly declared, and against incitements to rebellion or violence. Because men are passionate and prone to violence in defence of their superstitions, it may even be found necessary to prohibit the expression of beliefs, which are in themselves rational and harmless, when the expression of the beliefs is likely to lead to violence or likely to shatter the peace and social harmony in the society. Social harmony does not here mean convergence of opinion, but the absence of hatreds that are likely to lead to disorder. The preservation of public order and stable government was for Spinoza both the necessary and the sufficient condition of censorship, which is in itself bad, since it obstructs freedom of mind; but the evil is occasionally overridden by the supreme necessity of social stability and public order. This is so far a clear statement of a moderate liberalism, unusual in its date but still familiar in outline. There are two pecularities to be noted : first, that the rights of the citizen and of the sovereign or government are established by reference to natural laws and not by reference to moral laws, conceived as being distinct from natural laws. Second, Spinoza differed from most other liberal philosophers, and conspicuously from Mill, in not arguing that freedom of worship and freedom of expression were certain, or even likely, to lead in the long run to a general enlightenment and, through this enlightenment, to ever more harmonious and stable societies. His main justification for advocating freedom of expression was not found in its social consequences but rather in the natural desires and needs of individuals. Also he was not convinced that the social consequences of aiming at philosophical enlightenment are always and unconditionally desirable. On the contrary he argued that philosophical and scientific enlightenment may sometimes be in some of its aspects, though not in all, a threat to social peace and stability. Human nature is so constituted that the behaviour of the majority of men will always be largely governed by hopes and fears which are not founded on a clear and unsentimental view of their own interests, and of the interests of men generally, but on unrecognized ignorance, and confusion. Therefore they will cling to the superstitions of conventional morality and conventional religion, which imagines a moral law, and a set of moral commandments, backed by rewards and punishments. Given the necessity of keeping the peace, it is dangerous to allow enlightened opinions to undermine these superstitions, unless one is reasonably sure that the true and adequate reasons for conforming to ordinary moral principles are both understood and also will have sufficient emotional force. Once their fears of punishment and hopes of reward are shaken or undermined, unintelligent men may become lawless and irresponsible, because they are unable to understand morality as fully enlightened self-interest. There is therefore the continuing need to keep a delicate balance between rational thinking and conventional religion and morality. Secularization could be pressed too far and too fast without regard to the facts of human nature ; this Weberian thought is typical of Spinoza.

It is highly desirable that there should be a community of enlightened and learned men, who will be like-minded in their enlightenment and who can be of the utmost assistance to each other in developing clear thinking and rational inquiry. But they will not expect a whole society to be an ideal community.

[134]

With so much admitted, there remains a still closer connection between the two kinds of freedom : the freedom of mind which is a state of the individual, when his powers of thought are as fully developed as they can be, and freedom as a social ideal, when the citizens of a state are able, without threat of penalties, to follow an inquiry wherever it leads and to discuss with like-minded men ideas which are incompatible with established opinions. The connection is not merely that the freedom in society is an ancillary aid and an external means to freedom of mind. There is an internal relation between the two, which depends upon Spinoza's notion of individuality, central in his metaphysics.

Every individual thing, of whatever kind, strives to maintain itself as a distinct individual against the forces that impinge upon it and that would destroy its relative independence and coherence. This conatus, or striving, can be seen, in biological terms, as a tendency of living organisms to preserve an individual character, and this individual character provides, at the same time, the appropriate coherence within the organism and also an immunological reaction when there is an invasion from outside. The immunological reaction is the negative aspect of the creature's limited autonomy. Spinoza's account of individuality is intended to be entirely general, and similar drives to self-maintenance in less complex, non-living things could be described in physical terms. Reality, conceived as a domain of extended things, exhibits an indefinite variety of individuals, individuated by their self-maintenance and by their relative independence of their environment, all acting and reacting in accordance with the same fundamental physical laws.

In psychological terms, the drive to self-maintenance, and hence the individuality of the thinking person, exhibit themselves in his desires, which derive from this primary impulse of self-assertion complicated by all the thoughts associated with pleasure and with suffering in his experience. There is a coherence in the system of his desires and beliefs and emotions, and an individual make-up, as in his physical nature. Universal laws of thought govern his thinking and his emotions ; but he has some individuality in the system of his desires and beliefs. One may therefore say that there is a deeper reason why Hobbes was right to think of the untamed condition of men, without an imposed civil order, as one of necessary and continuous conflict. But he had not pressed his analysis far enough, and had not represented the war of all against all as only a special case of a universal

[135]

natural process. For this reason Hobbes's picture of the state of nature has seemed rather arbitrary and under-motivated. Within Spinoza's philosophy the clash between the drive of self-assertion, and the conflict between derived desires and ambitions, are neither arbitrary nor an uncompensated evil. Men must try to impose on the social and natural environment their own desires and ambitions, as a natural necessity; the competition is common to all creatures; and its positive aspect is the comparative autonomy and self-direction which men of high vitality may attain. They need to be persuaded that their natural drive towards greater power, and freedom from external influences, can only be satisfied by an intellectual grasp, and a theoretical understanding, both of themselves and of the external influences.

Spinoza lays emphasis on the quasi-logical principle *Omnis determinatio est negatio.* If an individual is to assert his independence and identity as an individual, which he naturally must, he will be establishing his own identity by denying and opposing anything that limits or threatens his independence. The egotism of powerful individuals, and of a powerful group of individuals, in pursuit of their own interests, as they conceive them, and of their own ambitions, is the negative face of their virtue, which is to manifest some distinct power of their own and to enjoy doing so. The same behaviour, which can be seen as aggressive and egotistical, from an external point of view, can also be seen, from the standpoint of the agent, as an unavoidable drive to establish his own freedom and identity, that is, his distinct existence as an individual satisfying a specific description that singles him out from other men. To adapt a phrase used in the Romantic Movement, particularly by Byron, a man is apt to "feel that he exists" when he defines his own individual nature by opposition to those around him : at a general level he may define himself as a Protestant in a Catholic environment, or as a Jew among Christians, as a Blue among Greens in Constantinople, and as a convinced member of any minority resisting the pressures of the majority.

The coherence of such groups, and the preservation of their identity over long periods, obey the same type of law that is applicable to individuals. They are unities of a looser kind, but they struggle to maintain themselves, and their distinctness, in opposition to their environment, whether they are nations or churches. Spinoza commented on the survival of the Jews as a distinct force and on their extraordinary coherence as a people; they conspicuously illustrated the maintenance of a distinctive character against all the external forces making for their disintegration. Spinoza comes very close to Machiavelli, and to Machiavelli's notion of *virtù*, when he praises both political realism and the vitality that preserves a people as a distinct force in the world.

So far Spinoza can correctly be interpreted as following a Heraclitean doctrine, which is a classical form of rational pessimism; that vitality, and the possession of a distinctive character, engenders, and is engendered by, endless strife. Social stability and harmony, in so far as they are attainable, will always rest upon a temporary balance of forces, not unlike the stand-offs that are normal in combat between animals and between populations of animals sharing the same terrain. In the competition for survival of persons, and of groups of human beings, the hostilities are reinforced by religious and moral beliefs, which cause useless wars; and Spinoza had reason to be particularly interested in undermining the intellectual errors associated with wars of religion.

III

So far freedom of the individual, which entails freedom of thought, has not been represented as naturally and immediately associated with social harmony and peace, which are the necessary conditions of freedom of mind. On the contrary, the prospect is apparently of perpetual conflict, which is a natural process in which virtue and vitality are expressed. Spinoza's solution is found in the climb up the ladder of grades of knowledge, a climb which is open to those who are able to reflect with some detachment from their immediate interests. The level of systematic knowledge that a man attains, and his understanding of rational methods of inquiry, are determined by the degree to which he is able to resist received opinions and immediate impressions, and actively to explore a subject matter for himself, until he arrives at the basic principles and underlying structure.

In the human sciences, as in physics, there is a deep structure of natural law to be discovered. The laws of thought, and the laws governing the emotions, are plainly different from the laws of physics and of the other physical sciences; but the laws governing thought and emotion can be understood if once we undergo a philosophical conversion and turn away from the superstitions of free will and from the belief that men are islands in nature or that the human soul is a monad. Human passions can be studied systematically, and

it is possible to understand the causes of religious and racial fanaticism and hatreds; and there can be a rational political science
founded on psychological understanding.

IV

Spinoza is eccentric as a political theorist, and in his theory of freedom, in virtue of being an unambiguous naturalist in moral theory.
Commentators on Hobbes have found it possible to argue whether
or not he takes the notion of right to have some distinctive moral
force; evidently there is ambiguity in his use of moral notions.
Spinoza is entirely clear and consistent in interpreting every moral
notion naturalistically, that is, as properly to be applied only on
the evidence of observable features of human dispositions and behaviour. There is no place for moral notions, in a Kantian sense.
For instance, to speak of a man's natural right to do something is
properly to speak of his desire and power to do it. The propriety
here is obviously not the propriety of ordinary habits of speech, but
the propriety of consistent theory. I shall not dwell on this point
because it has been made clearly enough by T. H. Green and A. G.
Wernham and many other commentators.

The philosophical conversion proposed is a drastic change of consciousness because it entails regarding one's own emotions, desires
and beliefs, including one's moral opinions, with detachment, as
natural phenomena to be explained as the regular effects of causes,
either in the order of the imagination or in the order of the intellect.
If the belief or desire is only to be explained in the order of the
imagination, it is on reflection discredited as confused and unfounded.
Freedom of the individual, which is freedom of mind, arises from the
ability to reflect on the causes and objects of one's desires and beliefs, and, by this reflection, to change them. Human minds may
form ideas of ideas indefinitely, and this added complexity in their
reflexive thinking is their distinctive power. I have elsewhere defended Spinoza's claim that beliefs, desires, emotions, and propositional attitudes generally, are modified by the subject's changing
beliefs about their nature and about their causes.

Consequently a conversion from a traditional doctrine of moral re-
sponsibility and free will, and from conventional theories of the nature
and causes of emotions, will result in a change in the emotions themselves, together with the desires and the behaviour associated with
them. That mental causality takes this form, through reflexive knowl-

edge, through ideas of ideas, is precisely the reality of human freedom, which is limited, and not absolute; it is limited by the limits
of the power of active thought, present to some degree in everyone.

V

The closer connection between freedom of thought and of expression,
on the one side, and freedom of the mind, can now be stated. The
drive towards autonomy and independence, which is also a drive
towards greater power and vitality, is expressed in intellectual activity,
and in attempts to master and control the environment, and also in
one's own feelings, desires and beliefs. Intellectual power consists
in systematic and theoretical understanding, and as medicine is a
practical application of physics and chemistry, so rational ethics and
rational public policy are, among other things, practical applications
of psychology and of the theory of the emotions. There is still a
crucial difference between the two applications of theory : the psychological theory acts directly on the mind in the case of self knowledge, while physical theory acts only indirectly on the body. It is
impossible for a man who has a systematic understanding of the
causes in his experience and imagination of his political and social
loyalties and hostilities, and of the causes of his moral prejudices,
and who sees them as features of the common order of nature, to be
at the same time altogether serious about them. He will not take
them to be binding on all men, except in so far as he takes them
to be rational principles which any clear-headed person must accept :
that is, except in so far as he can explain them within the order
of the intellect, and without reference to an association of ideas
formed within his own experience. So his attachment to any cause,
and to any group, that divides men by conflicting loyalties is loosened
by reflection.

Spinoza's reasoned hope was that when the secular inquiring habit
of mind spread, being a form of philosophical conversion, divisive
associations would lose their force and ferocity, and a new Machiavel-
lianism, a new political realism, would gradually take its place. The
two kinds of freedom, social and individual, are evidently connected
within the theory, in the sense that each is a condition of the advance
of the other; Spinoza believed that progress depended both upon
acceptance of political arguments, as set out in his two political books,
and also on the more refined arguments from metaphysics and the
philosophy of mind set out in the *Ethics*. Without freedom of dis-

[139]

cussion enlightenment would not spread; and without some diffusion of enlightenment in a population there would be fanaticism and resistance to freedom of discussion. Once the first steps along the liberal path had been taken, as they had been in Holland, the state, and the government of the time, may become entirely secular in their aims, and the evil of religious wars ended.

The limits within which he expected the enlightenment to spread were quite narrow. He did not think it possible that the mass of citizens would loosen their attachment to the established churches and their creeds, or that they would come to examine the usual conflicts in society between different creeds and moral prejudices in an inquiring, scientific spirit. On the contrary he thought that in the common order of nature unquestioning emotional allegiances, and the conflicts to which they lead, are to be expected. But there could be governing élites of new Machiavellians who would calculate the balance of political forces and reach accommodations on the basis of enlightened self interest, discounting their other differences. Rightly perceived self interest is naturally combined with an understanding of the self-interested motives of others, and this provides the necessary background to the deals and compromises that keep the peace. It is not altogether just that Spinoza should be criticized, as a political philosopher, for being excessively rationalistic, as he often is. He consistently insists that men are always governed by their emotions and desires, whether they are enlightened or not. But there can be a conversion of desire, and an enjoyment of knowledge, and of mental activity and inquiry.

VI

The strength of Spinoza's political theory is that he does not prescribe freedom of the individual in a liberal society as an ultimate and undemonstrated moral value, nor does he appeal to natural rights as ultimate and undemonstrated moral values. He argues that the universal drive to self-maintenance and comparative autonomy can be satisfied only by the kind of freedom of mind which requires liberal institutions as a necessary condition. Like many other defenders of liberal purposes, Mill was unclear and embarrassed in explaining why the freedom of the individual to follow his own desires, and to experiment, was the overriding value in politics: was it an instrumental value, necessary in discovering and promoting general happiness? If not, was the supremacy of this single end certified by intuition? Naturalism in moral theory circumvents these embarrassments. Men unavoidably pursue the extension of their own power and freedom, but they are confused in the pursuit. One may remove the confusions by argument, even though one could not alter the direction of their fundamental drives, even if one wanted to. Freedom of the individual, in Spinoza's sense, is the same as the individual's power to determine his own states, and is different from Mill's sense of freedom, identified as plenitude of choice. It is plausible to claim that freedom in the former sense is a universal and natural goal, while it would not be plausible to make this claim for freedom in the other sense.

On the other hand, my advocacy fails when one comes back to the notion of individuality; it seems that a person's sense of his own distinct nature as an individual is not naturally associated with detached intellectual inquiry and the use of rational methods. Rather, the pursuit of systematic theory, and of intellectual understanding, seems to entail that distinctive habits of thought, desires and beliefs, marking one individual off from all others, disappear : certainly not that the peculiar nature of an individual is more fully expressed.

Spinoza's own claim is that the sense of mastery and of vitality brings the pleasure that accompanies freedom and energy. There is also the peculiar pleasure of moments of insight, of *scientia intuitiva*, which is the culmination of intellectual activity. He does not claim that individual differences are expressed in the life of reason, nor does he imply that individual diversity is valuable or to be pursued for its own sake, as Mill sometimes implies. But he did argue that scientific and philosophical enlightenment, and the new self-consciousness that accompanies it, is both necessary and sufficient to prevent hatred and war between competing moral and religious believers. There can be no peace, and no civilized societies, until men are not divided by doctrines, but only by interests, which they recognize and conceive in common terms.

J. BEN-SHLOMO

Tel Aviv

Reply to Professor Hampshire

IN THE FOLLOWING remarks I shall have no argument with the excellent exposé put forward here. I would like, however, to emphasize some points and to suggest one additional aspect which was not touched upon, I think, in Prof. Hampshire's paper.

The concept underlying the whole of Spinoza's system is, in a certain sense, derived from political terminology: the concept of *Potentia* — the power of action, or, the power to dominate. No wonder it was Nietzsche, of all philosophers, who more than once expressed his admiration for Spinoza.

In the first place Spinoza's *metaphysics* is based on this concept. Ontologically we can truly say only one thing about God: that he is infinite power — "The power of God, by which he and all things are and act, is the same as his essence" (*Ethics* I, XXXIV Dem.). This is God's only essence, and it reveals itself to us only in thought and in extension: "All else that men ascribe to God beyond these two attributes... must be an extraneous denomination, such as that he exists through himself, is eternal, one, etc." (*The Short Treatise on God, Man and His Well-Being* [below: *S.T.*], I, 2, 29). All these are *propria*, i.e. properties or predicates which *we* (and that includes Spinoza's own philosophy) ascribe to God, but which are not real. The attributes, on the other hand, are the real actuality of God, and are identical with the Divine powers of action. A divine attribute and a divine power of action are one and the same thing. This dynamic conception is even more explicit in the early version of the *Ethics*, wherein the attribute of thought is called "the thinking *power*" (*S.T.* L, 2, 29) or 'potentia infinita cogitandi" (Ep. 32) and the attribute of extension is the "power to produce" (*S.T.* I, first dialogue, 11).

Power is also the real essence of the modal world: the body and the mind are modifications of the divine essence; i.e. a mode, or an individual, is but a certain manifestation of the divine power of

[142]

action. To be means to act. Hence, the concept of freedom — whether human or divine. Freedom is *not* a property of God, deriving from his essence; it is *identical* with God's essence; "true freedom is only, or no other than, the first cause" *(S.T.* I. 4, 5). This means that God's essence is "infinite activity, and an infinite negation of passivity and, in consequence of this, the more that, through their greater essence, things are united with God, so much the more also do they have of activity, and the less of passivity; and so much the more also are they free from change and corruption" *(S.T.* II. 26, 8).

The obvious conclusion is, of course, that "God alone is the only free cause", inasmuch as he is *causa sui.* Man, as a finite mode, cannot realize freedom unless he himself becomes, in a sense, *causa sui.*

Within the framework of the above terminology, the freedom of the individual is still defined in terms that carry political connotations, or should I say rather, a political flavouring. Freedom is a high degree of the power to act, autonomy, self-determination.

It is, however, possible to understand Spinoza's concept of freedom in quite the opposite meaning, a totally a-political one. Such a reading would rely not only on the utter lack of values and the absence of the very category of a moral imperative of any kind, which is a consequence of Spinoza's radical naturalism, as already noted by Prof. Hampshire. An additional reason for such an interpretation would be that Spinoza's concept of freedom can be formulated in terms which are typically religious or mystical. As a matter of fact, Spinoza deliberately chose such specific terms in his *Short Treatise.*

According to the well known Spinozistic concept of freedom, free is he who has the knowledge of the absolute necessity of his action, being a part of nature; he who conceives of his activity or essence as nothing other than a taking part in God's activity or essence. Human understanding knows itself to be a modification of God's infinite understanding and *nothing more.*

Now, this knowledge, which is also the love of God, is called in the *Short Treatise* 'The Service of God' : "We are truly servants, aye, slaves of God, and that is our greatest perfection, to be such necessarily." The free man is the servant of God by "being a part of the whole of Nature and unable of himself to do anything for his happiness and well-being". Indeed *all* things are truly such servants or tools of God, with the difference that Man can be *aware* of himself as such and therefore also know himself as a participant — albeit a finite one — in the infinite activity of God. Thus the awareness of servitude is at the same time an awareness of power : "We exist also as a part of the whole, that is, of him; and we contribute, so to say, also our share to the realization of so many skilfully ordered and perfect works, which depend on him" (*S. T.* II. 18, 2).

This awareness, which is human perfection, is defined as the love of God: "We offer ourselves up entirely to him; for the sole perfection and the final end of a slave and of a tool is this, that they duly fulfil the task imposed on them" (*S. T.* II. 18, 9).

This state of being like "a hatchet in the hands of a carpenter" is at the same time also a state of the fullest freedom. Spinoza ascribed the most radical and, of course, the most heretical meaning to the old Jewish saying: "None but the servant of God is truly a free man." The knowledge of necessity derives from the essence of man as a mode endowed with the power to think; therefore, it can be said that this knowledge is an action, the proximate cause of which is man's essence. To put it more precisely, human freedom is a state of mind in which God, in the attribute of thought, is known as cause of himself through this same state of mind, for God knows himself through the mediation of this individual human state of mind. In other words, the individual has an awareness that it is not he but God who is acting, because he himself is *not even an agent.* On the other hand, he is, in a certain sense, *causa sui,* and therefore free, according to the exact definition of freedom in the *Ethics* (I, Def. 7). This conception of freedom brings to mind certain radical Christian and Muslim mystics, not to mention eastern mysticism (to the exclusion, however, of Jewish mysticism). We may recall the scandalous saying of Meister Eckhart: "I am the unmoved mover, the cause of himself." In spite of the immense distance between the quietistic implications of such a view and Spinoza's general frame of mind, we must not forget that according to Spinoza God is always, and in any case, the immanent cause of *all* ideas, true and false, whether a man knows it or not. Thus, human freedom lies not in a certain state of affairs, nor even in the knowledge of it, but in the *experience* of the unity with God, when man feels himself to be no more than a part or tool of God's action. Hence the definition of human freedom in the *Short Treatise*: "True freedom is to be, and to remain, bound with the loving chains of his love" (*S. T.* II. 26, 5).

This kind of freedom is not achieved at the rational level of knowledge. This is only a stage on the way to full freedom: "Reasoning is not the principal thing in us, but only like a staircase by which we can climb up to the desired place, or like a good genius which, without any falsity or deception, brings us tidings of the highest good in order thereby to stimulate us to pursue it" (*S.T.* II. 26, 6).

True freedom is reached only at the level of *scientia intuitiva,* where man is aware of the identity of his psycho-physical existence with the unity of Divine extension and thought. At this point it is justified to speak of the mystical character of Spinozism. That does not mean that Spinoza's system is mystical, for it deals with real things — bodies, ideas, emotions, human beings, societies, states, religions — all of which are subject to discursive and rational discussion. As a matter of fact, these subjects of discussion take up the greater part of Spinoza's writings. Nevertheless, true and ultimate human freedom is only that experience of unity with God which is the love of God. Prof. Hampshire has confined his discussion to the kind of freedom which is achieved at the second stage of knowledge. As he says : "Freedom of mind arises from the ability to reflect on the causes and objects of one's desires and beliefs, and, by this reflection, to change them." It is an "intellectual power" which "consists in systematic and theoretical understanding", and which sees all things as "features of the common order of nature". Prof. Hampshire was quite right in so doing, as he was describing, with great precision, the relation between the freedom of the individual and that of the citizen. Within the boundaries of rational knowledge there indeed exists such a relation. However, Prof. Hampshire implies that there is a certain contradiction between the two meanings of Spinoza's concept of freedom. On the one hand freedom is "to assert the individual's independence and identity", in the words of Byron, "to feel that he exists". On the other hand "it seems that a person's sense of his own distinct nature as an individual is not naturally associated with detached intellectual inquiry and the use of rational methods".

My argument is, however, that such contradiction exists only for freedom at the *second* level of knowledge, whereas freedom at its highest level *transcends* the self-assertion of the individual and the individuality of the human mind itself.

In the highest state of freedom God alone is conceived as the true *individuum,* as an infinite organism, of which the human mind is but a limb. The finite individual is only an abstraction of that one totality. Here the human mind sees no more the "endless strife" of existence, but reaches a state of serenity and peace.

This is an ideal of freedom, common to all pantheists, and it poses a problem for Spinoza, one common to all pantheistic mystics : intuition is still a grade of *Knowledge,* a state of *awareness,* and not a real annihilation of the individual mind, Nirvana. Nevertheless, it is certainly a state of freedom which transcends the social and political dimension, and which bears no relevance to the freedom of the citizen. From this point of view we can also understand Spinoza's attitude to time and to historical time, his deep-down indifference to history. Although Spinoza has a political philosophy (for the political dimension is part and parcel of the real modal world) he does not have a serious philosophy of history (as can be discerned in his many misunderstandings of the history of his own people). In this respect he is truly an un-Jewish (and, for that matter, an un-Christian) philosopher. His thought belongs rather to the Classical Greek type.

Aristotle said that "he who has no need of society, because he is sufficient for himself, must be either a beast or a god, he is no part of a state" (*Politics* 1253a). Spinoza would have said that the freedom of he who knows himself *sub specie aeternitatis* does indeed liberate himself from the political bond, for it places him in the status of God himself.

S. PINES

Jerusalem

On Spinoza's Conception of Human Freedom
and of Good and Evil

THE TERMS free (*liber*) and/or freedom (*libertas*) are used by Spinoza in various contexts — for instance in reference to God as well as to man — and their functions within the context of Spinoza's system vary accordingly. There also appear to be certain differences of meaning; but this is a matter for semantic analysis, and its detailed discussion is beyond the scope of the present paper.

The paper will discuss Spinoza's notion of a free man, a topic dealt with in the last section of the fourth part of the *Ethics,* entitled "On Human Bondage". The fifth part, "On Human Freedom", and several passages in the *Tractatus Theologico-Politicus* are also relevant.[1] In treating of free man Spinoza refers to the concept of good and evil on the one hand and to knowledge of truth or, as he puts it, having adequate ideas on the other. A portion of the paper will be devoted to an attempt to elucidate the relation between these three notions.

Sources which Spinoza probably, or, in the case of Maimonides and some others certainly, drew upon, will be occasionally named; the point being that a comparison of the texts may help to determine the precise meaning of a concept or the affective value which Spinoza attached to it. Such an historical perspective may also be useful in tracing the fortunes of some of those concepts after Spinoza's time.

The expression "a free man" first occurs in Part IV of the *Ethics,* in Prop. LXVII. It begins: "There is nothing a free man thinks less about than death". The sentence has a near parallel in a treatise of Philo's predominantly influenced by Stoic doctrine; for the Stoics considered that only the good or superior man, who following in his conduct the dictates of reason is not a slave to the bodily passions,

---

1   However the context of the fifth part of the *Ethics* is in the main outside the scope of the present paper.

may be fitly termed free. Such a man has no thought of death.[2] Numerous moralistic philosophers took over these (or cognate) truisms. So did Spinoza. But his context was somewhat different and he introduced a new point of view, which may account for his preferring the term "free" to the equivocal term "good".

In the demonstration of Prop. LXVII, "the free man…" whose conduct is not determined by the fear of death is described as directly desiring the good; which means being active, living, preserving one's being, (all) this being based on one's seeking what is useful for oneself.

In this passage the term good can be taken as interchangeable with living and being active.[3] It may be remarked in this connection that the impulse (*conatus*) to preserve oneself is according to Spinoza[4] the essence of a thing. The assimilation of the good to what is useful[5] is Stoic doctrine. Spinoza clarifies it[6] by explaining that seeking what is useful to oneself is tantamount to seeking to preserve one's being. All this may be summed up in the statement that the good is the affirmation of one's being and the effort to preserve it. Quite evidently there is no opposition between this concept of good as understood in Prop. LXVII and the concept of truth.

A wholly different concept of good is a main subject in Prop. LXVIII. The proposition and its demonstration reads: "If men were born free, they would, as long as they were free, form no concept of good and evil."

Demonstration: I have said that a man that is guided by reason only is free; (it follows) that he is not born and does not remain free unless he has adequate ideas and hence has not the concept of evil. In consequence — (given the fact) that good and evil are correlative (terms) — he does not have the concept of good.

A clarification of two expressions is called for.

---

2   See Philo, *Quod Omnis Probus Liber Sit*, 22–23, Philo, Loeb Classical Library, IX, London–Cambridge (Mass.) 1954, p. 23, F. H. Colson's translation: "Some praise the author of the line: *What slave is there who takes no thought of death,* and think that he well understood the thought that it involves. For he meant that nothing is so calculated to enslave the mind as fearing death through desire to live. But we must reflect that exemption from slavery belongs to him who takes no thought (*aphrontis*) not only of death, but also of poverty, disrepute and pain and all the other things which the mass of men count as evil."
3   Cf. *Ethics* IV, Prop. XXIV.
4   *Ethics* III, Prop. XXII, *Demonstration.*
5   Cf. the definition of the good at the beginning of Part IV of the *Ethics.*
6   *Ethics* IV, Prop. XX.

Prop. XXXIV of Part II of the *Ethics* shows that in Spinoza's usage an "adequate idea" and a "true idea' are interchangeable terms.
Knowledge of evil is, as shown in *Ethics* IV, LXIV, inadequate (i.e. false) knowledge.[7]

In the Scholium to Prop. LXVIII Spinoza first indicates in rather obscure language that the hypothesis that men are born free (and hence lack, as long as they remain in that state, the concept of good and evil) is false because it presupposes that man is only subject to changes of which he himself is the adequate cause. This presupposition is false because it entails the absurd consequence that a man (i.e. a human individual) must necessarily exist for ever. Hence man being a part of nature is subject to changes that are not caused by himself.

In other words, the freedom of man from the notion of good and evil is not a habitual, normal state; it is a philosophical imperative.

The second part of the Scholium contains an interpretation of a biblical story, the fall of Adam. It has in common with Maimonides's interpretation[8] — which is modified by Spinoza — the unbiblical assumption that the knowledge of good and evil marks in itself — with no reference whatever to the punishment which it provoked — man's decline from his perfect state, which according to Maimonides consists in thinking about what is true and false rather than about what is good and evil; for the specifically moral judgements are concomitant with and necessitated by the need to exercise some control over the appetites and passions of the human individual.

The origin of the comparison instituted by Maimonides between the notions of true and false on the one hand and of good and evil on the other goes back to a passage in Aristotle's *De Anima* dealing with the difference between the theoretical and the practical intellect. Commentators of Aristotle, such as Themistius, whose works were doubtless known to Maimonides, point out that what is true is the end of the theoretical intellect and what is good of the practical. John Philoponus remarks on the superiority of the former intellect over the latter.

According to Spinoza knowledge of good and evil brings with it in the first place fear of death; then, as it seems, the imitation of the

---

[7] Being awareness of sadness, i.e. a transition to a lesser perfection. According to the *Praefatio* of the Part IV of Spinoza's *Ethics,* good and evil do not indicate something positive (existing) in things if these are considered in themselves; they are nothing but modes of thought, or notions that we form in comparing things with one another.

[8] *Guide of the Perplexed,* I, 2.

affects of beasts and the loss of freedom. The latter was recovered by the Patriarchs, who were guided by the spirit of Christ, i.e. the idea of God. Man's freedom and his wish that other men should obtain the good that he wishes for himself depend on this idea.

Two conceptions of good are discussed in this proposition.[9] (1) The ethical one which is correlative with evil entails the loss of human freedom. (2) The one predicated upon the idea of God, i.e. the cognition of true reality, goes hand in hand with the achievement of freedom. It is, however, not self-evident that the free man must desire that all men should enjoy the good he wishes for himself.

A very similar interpretation of the story of Adam's fall is propounded in Chapter IV of the *Tractatus Theologico-Politicus.* [10] According to this interpretation, the prohibition to eat of the tree of knowledge of good and evil signifies that Adam was enjoined to do and to seek what is good *sub ratione boni,* and not because it is the contrary of evil : whoever does what is good because of his love and knowledge of good, acts freely and steadfastly; he is the opposite of the man who acts out of fear of evil. The latter being constrained by evil, acts in servile fashion and is under the domination of someone (or something) other than himself.

The biblical story is also mentioned in another passage of Chapter IV of the *Tractatus.*[11] Spinoza observes there that if God had (in fact) told Adam that he did not wish him to eat of the tree of good and evil, his eating of it would have involved contradiction (for the identity between God's Will and Intellect entails the conclusion that everything that he wills, i.e. affirms or negates, involves some eternal verity, and consequently must of necessity be realized). Hence the scriptural version of the story must mean that God had only told

---

9   Because of this apparently Christian theological tag H. A. Wolfson (*The Philosophy of Spinoza,* II, Cambridge [Mass.], p. 256) considers that "some Christian theological exegesis of the story of the fall of Adam ... is undoubtedly the direct source of Proposition LXVIII". Rather surprisingly he makes no allusion to the obvious points of resemblance between Spinoza's interpretation and that of Maimonides. In this connection the fact that both philosophers are of the (by no means commonly accepted) opinion that knowledge of good and evil is in itself a defect is to my mind of great significance. The fact that both Maimonides and Spinoza refer to Adam's having become after the fall similar to the beasts may also be mentioned, as this remark is not taken from the story of the Book of Genesis. But the points of resemblance between Adam and the animals stated by Maimonides are not identical with those found in Spinoza's text.

10   C. Gebhardt's edition of Spinoza's *Opera,* III, p. 66.

11   *Ibid.,* p. 63.

Adam that evil will follow upon his eating of the fruit of the tree, but had not revealed to him the necessary character of this consequence. Because of this Adam regarded this revelation (i.e. God's command) not as a necessary truth, but as a law which lays down that advantage or disadvantage will result not in consequence of necessity and of the nature of the action that is committed, but because some prince who exercises absolute rule wills it so. It was because Adam's faculty of cognition was at fault that the revelation in question was transformed into a law and God, as it were, into a legislator and a ruler. The same holds for the Decalogue; because the faculty of cognition of the Hebrews was at fault, God's existence and his being the sole object worthy of worship taught in the ten commandments were regarded by the people not as eternal truths but as laws.

The opposition between the religious laws conceived as ordinances of an imaginary God regarded as a ruler and legislator on the one hand and the eternal verities and the dictates of reason on the other is what the *Tractatus Theologico-Politicus* (or a considerable part of it) is about. Religious laws are essentially laws not promulgated by the people who are called to obey them, but by an external authority. Those who obey such an authority are said to live under the law and appear to be slaves.[12] They cannot be called just for it is only out of fear of punishment that they give everyone what is his due. According to Spinoza Paul seems to have had this in view when he states that those who live under the law cannot be justified by the Law.[13]

Our discussion to this point may be re-stated as follows: The term freedom (*libertas*), as applied to men in a non-political context, has as used by Spinoza in the *Ethics* two valid connotations. One of them which apparently goes back to the Stoics is essentially a metaphor: The human individual who dominates his passions and has adequate knowledge may be termed free. The adjective describes a happy stage; it carries no programmatic significance. In using it Spinoza followed a venerable philosophical tradition.

The second connotation of "free" may be due to a linguistic innovation of Spinoza. But this innovation occurs in a philosophical context which forcibly calls to our mind the fact that Spinoza was familiar with a work of mediaeval Aristotelianism, namely Maimonides's *Guide of the Perplexed*.

---

[12] *Tractatus*, Chap. IV, ed. Gebhardt, p. 59.
[13] *Romans* iii, 19–20.

The new conception of freedom is from the historical point of view clearly connected with certain development of Peripatetic theory, which Spinoza uses for his own purposes; the conclusions that he reaches and the philosophical programme that he suggests or implies are all his own.

Aristotle's differentiation between the theoretical and the practical intellect may, in our context, be taken as a starting point.[14] Themistius provides an apparently correct clarification of this distinction. As he understands it,[15] the theoretical intellect has truth as its end whilst the end of the practical intellect is the good. It may be taken for granted that in this connection "good" does not refer to the *summum bonum* of the philosophers, but to something relative, in the spirit of Aristotle's remark[16] that what is good for man is not good for the fishes.

John Philoponus explains the distinction between the two intellects in a similar way. In point of fact, according to him these constitute one and not two faculties; they differ because of the difference in their ends. John Philoponus states with some emphasis that truth which the theoretical intellect endeavours to attain is superior to good which is the end of the practical intellect. Man's intellect is practical only during the union of the soul with the body. After the cessation of this union it is exclusively theoretic.[17]

Maimonides modifies this Aristotelian theme which he employs in his interpretation of the story of Adam's transgression.[18] In accordance he speaks of the perception of good and evil (and not, as the Aristotelians did, only of good) ; and he does not dignify this perception by ascribing to the activity of the practical intellect a term which he does not mention in the *Guide*. Good and evil are not intellectual concepts; they are merely commonly accepted notions. The inferiority of judgements based on these notions to propositions which deal with truth and falsehood is dwelt upon with a vehemence which as far as I can see has no parallel in the Aristotelian tradition prior to Maimonides. The latter, nevertheless, appears to consider that, given the human condition, recourse to these judgements is unavoidable; at any rate this conclusion may, as it would seem, be legitimately drawn from the chapter to which I am referring.

14 *De Anima*, 433a, 14–15.
15 See Themistius, *De Anima*, ed. L. Spengel, Leipzig 1866, p. 209.
16 See *Nicomachean Ethics*, 1141a, 23.
17 See G. Verbeke, Jean Philopon, *Commentaire sur le De Anima d'Aristote*, traduction de Guillaume de Moerbeke, Louvain–Paris 1966, p. XLVIII.
18 See *Guide of the Perplexed*, I, 2.

Spinoza's position is quite different on this point. According to him, as we have seen, having the notion of good and evil is incompatible with having adequate ideas; i.e. true knowledge. The fact that man, according to Spinoza's *Ethics,* is capable of having adequate ideas, thus entails the consequence that he can dispense with the notion of good and evil.[19] Further on an attempt will be made to show what this means in terms of Spinoza's system. In this context another point should be mentioned on which Spinoza differs from Maimonides. The former but not the latter employs the word "free" to describe the man who does not have the notion of good and evil. This meaning of the adjective apparently does not occur in any philosophical system that I have mentioned up to now. As it seems to me, the internal evidence of Spinoza's writings — I refer to the indications that can be discovered by comparing the *Ethics* to the *Tractatus Theologico-Politicus* — points to his having made use, as far as this particular is concerned, of quite a different source. In various significant passages in the *Tractatus* we find quotation from and references to New Testament texts, notably the Pauline Epistles in which the terms "yoke", "to free" and cognate words occur. The yoke which, according to this interpretation, Paul as well as Spinoza has in mind is the yoke of the Law, particularly the Mosaic Law, and the freedom which they recommend is freedom from the Law.

The following quotations from the *Tractatus* (Chap. III[20]), may serve to illustrate Spinoza's use of Pauline theology[21] for his own purposes:

> God therefore sent his Christ to all the nations, in order that he should free all of them from the bondage of the law, so that they should no longer perform good actions because of the command of the Law, but because of a steadfast decision of (their) mind.

In this passage not only the Mosaic Law, but also the Laws of the nations are regarded as instruments of bondage. This may also be true of the following text,[22] though the quotation from Paul may show that the Mosaic Law was foremost in Spinoza's mind:

19 This conception is of help in placing in the right context Spinoza's famous remark in the letter to Albert Burgh (Letter LXXVI): "I do not claim to have discovered the best philosophy, but I know that I grasp the one that is true."

20 Ed. Gebhardt, p. 54.

21 These verses are not cited by Spinoza.

22 *Tractatus,* Chap. IV; ed. Gebhardt, p. 5.

In truth, (a person) who gives everyone his due (only) because of the gallows, performs his actions because he is under the domination of someone (or something) other than himself[23] and because he is forced (to do what he does) by (fear of) evil;[24] he cannot be called just. On the other hand he who gives to everyone his due because he knows the true reason for and the necessity of the laws, acts with a steadfast spirit and because of his own decision and not that of another, and deserves therefore to be called just. I believe that Paul wanted to teach this when he said[25] that those who live under the law cannot be justified by the law, for justice, as usually defined, is a steadfast and permanent will to give everyone his due.

The words *malo coactus*, literally "forced by evil", appear to indicate that in heteronomous moral systems observance of the law is motivated by a certain notion of evil, the evil that befalls the transgressor.

Spinoza's ideas on the servitude that is imposed by the Mosaic law are summed up in a passage occurring in Chapter II of the *Tractatus.*[26]

> ... It cannot be believed that ignorant men accustomed to Egyptian superstitions and brought up in a most miserable bondage (could have) conceived a sound (idea) about God, or that Moses taught something other than a way of life; (he did this) not as a philosopher, so that they should have a good life because of their freedom of mind, but as a lawgiver so that they should have such a life because they are constrained to it by the rule of the Law. Hence the way to live well, or the true life, the worship and love of God (constituted) for them bondage rather than freedom, a grace and a gift of God... Furthermore he terrified them by threats (dealing with what would happen to them) if they should transgress these commandments; as against this he promised many good (things[27]) if they should keep them .... Hence it is certain that they were ignorant of the excellence of virtue and of true happiness.[28]

Spinoza's sharpest criticism is undoubtedly directed against the Mosaic law, but it is equally valid if directed against all religious systems of

---

23 *Ex imperio alterius.*
24 *Malo coactus.*
25 *Romans* iii : 19–20.
26 Ed. Gebhardt, pp. 40–41.
27 *Multa ... bona.*
28 *Veram beatitudinem.*

legislation which draw their authority from a God conceived as a ruler and lawgiver. All such systems contain a series of commandments and prohibitions and are founded upon the (inadequate) concepts of good and evil.[29] They lead men into bondage or keep them there. These remarks based primarily upon texts of the *Tractatus* have quite evidently, as it seems to me, a bearing on Part IV, Prop. LXVIII, which has been discussed above. The free man is referred to in that proposition as having no concept of good and evil; in other words, he is, if we accept Spinoza's position, a man who rejects in the name of true knowledge all the religious laws and all religious morality.

It may be argued that Spinoza was the first philosopher to give the adjective "free" the meaning we have been discussing and to state more or less explicitly that the achievement of the "freedom" in question should be one of the main goals of rational man.[30]

If we take this position of Spinoza as a starting point, it is easy and tempting to go further and make the assumption that, given the spuriousness of the traditional systems of morality, this "freedom" is the only characteristic of man that has some validity, and authenticity. It is not impossible that Spinoza is to some extent a direct or indirect source of this tendency in nineteenth and twentieth century thought. Admittedly, this is, unavoidably in this context, a rather vague remark.

The following brief observations on Nietzsche concern the history of the antithesis between the good and the true, which was first formulated, as we have seen, within an Aristotelian framework. Nietzsche was doubtless unaware of this origin of this antithesis which plays a considerable part in his thought and to which mainly in his final period he gives a new twist. To cite but one example, he states in *Ecce Homo* that the fact he "the first immoralist" chose Zara-

---

29 And also on the concepts of sin and of (religious) merit (*peccatum et meritum*). These two concepts are mentioned in the Appendix to Part I of the *Ethics*. They arise from the (mistaken) idea that men have freedom of action (i.e. are not subject to natural necessity). The concepts of good and evil are also mentioned in this Appendix, but not as applied to men's behaviour, but to what occurs (in the universe). They stem from (the baseless) idea that it is for the sake of men that everything happens. These and various concepts should be regarded as modes of the imagination. Cf. also below.

30 In the beginning of Part V of the *Ethics*, *De Libertate Humana*, freedom (*libertas*) is used as an equivalent of *beatitudo*. But this may be a higher sort of freedom than the one alluded to in Prop. LXVIII of Part IV; for it is consequent upon intellectual love of God.

thustra (as his spokesman) is due on the one hand to the fact that this Persian was the first to consider the struggle between good and evil as the decisive factor in the course of events, that "he created morality, this fatal error". On the other hand it is due to the fact that truthfulness is regarded by Zarathustra as the supreme virtue. This virtue overcomes morality. The transformation "of the moralist into his contrary — into myself — that is the signification of the name of Zarathustra" as used by myself.[31]

In the same work he remarks that a lie, in other words the reluctance... to see reality as it really is, is a condition for the existence of good men.[32] In a letter written to Franz Overbeck on 30 July 1881,[33] Nietzsche expresses his astonishment at the kinship which he perceives between Spinoza's position concerning morality and cognate topics and his own.

> I am astonished and charmed! I have a forerunner, and what a forerunner. I hardly knew Spinoza... Not only his general tendency is similar to my own, namely to regard (*zu machen*) cognition as the most powerful affect, I recognize myself in five main points of his doctrine. As regards these matters this very abnormal and solitary thinker is very close to me: he denies freedom of will; final ends (*Zwecke*); the moral order of the world; that which is the unegoistic (impulse);[34] evil. Though admittedly the differences are immense, they are mainly due to differences of the periods (or difference in) culture and science.[35]

The points which struck Nietzsche in Spinoza's doctrine are quite different from those which exercised an enormous influence on

[31] *Ecce Homo, Warum ich ein Schicksal bin,* § 3.
[32] *Op. cit.,* n. 4.
[33] *Friedrich Nietzsches Briefwechsel mit Franz Overbeck,* Leipzig 1916, p. 149 f.
[34] *Das Unegoistische.*
[35] Nietzsche, *Aus dem Nachlasse der Achtziger Jahre,* Werke in drei Bänden, ed. K. Schlechta, III, p. 486: "Wie erklärt sich Spinozas Stellung, seine Verneinung und Ablehnung der moralischen Werturteile? (Es war *eine* Konsequenz seiner Theodizee!)" This explanation does not fit Spinoza's conception of God, but it fits to some extent mediaeval theories from which Spinoza's views derive. Nietzsche's interpretation of the biblical story concerning man's first transgression differs from that of Spinoza (and from that of Maimonides). In a sense it is more conventional. According to him the knowledge that man is supposed to have acquired in eating fruit of the tree is science (*Der Antichrist* 48, ed. Schlechta, II, pp. 1212 ff.).

German thought in the eighteenth century and the beginning of the nineteenth.

However Nietzsche's position with regard to the antithesis : true and good was in some of his writings different from Spinoza's (and from that of the Aristotelians mentioned above). The reason was that he had renounced the notion of truth (as conceived, for instance, by Spinoza when he refers to adequate ideas) and questioned the value-judgement that prompts the wish to grasp the truth. A philosophy that is beyond good and evil should not entertain the preconception that truth is preferable to falsehood.[36] In other words, "true and false" derive from, and are variations upon, "good and evil". This is a quite different perspective from the one pre-supposed in Spinoza's statement according to which he does not claim that his philosophy is the best, but knows, on the other hand, that it is the true philosophy.

In conclusion some comments will be made on a remark of Spinoza concerning a "free man's" behaviour in society, *Ethics* IV, Prop. LXXII : "The free man never acts by fraud,[37] but always honestly".[38]

Demonstration

> If a free man, qua free, were to do something by fraud, he would do it following the dictate of reason, so that acting by fraud would be a virtue...; consequently... it would be advisable to act by fraud in order to preserve one's being; this means (as is evident in itself) that it would be advisable for men to agree in words only while being in fact opposed to one another, which... is absurd...

Scholium

> If it should be asked whether, given the case that a man can by (an act) of faithlessness[39] free himself from a present danger of death, the reason (that requires him) to preserve his being would not in any way advise him to be faithless, the following answer should be given after the same manner, namely that if

---

36 Cf. *Jenseits von Gut und Böse*, I, 1–4, ed. Schlechta, pp. 567–570. Cf. *Die Fröhliche Wissenschaft*, 344, ed. Schlechta, II, pp. 206–208. The attitude to truth and to the search for truth which is expressed in *Jenseits von Gut und Böse* and elsewhere is hardly compatible with the passage on Zarathustra quoted above.

37 *Dolo malo.*

38 *Cum fide.*

39 Or treachery; *perfidia.*

reason would advise this (this would mean) that it would give this advice to all men. Hence reason would in every way advise men by no means to join forces and have common laws unless they conclude a mutual pact by fraud. (This means that) in fact (it would advise them) not to have common laws, which is absurd.

The mention of virtue in the first part of the demonstration is explained by a reference to *Ethics* IV, Prop. XXIV, in which acting in accordance with virtue on the one hand and with the dictates of reason on the other are equated. Acting in this way is identical with preserving one's being.

There is an at least apparent contradiction between this position and the text of the Scholium of Prop. LXXII according to which reason requires to adopt a course of action leading to the danger of present death, i.e. the non-preservation of one's being. One may consequently ask what was Spinoza's motive in inserting Prop. LXXII. It seems probable that he was guided by an overriding reason : The necessity to render life in society possible, and to prevent a return to the state of nature with its perils and terrors. Spinoza seems tacitly to imply that, faced with mortal danger, a "free man" would not let his course of action to be determined by such notions as right and wrong (*iustum et iniustum*) which are a product of society,[40] but by the persuasion of reason. The latter's advice bids free man who is in mortal danger not to commit an act of treachery or deception, because his doing so, if legitimated by reason, would mean that the common laws should permit treachery or deception. This calls to our mind a formula which as enunciated by Kant in the *Critique of Practical Reason*[41] reads : "Handle so dass die Maxime deines Willens jederzeit zugleich als Prinzip einer allgemeinen Gesetzgebung gelten kann." In other words the Scholium of *Ethics* IV, Prop. LXXII, contains a clear application *avant la lettre* of the Kantian categorical imperative. The fact that Spinoza speaks in this connection of the dictates of reason without differentiating between theoretical and practical reason, while Kant uses the originally Aristotelian term *praktische Vernunft,* which is given by him a new signification, is in itself interesting, but does not affect the resemblance referred to above. It would seem that Spinoza's Scholium should be taken into account when the genesis of the notion of categorical imperative is investigated. If Kant was not directly or

40 Cf. *Ethics* IV, Prop. XXXVII, Scholium II.
41 See *The Critique of Practical Reason,* I, 1, 7.

indirectly influenced by Spinoza's text, which is by no means certain, the text shows that ideas anticipating the categorical imperative were propounded in the seventeenth century intellectual climate.

I shall add a final observation. A comparison between Spinoza's doctrine and Kant's ethical and religious philosophy might help to solve certain problems posed by the latter. Some of the differences existing between the two philosophers seem to me to be as significant for the relation between them as the similarities. The importance assigned by Kant to the notion of radical evil[42] and his conception of God as a lawgiver[43] may possibly be accounted for by the need to put forward an antithesis to the theories of Spinoza.

---

[42] Cf., for instance, Kant, *Die Religion innerhalb der Grenzen der blossen Vernunft*, I, 3. Cf. Spinoza, *Cogitata Metaphysica*, I, VI: *"Malum autem absolutum nullum datur, ut per se est notum"*.

[43] Cf. Kant, *op. cit.*, III, 5.

ARNE NAESS

Oslo

Spinoza and Attitudes Towards Nature

I

THIS PAPER is not a report on pure research, but research in the service of the deep, philosophically oriented international ecological movement. More specifically it takes seriously the thesis that in the long run our strange human species can avoid major crises only if the attitudes towards nature, prevalent in the industrial states, are changed. A key term today in so-called 'green' philosophy and politics is 'society in dynamic ecological equilibrium'. This thesis maintains that one of the necessary conditions of ensuring a 'soft landing' in such a society is change of dominant attitudes.

I am concerned with how to achieve a soft landing without dictatorship or other immense catastrophies. Near-equilibrium might be obtainable through harsh dictatorship, by using ecological experts and *forcing* changes of economic and other policies upon a world populace which has no regard for nature except as a realm of resources for humans.

A salutary change might develop without much philosophical reflection. There is, however, a chance that some of us, in our capacity as academic philosophers, might contribute in a modest way to such a change by pointing to *philosophies of nature which are in harmony with a sane ecopolitical outlook.*

Some have pointed to Schelling, others to other philosophers. I point to Spinoza.[1] Not that I think his extremely complex views can be

---

1 Some may judge that what I say is unhistorical. Or that I make Spinoza modern. But I look at a text of Spinoza as a score of Bach, open to many interpretations. In all humility I will say that while my interpretations of the *text* of the *Ethics* can be upheld, they are certainly not the only plausible interpretations. I make a distinction between talking about

conveyed to large numbers of people today, or even be thoroughly understood by a small learned minority. The availability of Spinoza's thought is limited today, but his personal appeal is immense and practically universal among all who study philosophy.

I shall try to formulate how I conceive our historical situation in relation to nature.

In the Hellenic period a religious movement towards inwardness eventually had the effect of downgrading the status of the physical universe, including the human body. In Europe in the Middle Ages there was a dominating tendency to concentrate value in God and the Spirit *at the cost of* the body and the physical universe. The attitude of a Francis of Assisi did not prevail.[2] An overly lofty estimation of 'the world' was generally considered a temptation, and one had to fight the flesh. Naturalness tended to be identified with sinfulness and crudeness; everything natural came under suspicion. Individuality, or, in the terminology of Spinoza, particular things, were downgraded in their ontological and axiological status. All value was absorbed in God, the creation only imperfectly reflecting the qualities of a *spiritual* world order.

The renaissance and the new natural science eroded God and Spirit as the mansions of all value, *but did not reinvest nature*. On the contrary, nature was given the rather passive, profane job of serving as stuff and machinery. Holy places, the closeness and the religious veneration of nature were not restored.

The situation is now one of indifference and poverty : the transcendent God is gone, and nature is divested of any attribute that could foster a natural, deep reverence or fruitful personal interaction. (The hunter-gatherer interaction is today considered 'technically backward', and also there is less and less to hunt and gather !)

What is left of nature is seen as *materials* for satisfying human needs, or, in the industrial states, for the proliferation of wishes. Nature is seen as something neutral or hostile which has been largely, but not yet completely, subdued and conquered. What is left of comparatively untouched nature is the subject of superficial aesthetic or recreational

the historical Spinoza as a person and presenting an interpretation of one of his texts. This, again, is different from presenting a reconstruction inspired by Spinoza.

2 Even Francis of Assisi, the saint of ecology, was no friend of the body : *"Nous devons avoir en haine nos corps, avec les vices et les péchés, . . ."* (*Documents,* Paris 1968, p. 118). As used by Spinoza, the term *corpus* permits one to ask Francis : what about the **corporeal events corres-**ponding to your faith ? And what about *"les vices et les péchés"* of your spirit?

attitudes. Life and work in and with nature is a rare privilege. So much for a nut-shell formulation of our predicament.

In this situation the philosophy of Spinoza provides a potentially vast source of inspiration. The following enumeration of traits does not presume to convince those who feel comfortable in the present era of fast and vast changes on the surface of the earth, or those who feel at home with the so-called 'modern' life-style. It is, however, aimed at mobilizing those who feel otherwise, and to induce them to make themselves better heard in the social and political debates.

II

1. The completely immanent God: *Deus sive Natura.*
One of the very basic ideas of Spinoza is the immanence of God in Nature. "God is the immanent, not the transcendent cause of all things" (*Ethics,* Part I, Prop. XVIII).[3] God's role as the cause of all things does not preclude the infinite number of particular things themselves from causing infinitely many things. God as cause cannot be distinguished, except conceptually, from what the particular things themselves cause. He is, in a sense, helpless without the essences of particulars! Without our essence there is no God; without God we are nothing. While Spinoza places stress on the second part of this assertion, the first is also implied in his philosophy of immanence.

The Spinozic *identification* on the level of denotation or extension or reference (not on the conceptual or connotational level) of God with Nature means reinvesting Nature with perfection, value and holiness. Spinoza explicitly rejects degrading nature in the way of some of his contemporaries.

The expression *Deus sive Natura,* God or Nature (with a capital N) occurs twice in the preface to Part IV of the *Ethics.* Here Spinoza

---

[3] The mediaeval users of the distinction *natura naturans / natura naturata* and *naturare/naturari* may be said, with Geroult and others, to have introduced the concept of immanence of the divine cause in its effect. Characteristic of Spinoza is that he uses the distinction "to express his concept of absolute immanence, which those terms never had signified" (M. Geroult, *Spinoza, I: Dieu,* Paris, Aubier, 1968, p. 567). Speaking about the immanence of God in Nature (and Nature in God) as a Spinozic conception, I take it to be absolute at the level of denotation or extension. At the narrower level of connotation or intention, immanence — if the term can be used at this level at all — is not absolute. If it were, we would have general substitutability of *Deus* and *Natura* in the *Ethics.* This is hardly Spinozic. See here, pp. 125 f.

talks about "the entity which we call God or Nature" and of the "actions" of God or Nature. The expressions *Deus sive Natura* and *Deus seu Natura* also occur in the proof of Part IV, Prop. IV :

> The power through which particular things, and as a consequence, man, preserve their essence, is God's, or Nature's power, not in the role of (*quatenus*) being infinite ; but in the role of being explicable (*explicari potest*) through the actual human essence. The power of man, in the role of being explicated through his own actual essence, is part of God's or Nature's infinite power, that is, essence.

As individuals we are, as are all other particular things, invested with part of God's or Nature's infinite power.

If the idea of God's immanence is taken seriously, the two roles of God or Nature are equally basic : the role of being infinite and non-explicable through particular finite things and the role of being thus explicable. Part I of the *Ethics* speaks about *Deus quatenus infinitus,* the other parts mainly about *Deus quatenus non-infinitus.* These other parts are as genuine an expression of Spinoza's system as is Part I.[4]

I have translated the central but little studied term, *quatenus,* 'in the role of'. Other translations are of interest, for instance : 'in the capacity of' ; 'functioning as' ; 'as', and the very common translation 'in so far'.

Using the extensional equivalence of 'god' and 'nature', we obtain an intuitively acceptable theorem : Nature does not exist apart from particular finite things. Nature or *natura naturans* is immanent in nature as *natura naturata.* Immanent in particulars : particularity and divinity may perhaps be said to be equally basic aspects of 'The Whole'.

But let us go back to the four occurrences of *Deus sive* (or *seu*)

---

[4]   Some researchers seem to attribute the logical superstition to Spinoza, that the content of Parts II–IV of the *Ethics* can be deduced from Part I. But all the way through the *Ethics* new insights are communicated :

1.   The definition of God in Part I does not refer to the non-infinite aspect of God. The aspect is something new, although it does not contradict what is said in Part I. Its heading may be read *De Deo quatenus infinito.*

2.   In general, a certain freedom in our attitude towards the *exposition* of Spinoza's system is called for, as long as we do not postulate that every one of its formulations and its order of presentation directly express insights of the third kind. G. Fløistad warns against any such assumption.

Natura in the *Ethics*. In these occurrences one might plausibly interpret the terms *Deus* and *Natura* as having identical intension or connotation. If that were so in the rest of the *Ethics,* we should, without disturbing the meaning, be able to substitute one for the other in the text. However, while such a substitution leads to an interesting new Spinoza text, well worth considering today, it can sometimes lead to theorems which Spinoza himself would hardly subscribe to.

If *Natura* is substituted for *Deus* in Part V, we get, among others, the following theorems :

> Prop. XVN : He who clearly and distinctly understands himself and his affects, loves Nature, and the more he understands himself and his affects.
>
> Prop. XVIIIN : Nobody can hate Nature.

When we contemplate God, that is Nature, says Spinoza, in his proof, we are active (and enjoying an active affect), and this excludes hating.

(When dragged along on still another botanical excursion by her parents — both botanists — a very young Norwegian girl exclaimed "I hate nature". How are we to interpret this ?)

The introductory passage to the proof of Prop. XX, Part V, is worth quoting :

> This love of Nature is the highest good we can strive for in harmony with the dictate of reason, and is common to all humans, and we wish all would enjoy it. As a consequence it cannot be polluted through jealousy.

Prop. XXIV of Part V is basic concerning particulars :

> Prop. XXIVN : The more we understand the particular things, the more we understand Nature.

This proposition regarding the (qualitative) increase of our understanding of God seems to be intuitively obvious to Spinoza : he offers no extended proof, but merely refers to the Corollary to Prop. XXV in Part I, a rather flimsy basis for such an unconventional conception. Presumably he would accept the reverse of XXIVN :

> The more we understand Nature, the more we understand the particular things.[5]

---

[5] Prop. XXIV may be interpreted in a quantitative manner : more things are understood ; or in a qualitative one : a higher degree, things are understood in the third way ; or in a way combining both aspects. The

Clearly we cannot identify Nature (with a capital N) simply with the (infinite) set of particular physical and non-physical things. Such an atomistic view is scarcely consistent with Nature as a whole, being an individuum.

Gestalt thinking and the concept of 'inner relations' are useful in making precise the interconnectedness of parts and whole.

We can now get a feeling of how the propositions of the *Ethics* read when the term God is replaced by the term Nature. Let us inspect the relation between our highest aims in life and God or Nature.

In the following quotation from Part V, Proof of Prop. XXVII, 'God or Nature' is substituted for God :

> The highest virtue of the mind is to understand God or Nature, or to understand things in the third way.

The 'or' (*sive*) directly connects understanding God with understanding things. For validity Spinoza refers to the just-quoted Prop. XXV. If we focus on God *rather than* on Nature, the lofty status of understanding particulars seems to reveal an inconsistency.

According to the *Ethics* the highest good that the intuitive way of cognition can lead us to is the understanding of particular things in the light of God or Nature. In Section 13 of Spinoza's work on the Understanding, he identifies the highest good with the understanding of the unity of mind with total Nature (*cum tota Natura*). The difference in formulation is instructive. The latter refers to 'Nature', not to 'God', but achieves the same as the first through the terms 'unity' and 'total'.[6] According to the interpretation of Spinoza's system suggested in the foregoing pages it is beyond the scope of our reason or language to describe *exactly* what the relation *is* between God, perfection, Nature and individual things, e.g. living beings.

second sentence of the proof of Prop. XXV provides evidence for a qualitative interpretation. On the other hand, Spinoza, especially in connection with the many parts of the body and the many (more than eighty) classes of emotions, *stresses multiplicity and diversity*. It is also important that understanding God or Nature includes understanding of the third kind, intuitive understanding of *particular* things. It is implausible that it is equivalent to a qualitatively more and more perfect understanding of one particular thing.

6   The adjective *totus* is perhaps better rendered by 'totality' than by 'whole', if we wish to stress that the third way of understanding is that of seeing *single particular* things from the point of view of the whole. If we wish to stress the unity of the mind with a whole which has an aspect of undivisibility and changelessness, then 'whole' may be a better translation than 'totality'.

But the interpretation clearly has affinities with an attitude towards nature found among a significant subgroup of researchers, poets and people with no special status. Here we are concerned with ecology.

The philosophical aim of the deep ecological movement may be formulated in a way not very different from that of Spinoza when he speaks about God or Nature and the role of particulars. Quite central to both is Spinoza's pronouncement, just referred to :

> This is the goal I seek (*tendo*), namely to acquire such a nature[7] (i.e. a nature which involves the understanding of the unity of the mind with total Nature) and to strive that many with me acquire it.... To do this it is necessary to understand so much of nature as is sufficient to acquire such a nature; and then to form a kind of community (*societas*) that is required in order that as many as possible in the most easy way can safely reach it (*Tractatus de intellectus emendatione*, Sect. 14).

There is a wide gap between Spinoza's *credo*, strictly interpreted from a historical point of view, and that of the deep ecological movement. Yet although man's predicament today differs from that in the seventeenth century, there are some similarities which suggest a basic continuity through the centuries.

Nature as conceived by field ecologists is not the passive, dead, value-neutral nature of mechanistic science, but is akin to the active, perfect *Deus sive Natura* of Spinoza. It is all-inclusive, creative (as *natura naturans*), infinitely diverse, and is alive in the broad sense of Spinozic panpsychism. It manifests structure, namely the laws of nature, but, because 'all things hang together', we cannot predict the long-range effects of our particular actions and policies. This is in harmony with Spinoza's warning that we should not think man capable of ever fully understanding the 'common order' of Nature.

Nature (with a capital N) is *intuitively* conceived as perfect in a sense that Spinoza and ecologists hold more or less in common : it is not a narrowly moral, utilitarian or aesthetic perfection. Nature is perfect 'in itself' and not in so far as it serves specifically human needs. Spinoza does not *argue* in favour of Nature's perfection.

'Perfection' has to do with *per* and *factum*, something already accomplished and completed. 'Perfection' in Spinoza means *completeness* and *realness* (cf. *Ethics*, Part IV, Preface) of some sort when applied in general, and not only to specifically human achievements.[8]

---

7 Is *'natura'* here identical extensionally with 'essence'? This would imply that one's essence may be changed through self-causation.

8 'Perfection' is not a term which is introduced in the *Ethics* by means of

In the latter case it means reaching what has been consciously intended. The concept of completeness is related to the concept of a *mature ecosystem*. Completeness suggests maximum diversity, maximum self-reliance, maximum dynamic equilibrium.[9]

2. The value-dualism spirit / matter, soul / body is eliminated in the *Ethics*. The same is true of the basic attitude of field ecologists. Perfection characterizes both realms.[10]

In view of the tendency to look upon the body as something more crude than the spirit, both field ecologists and Spinoza oppose most forms of spiritualism and, of course, moralism. Their realism does not, however, exclude the possibility of future societies characterized by generosity, justice and non-violence.

3. According to Spinoza Nature (with a capital A) is not *in* time. As an *absolutely* all-embracing reality, Nature has no purpose. If it had a purpose, it would have to be part of something still greater, for instance a grand project. Time and, therefore, purpose are only definable *within* the network of relations of Nature; therefore Nature as a whole cannot have aims or goals which refer to time. There is no all-embracing *progress* from the point of view of eternity or timelessness.

In ecological thought there is a marked reaction against facile

a separate definition. When not applied to Nature it admits of degrees. Joy is an emotion through which mind is said to become *more* perfect (Part III, Scholium to Prop. XI). Whatever its connotation, 'more perfect' cannot be separated in denotation from 'more powerful'. Compare proof of Prop. XLI: "Joy... is the emotion through which the power of the body to act, increases or is furthered." The relation to action, and therefore to understand, is intimate. The more perfect is the more active and the less passive (Part V, Prop. XL). In short, 'more perfect than' cannot, in denotation, be separated from a number of other basic relations. The application of the term to Nature or God clearly is on par with the application to God of terms like 'love' (*amor*), 'intellect', 'mind', that is, it cannot be taken in any precise sense known from phenomena *in* Nature.

9   The term 'maximum' rather than 'optimum' diversity presupposes a concept of diversity that is common, but not universal, among ecologists.

10   Unconditional acceptance of the axiom of perfection is not possible for me. Or, more precisely, it is only possible through dubious interpretations of the terms 'perfection' and 'Nature'. Spinoza helped himself with his theory of non-existence of *adequate* ideas about evils. Although I find that theory dubious, as well, I have not come across any better one. What follows (pp. 167–175) is a thoroughly revised version of parts of my article "Spinoza and Ecology", in: S. Hessing (ed.), *Speculum Spinozanum 1677–1977*, London 1978.

finalism. The development of 'higher' forms of life does not make field ecologists less impressed with the 'lower' forms, some of which have flourished for countless millions of years and are still 'going strong'.

In time there is no 'purpose' of the type that would eradicate the function or value of bacteria after 'higher' forms have developed.

4. There is no established moral world-order. Human justice is not a law of nature. Concurrently *there is no natural law limiting the endeavour to extend indefinitely the realm of justice and mercy as conceived in a society of free human beings.*

These Spinozic thoughts are important for striking a balance between the submissive, amoral attitude towards all kinds of life struggles and the shallow, moralistic and antagonistic attitude. Future societies in ecological equilibrium presuppose such a 'third way'. Humans have a right to self-fulfilment, but when free and rational they desire the same for all life forms.

5. Good and evil are predicated in relation to beings *for* whom something is good or evil, and *for* a purpose. Something is good or bad in the sense of its being useful or detrimental. When they are not related to subjects and purposes, the terms are meaningless.[11]

Thus interpreted one may say that for the utilitarian Spinoza the expression 'x is useful for y' is equivalent to 'x causes an increase in y's power', 'x causes an increase of y's freedom' and 'x causes an increase of y's perfection'.

This accords well with the effort of field ecologists in general and social anthropologists in particular to understand each culture 'from within', as well as with mild forms of sociological functionalism. It contrasts with absolutistic moralizing on the basis of an unquestioned

---

11 The occurrences of the words *bonus* and *malus* in the *Ethics* admit of various conceptualizations. According to Part IV, Def. I, 'x is good for y' does not mean more than 'x is useful for y' or 'x is known by y to be useful for y'. Spinoza does not *say* anything to the effect that freedom, perfection and the other 'in-itself' states are good. They enter the system both as something that things actually or in fact or with necessity strive to realize and as unquestioned desirables.

An extreme naturalism is consistent with one particular well-known set of equivalences in Part III, Prop. XXXIX, Scholium : "... we strive after nothing because it is good, but on the contrary we call that good which we strive for." It is to be noted, however, that Spinoza does not say that we call something good *because* we strive for it. Good is not an effect caused by striving. And the striving is not just for self-preservation in the narrow sense, but for freedom, virtue and power. See also n. 12, below.

value code which predominates in some (mostly industrial) societies. It does not *exclude* that some states of affairs are better than others for all persons or sentient beings, and that some purposes define goals with the status of autotelic value.

For Spinoza the 'in-itself' predicates express such values : 'in it-self', 'free', 'virtuous', powerful', 'self-caused', 'active'.[12] In *general* social anthropology, I suspect similar values are recognized or will be increasingly recognized.

6. Every thing is connected with every other thing. There is a net-work of cause-effect relationships which connects everything with everything else.

The ecologist Barry Commoner has called 'All things are connected with all others' the first principle of ecology. Interconnectedness in the sense of internal rather than external relations characterizes ecological ontology. The maxim is misleading except when things are ultimately conceived as *gestalts.*

7. Nothing is causally completely inactive, nothing is wholly with-out an essence which it expresses through being a cause. In a limited sense the whole of Nature is alive and one individuum (one *gestalt*).

Every being strives to preserve and develop its specific essence or nature.

Every essence is a manifestation of God or Nature. There are in-finite ways in which Nature thus expresses itself. And there are infinite kinds of beings expressing God or Nature.

The pervasive basic striving is no mere effort to adapt to stimuli from the outside. It is an active shaping of the environment. Success-ful acts create new wider units of organism/environment. The basic urge is to gain in extent and intensiveness of self-causing. The term 'self-realization' is therefore better than 'self-preservation', as the former suggests activeness and creativity, while the latter denotes a passive conservative or defensive attitude.[13]

8. Another name for the ability to act out one's nature or essence is 'power', *potentia,* the substantivation of the verb 'to be able', *posse.* It is not the same as to coerce others.

---

12 For a detailed exposition of the equivalence of these terms, see my *Freedom, Emotion and Self-subsistence* and *Equivalent Terms in Spi-noza's Ethics,* Oslo, Universitets forlaget, 1975.
13 According to Part III, Prop. VI, *every* thing, as far as it is in itself, strives to preserve its being. I take the term *perseverare,* translated as 'preserve', to mean something much more active than just to survive. Therefore, I accept as equivalent '*x* increases in power' and '*x* increases in level of self-preservation'.

The power of each thing is part of God's power. God or Nature has no other powers than ours. "Each and every existing thing expresses God's nature or essence in a certain determinate way... that is,... each and every thing expresses God's power..." (Part I, Proof of Prop. XXXVI). Without particulars, Nature's essence or power is not expressed. Nature is totally dependent upon the particulars.

The above may be said to go against any hierarchical conception of existence. No subgroup of particulars expresses more of God's essence than any other. But this is perhaps somewhat misleading, as Spinoza considers men to have more power than animals, and therefore they may be said to express *more* of God or Nature's power. But Nature's power being infinite, the distance remains the same, namely infinite, for all particular things.

All beings strive to maintain *and gain* power. This need not be a striving to dominate, subdue or terrorize. The establishment of symbiosis, 'living together', rather than cut-throat competition marks a gain in power. At higher levels of self-realization, the self in some ways encompasses others in a state of increasing intensity and extension of 'symbiosis'.[14] The freedom of the individual ultimately requires that of the collectivity.

9. If one insists upon using the term 'rights', every being may be said to have the right to do what is in its power. "Everybody exists through Nature's highest right (*summo naturae jure*), and consequently everyone, through Nature's highest right, does that which follows from the necessity of his Nature..." (Part IV, Prop. XXXVII, Scholium II).

'The Ethics of Ecosystems' and 'Environmental Ethics' as proposed by ecologists tend towards the acceptance of a philosophy of Natural Right. The same holds true of the movement among jurists to accept 'legal rights for natural objects'. Justice William O. Douglas of the U.S. Supreme Court wrote in his 'Opinion' that legal standing should be accorded to "valleys, alpine meadows, rivers, lakes, estuaries, beaches, ridges, groves of trees, swampland, or even air that feels the destructive pressures of modern technology and modern life".[15]

Animals have the same kind of right to self-expression that we have.

---

14 Good relations to others are obtained, according to Part IV, Prop. XLVI, 1 (Scholium), LXXII, *inter alia,* through generosity and other forms of non-injury (*ahimsa*). According to Part IV, Prop. XLV, "Hatred can never be good", that is, according to Part IV, Def. I, it can never be useful to us. Therefore it cannot cause an increase in power or understanding.

15 Chr. D. Stone, *Should Trees Have Standing*, Los Altos 1974, pp. 74–75.

"That right which they have in relation to us, we have in relation to them" (Part IV, First Scholium to Prop. XXXVII).[16] Rights as part of a separate moral world order is a fiction.

Field ecologists tend to accept a general 'right to live and blossom'. We have no *special* right to kill and injure, *Nature does not belong to humans or their states.*

10. There is nothing in human nature or essence, according to Spinoza, which can *only* manifest or express itself through injury to others.

The human attitude of violence and hostility towards some species of animals has made it impossible to study realistically their life and function within the whole. The field ecologist who deeply identifies with the species studied is able to live peacefully with any kind of 'wild' animal. Even with vicious sharks! This attitude harmonizes with Spinoza's view concerning the free man (*homo liber*). His doctrine on the development of affects (Parts III–IV of the *Ethics*) makes the field ecologist's symbiotic attitude *inevitable* if the development proceeds far enough. It is prescribed in the very nature of humans.

In what follows other Spinozitic thoughts are mentioned which harmonize with those of field ecologists, even if the latter do not often develop them consciously.

11. The realization of union with the whole of Nature is made through the understanding of the particular things as a manifold of expressions or manifestations of Nature.

Ecological thinking presumes an identification with particulars in their internal relations, or *gestalt* relations, to others. The identification process leads deeper into Nature as a whole, but also deeper into unique features of particular beings. It does not lead away from the singular and finite. It does not lend itself to abstract thinking or contemplation, but to *conscious, intuitive, intimate interaction.*

Many astonishing discoveries by field ecologists are due to intensive studies of particular *individual* animals which they give names to and in many ways perceive intuitively as individuals. Those who hire ecologists and those who use their publications have little interest in

---

16 It must be conceded that Spinoza holds that we cannot be the friends of animals or include them in our society. Only humans can be friends of humans and be members of our societies (see Part IV, Appendix, Chap. XXVI). And because we are more powerful than animals, we have in a sense more rights. We are able to *use* animals as we see fit, and one cannot issue laws against killing them. Most animals lack the power to use us (cf. Part IV, Scholium I to Prop. XXXVII, and Appendix, Chap. XXVI).

these individuals. Judged on the basis of *publications* field ecologists seem on the whole to be contributors to nomothetic science and to concentrate on narrow 'environmental' problems and 'nature management'. In this respect field ecologists can be compared to artists who, for the sake of earning a living, are part-time art dealers. They are perhaps only quoted when talking about prices.

12. 'Rationality' is wise conduct maximizing self-realization. It cannot be separated from perfection, virtue and freedom. "Since reason does not demand anything contrary to Nature, it demands that everyone love himself, look for what is useful, . . . and that he strives to obtain all which really leads man to greater perfection . . ." (Part IV, Prop. XVIII, Scholium). Since self-realization implies acts of understanding with increasing perspective, rationality and virtue increase with the development of understanding. The maximum is 'an understanding love of Nature', *amor intellectualis Dei*. This implies acts of understanding performed with the maximum perspective possible, or loving immersion in and interaction with Nature.[17]

An attitude towards nature as judged in terms of the behaviour of industrial nations is rational in a very different sense. It is cleverness relative to extremely short-sighted, narrow interests. Many people assume that rationality is cold calculation in the service of such ends. Acquaintance with Spinoza's conception means an immense widening and deepening of the conception of rationality.

13. Because of the interaction of things and understanding — things cannot be separated. The units of understanding are not propositions but acts. To the content of ideas in the "attribute of non-extension" there corresponds an act in the "attribute of extension". Ultimately these attributes are attributes of the same thing, but the human way of understanding is such that we have to treat them separately.

The increase of rationality and freedom is, according to Spinoza, proportional to the increase of activeness, each action having the aspects of understanding and of a behaviour of interaction. Relations to Nature are interactions; doing ethology or social anthropology exemplifies active relations on the level of cognition.

[17] The basic position of 'understanding', *intelligere*, in Spinoza's system is seen from its relation to 'causing'. If something is caused adequately through something else, it is adequately understood through this something, *and* vice versa. Activeness is internally related to understanding because the specific activity of the mind *is* understanding. It is also related to increases in power and freedom. In this way not only intuitive understanding of the highest (third) kind, but also the understanding of nature, promotes power, freedom, joy and perfection.

14. Since to gain in understanding expresses itself as an act, it is in its totality a process within the extended aspect of Nature and can be studied as such.

This point is of prime importance to the methodology of ethology : the 'world' of a living being is investigated through study of its manifest ('molar' and 'molecular') behaviour. Spinoza furnishes ethology with a frame of reference completely devoid of the kind of uncritical 'mentalism' and 'introspectionism' that has often obstructed the study of cognition in animals and men.

The framework of relating Spinoza to general ethology is also suited to counteracting the tendency to conceive human knowledge as something existing independently of acts of particular human beings in particular situations — and stored wholesale in libraries.

The formulation of Spinoza does not point to any definite form of 'behaviourism'. We are free to inspect critically any contemporary version. There is no reason to identify the concept of 'behaviour' with that of J. B. Watson or B. F. Skinner.

15. Most of the basic concepts used in the *Ethics* to characterize the human predicament are such as can be used whatever the cultural context. They are, furthermore, adapted to general characterizations covering smaller or greater parts of the animal, plant and mineral kingdoms. Some of these concepts have already been mentioned.

Spinoza rarely touches upon questions concerning animals, but, where he does, he shows that his main concepts are not intended to apply only to humans.[18] He warns, however, against thinking that the joys of insects are the same as those of humans. Each kind of living being is content with and delights in what corresponds to its nature or essence. But they *have* joys and, therefore, presumably also sorrows.

Among the important concepts which have an application wider than to the human species, one may note the following :

perfection (cf. point 1)
good and evil (cf. points 4–5)
striving to express one's nature or essence (cf. points 7–8)
self-preservation, self-realization (cf. points 7–12)

---

[18] The panpsychism of Spinoza is expressed in the *Ethics*; see Scholium to Prop. XIII, Part II. Individuals other than humans are animated, *animata*, but in different degrees, *diversis gradibus*. Spinoza even (in the proof of Part III, Prop. I) uses the expression "the minds of other things", *aliarum rerum mentes*. About the difference in appetites and joys between various kinds of animals, see the Scholium to Prop. LVII, Part III.

power (cf. points 8–10)
rationality (cf. points 12–13)
rights (cf. point 9)
virtue (cf. point 12 ; cf. the expression *'potentia seu virtus')*
freedom (cf. points 12–13)
understanding (cf. points 13–14)
feeling (see Scholium to Prop. LVII of Part III)
emotion (the passive ones are confused *ideas)*
confused idea (see General Definition of Affects, *Ethics,* Part III)

For all these terms it is true that Spinoza's definitions are *open as regards their exact range.*[19] Some are clearly intended to be applicable at least to a major part of the kingdom of animals. Because of equivalences between many of them the range of all of them can, without doing violence to Spinoza's texts, be made as large as suitable within ecology and the theory of evolution.

The wide applicability of Spinoza's *concepts* does not imply uncritical *statements* about similarities between humans and other living beings. It ensures a broad continuity of outlook and the possibility of fighting human haughtiness and cruelty.

III

Main conclusions :

1. Spinoza's fundamental conception of an all-embracing reality and man's place within that reality is today the most adequate conception in the light of ecological research.

2. It is congenial to the basic attitude of field ecologists towards forms of life and the various species.

3. Its wide acceptance, or the acceptance of conceptions consistent but not necessarily identical with it, could promote the aims of the ecological movement.

These conclusions are, of course, in need of some warnings against uncritical enthusiasm :

---

[19] Spinoza does not say so directly, but I think he would deny rationality of any kind to beings other than humans. He speaks, however, about the 'virtue or power' of animals, and he more or less identifies virtue and rationality "...to act virtuously is nothing else than to act according to reason : ..." (Part IV, Proof of Prop. LVI).
While Spinoza may be interpreted in various ways as regards the relation of animals to man, we have been interested in the main trend of his reasoning.

a.   Spinoza's system with its complicated details is scarcely thoroughly comprehensible to anybody today and has no chance of being accepted by any substantial group of people.

b.   Some of his opinions on animals and on other subjects of ecological concern are neither in agreement with research nor congenial to basic ecological attitudes.

c.   His texts lend themselves to various interpretations. They can be used in a variety of reconstructions of his systems, some of which might go against or be indifferent to basic conceptions and attitudes of field ecologists.

d.   There is no complete consistency of attitudes among field ecologists. The present paper cannot speak for all, though it speaks for a substantial subgroup.

L. KOŁAKOWSKI

Oxford

Spinoza : Selbstmord oder Selbsterhaltungsmetaphysik ?

MEIN HAUPTGEDANKE IST in dem Titel enthalten. Ich glaube, dass Spinozas Moralphilosophie auf zwei gegeneinander begrenzende Prinzipien aufgebaut ist : die moralische Bejahung der Individualität oder das Selbsterhaltungsprinzip und eine Tendenz, die auf ihre Zerstörung oder metaphysische und moralische Entwirklichung abzielt. In der spinozistischen Weltauffassung ist dieser Widerspruch, glaube ich, nicht zufällig; er ist in den zwei widerstreitenden Tendenzen seiner Seinslehre eingewurzelt; er darf auch als Konflikt zwischen Ontologie und Physik gedeutet werden und lässt sich — in bezug auf historische Quellen — auf den Widerspruch zwischen der neuplatonischen Theorie des Absoluten und der kartesianischen Naturphilosophie zurückführen. Wenn ich jetzt auch diese Interpretation durch keine detaillierte Textanalyse begründen kann, wird mein Standpunkt, hoffe ich, für alle, die mit dieser Philosophie vertraut sind, vollkommen verständlich sein.

Spinozas Metaphysik kann als Fortsetzung einer Strömung gelten, der in der europäischen Philosophie Parmenides den ersten Anstoss gegeben hat. Und wenn wir an die religionsphilosophische Theorie von Mircea Eliade glauben dürfen, nach der jede religiöse Tätigkeit sich endgültig auf den Versuch die Zeit unbeweglich zu machen oder das zeitlose Sein zu ergreifen, zurückführen lässt, dann darf auch diese Metaphysik als eine Fortsetzung dessen betrachtet werden, was immer im Zentrum der religiösen Erfahrung gestanden hat. Sie versuchte aber in abstrakten Begriffen etwas auszudrücken, was einst in mythologischer Narration und in anschaulichen Symbolen ausgedrückt zu werden pflegte; das konnte sie nicht, wie es scheint, ohne in Widersprüche zu geraten.

Was in der Fundamentalidee dieser, bis auf Parmenides zurückgreifenden Metaphysik vorausgesetzt wurde, war nicht nur der Glaube, dass wir sinnvoll von dem zeitlosen — im Unterschied von einem

[176]

immerwährenden — Sein reden können ; sie setzte überdies voraus, dass "sein" im eigentlichen Sinne soviel wie "zeitlos sein" heisst oder, um dasselbe auf die umgekehrte Weise auszusagen, dass "in der Zeit sein" so gut wie "nicht sein" ist. Dass das absolute Sein zeitlos (und nicht immerwährend) bleibt, ist definitionsmässig wahr, da zu seiner Absolutheit notwendigerweise auch seine vollkommene Aktualität gehört ; es gibt in ihm folglich keinen Unterschied zwischen *potentia* und *actus*. Ein zeitliches Seiendes dagegen, wenn es sogar ewig (im Sinne von immerwährend) wäre, müsste doch sein Verhältnis zu sich selbst mit Hilfe des Gedächtnisses oder der Vorwegnahme vermitteln und folglich könnte es kein "*totum simul*", könnte es keine reine Aktualität sein.

Und hier liegt die Schwierigkeit : falls das zeitlose Sein wirklich ist, ist es überhaupt möglich, dass es doch nicht das *einzige* Sein ist ? Ist es nicht so, dass unter Annahme seines Bestehens alle partikulären Seienden (und das heisst : alle begrenzten, zeitlichen Wesen) in einem nebelhaften Sinn irreal oder eine Täuschung sind ? Dann erhebt sich aber natürlich sofort die Frage : wessen Täuschung ? Des Absoluten selber ? Es kann doch keiner Täuschung unterliegen. Sind sie also ihre eigene Täuschung ? Sie müssen doch sein, um der Täuschung zum Opfer zu fallen. Und so kehren wir zu der scheinbar widersinnigen, lächerlichen und schwindelerregenden Frage des armen Arztes von Anton Tschechows *Drei Schwestern* zurück : "Vielleicht existieren wir überhaupt nicht, vielleicht scheint es uns nur, dass wir existieren ?" — eine Frage, der wir im Rahmen der normalen logischen Disziplin keinen klaren Sinn zu geben imstande sind, die aber psychologisch, empathisch, verständlich ist.

Dieselbe Zweideutigkeit entsteht auch auf dem Boden der christlichen Philosophie, falls man ihr eine vollkommene Konsequenz geben will. Dass *Deus est quodammodo omnia*, dass Gott auf eine gewisse Weise alles ist, wird in dieser Philosophie vertreten ; tatsächlich kommt dieser Ausdruck von Thomas von Aquino her. Wenn wir aber weiter zu dringen versuchen und wenn wir fragen "*quo modo ?*", auf welche Weise ? kommen wir leicht zu dem Schluss, den Meister Eckhart formuliert hat : Gott und Sein sind dasselbe ; folglich sind alle Geschöpfe nichts, also nicht etwas Unbedeutendes und überhaupt nicht Etwas, sondern das reine Nichts, *purum nihil* (die Formel, die bekanntlich vom Papst Johann XXII 1329 als häretisch, frech und schlecht klingend verurteilt wurde). Es folgt überdies daraus — da die gesamte in der Welt wirkende Energie göttlicher Herkunft ist — dass auch das Böse von Gott stammt oder vielleicht, dass der Unterschied zwischen dem Guten und dem Bösen keine Begründung im Sein hat.

[177]

Diese philosophische Zerstörung der kontingenten Wesen, das heisst der ganzen Schöpfung, schliesst auch die Zerstörung der menschlichen Subjektivität ein. Damit aber kann die ganze Vielfältigkeit der Welt der geschaffenen Dinge nicht einmal als Täuschung bezeichnet werden und wird völlig unbegreifbar ; es gibt keine Lösung ausser etwa der Hinnahme des Widerspruchs, das heisst ausser der Anerkennung, dass unsere Logik für die Betrachtung des unendlichen Seins unanwendbar sei, und zwar deshalb, weil unsere Sprache in diesem Bereich keine Genauigkeit erreichen kann, und wenn sie nicht genau ist, unausweichlich in Widersprüche verfällt. Es kommt aber nur selten vor, dass die Philosophen diesen letzten Schluss ausdrücklich anzunehmen wagen, wie es Cusanus tat.

Dies ist nun die Kernfrage des Neuplatonismus : was für einen ontologischen Status kann der Welt der endlichen Dinge (die Subjektivität eingeschlossen) gegeben werden, unter der Voraussetzung, dass *sein* soviel heisst wie *unendlich sein*, und dass es uns erlaubt ist, den Begriff der aktuellen, der erfüllten Unendlichkeit zu benutzen ? Und das ist auch *die* Frage Spinozas par excellence : eine Frage, die er nie gelöst hat und die er sich bewusst war, nicht gelöst zu haben. Er brauchte freilich nicht die hoffnungslose Frage zu beantworten, was eine unendliche Subjektivität sei, da es diese für ihn nicht gab, statt dessen stellte er aber eine andere, genau so hoffnungslose Frage auf : was ist das Attribut des Denkens, das keine Subjektivität ist und das dem absoluten Sinn zugeschrieben wird ?

Nun ist bei Spinoza diese, von Hegel in bezug auf Spinoza "Akosmismus" benannte Tendenz, die geschaffene Welt zu entwirklichen, äusserst stark. Wir spüren hier, in der *Ethik*, eine unausweichliche Konsequenz, der jedoch ein umgekehrter Gedankengang entgegentritt. Zu sagen, dass die Welt Gott ist, läuft, wie Thomas Hobbes bemerkte, auf das gleiche hinaus, wie zu sagen, dass es keinen Gott gibt ; man könnte diesen Satz vielleicht auch umkehren und sagen : Zu sagen, dass es keinen Gott gibt, heisst, dass es keine Welt gibt. Was kann dies aber eigentlich bedeuten ?

Dass es bei Spinoza keinen logischen Übergang von der Substanz bis zur Welt der modi (unendliche modi eingeschlossen) gibt, erscheint, in der Architektonik seiner Metaphysik, als eine Konsequenz seines Beweisensstils, spezieller gesagt : des ontologischen Gottesbeweises. Dieser kommt hinaus auf den Satz, dass die Existenz analytisch erschlossen werden kann und damit zur Wahrheit erhoben wird (einzig im Falle des absoluten Seins). Der ontologische Beweis ist nicht weniger als ein Satz, der zugleich existenziell und analytisch sei : eine Verbindung, die sowohl für Kant, als auch für die ganze empiristische Philosophie logisch unmöglich ist. Nun begründet bei Spinoza dieser Beweis nicht nur eine logisch zwingende Notwendigkeit des Seins der Substanz, sondern auch die Tatsache, dass es nur eine einzige Substanz geben kann. Der Grund dafür ist, dass durch sich selbst sein, *per se esse,* dem *per se concipi posse* (durch sich selbst begriffen werden zu können) gleicht — eine Gleichung, die aus der charakteristisch spinozistischen Identifizierung der ontischen und der logischen Ordnung folgt. Auf der anderen Seite heisst, 'nur durch sich selbst begriffen werden zu können', *per se solum concipi posse,* soviel wie 'durch keine andere Begriffe bestimmbar zu sein'. Es scheint, dass diese Voraussetzung besagt, dass Gott als *das* bestimmt wird, was nicht bestimmt werden kann (also eine Antinomie, die der von Poincaré aufgezeigten Antinomie analog ist : der Antinomie der kleinsten Zahl, die unmöglich mit Hilfe von weniger als hundert Worten definiert werden kann).

Um gültig zu sein, setzt dieser Beweis den hergebrachten nominalistischen Gedanken voraus, nach dem das Attribut mit der Substanz (und überhaupt, jede Eigenschaft mit dem Ding, dem sie gehört) identisch ist, dass heisst, dass es keinen besonderen ontologischen Status hat. Es ist aber gleichzeitig vorausgesetzt, dass der Unterschied der Attribute keine *distinctio rationis,* kein nur vernunftmässiger Unterschied ist, da man in diesem letzten Fall annehmen müsste, dass jedes Attribut, um wirklich zu sein, die Existenz der menschlichen Vernunft, also eines *modus,* verlangt ; das letzte ist aber unmöglich ; darum scheint mir die Deutung, die Spinoza in diesem Punkt der Lehre des Maimonides zuschreibt, unhaltbar. Diese Verneinung des ontischen Unterschiedes zwischen der Substanz und den Attributen ermöglicht es Spinoza zu argumentieren, dass ein mit unendlich vielen Attributen ausgestattetes Sein nur ein einziges sein könne ; da es sonst mehrere Wesen geben müsste, die dieselben Attribute teilen, diese Wesen aber, kraft derselben Identifizierung, auch identisch sein müssten. Dass es, auf der anderen Seite, unendlich viele Attribute geben muss, ist uns kraft des Begriffes des vollkommensten Seins bekannt, und dass wir von jenen nur zwei kennen, soll daraus folgen (wie Spinoza im Briefe an Schuler erklärt), dass sich unsere Denkensfähigkeit nur auf das erstreckt, was in der Idee des Körpers enthalten ist und diese Idee nur zwei Attribute begreift ; diese Erklärung scheint aber der sonst ausdrücklich aufgestellten Behauptung entgegenzustehen, nach der die Ursache aller Dinge Gott als das aus unendlich vielen Attributen zusammengesetzte Wesen ist.

Wenn wir schon wissen, dass jedes endliche Ding an beiden Attributen teilhat, das heisst, dass alles was ist, zugleich Körper und Idee ist, ohne aufzuhören, dasselbe Ding zu sein, und dass dabei diese zwei Aspekte jedes Dinges voneinander völlig unabhängig bleiben, wissen wir weder, worin diese Teilnahme besteht, noch auf welche Weise es möglich ist, dass endliche Dinge irgendeinen eigenen Seinsstatus haben. Wir wissen zwar, dass jede Erkenntnis, die Gewissheit bringt — also die einzige, die verdient, ausgeübt zu sein — *von Gott* zu den Dingen und nicht umgekehrt fortschreitet, dass also Gott keineswegs aus seinen Wirkungen erkannt werden kann, oder — was das Gegenstück desselben ausmacht — dass die Dinge ohne Gott nicht erkannt werden können. Spinoza nimmt das Prinzip an, das einst Descartes in Antwort auf Gassendis Einwände hin formuliert hatte, das aber bei Descartes keine grosse Bedeutung hat, sonst aber in der früheren pantheistischen Tradition (z. B. bei Eriugena) bekannt war : ein Prinzip, nach dem das unendliche Sein kein negativer Begriff, kein Mangel an Grenze sei (wie z. B. Hobbes behauptete, der aus diesem Grunde diesen Begriff für wesentlich unverständlich erklärte), sondern umgekehrt eine Bejahung, ein Positivum darstellt ; jede Begrenzung erscheint gerade als Negation des Unendlichen, nicht umgekehrt. So steht es bei Spinoza mit den Dingen in ihrem Verhältnis zu Gott.

Auf den ersten Blick ist es gar nicht klar, was es bedeutet, dass die Dinge Modifikationen der einzigen Substanz, d. h. ihre Begrenzung *(determinationes* bei Spinoza oder *limitationes* bei Descartes) sind ; gewiss hat dieser Begriff der Begrenzung, wie alle Kategorien der Metaphysik Spinozas, einen sowohl räumlichen wie logischen Sinn, aber sogar der räumliche Sinn ist nicht ersichtlich. Es ist nicht klar, was der Gedanke besagt, dass die Dinge nicht einfach begrenzt sind, sondern als Begrenzung der unendlichen Substanz definiert werden sollen. Es ist klar, dass für Spinoza Dinge keine Teile der Substanz sind ; Substanz ist keine Ansammlung von Dingen, sie ist unteilbar ; die Dinge sollen als Teile des unendlichen modus gelten, der letzte aber, wie wir sonst wissen, gehört der *natura naturata* zu. Die ausgedehnte, die körperliche Substanz ist ebensowenig aus Teilen zusammengesetzt, wie eine Linie aus den ausdehnungslosen Punkten zusammengesetzt ist. Auch ist sie keine *materia prima*, da in ihr keine Potentialität besteht, da sie vielmehr reine Aktualität ist. Sie ist ein unteilbares und zeitloses Ganzes, ein Individium ; in ihr Teile zu unterscheiden, d. h. besondere Dinge in der Erkenntnis zu ergreifen, ist die Aufgabe der empirischen Anschauung, die aber gerade ein Resultat der Abstraktion ist ; das abstrakte Wissen, das darin besteht, Dinge als begrenzt und abgesondert zu betrachten, ist zwar für praktische Zwecke unentbehrlich, sonst aber eine wesentlich entstellende Erkenntnisweise.

Diese Doktrin war besonders den Angriffen der Rationalisten als widersinnig ausgesetzt. Seit Pierre Bayle konzentrierte sich die rationalistische Kritik auf diesen Punkt : es folge daraus, schrieb Bayle, dass alle Dinge wesentlich dasselbe seien, dass dieselbe Substanz ein Substratum der Inhärenz der einander widersprechenden und unvereinbaren Eigenschaften sei, und zwar in ihren beiden Attributen : dasselbe Ding sei gleichzeitig rund und quadratisch, derselbe Gott als Henker töte sich selbst als Opfer, und derselbe Gott, modifiziert in die deutsche Armee, mache sich selbst in Form der türkischen Armee nieder ; jede Verschiedenheit der Dinge werde aufgehoben, das Widerspruchprinzip werde für ungültig erklärt und damit offenbare sich die ganze Konstruktion als leeres Hirngespinst.

Hirngespinst oder nicht, gehört diese Idee jedoch zu dem eigentlichsten Gedankengut der neuplatonischen Überlieferung und auch zu der Tradition der niederländischen Mystik ; tatsächlich ist sie älter als die Philosophie und kann in der klassischen religiösen Literatur Indiens gefunden werden, wenn sie auch bei Spinoza in einer teilweise scholastischen, teilweise kartesianischen Sprache ausgedrückt ist. Sie besagt : es gibt nur ein einziges Konkretum und dieses hat keine Teile ; was uns Teile zu sein scheint, erscheint so nur im Resultat der empirischen, d. h. abstrakten Erkenntnis, einer solchen, die die Wirklichkeit künstlich in abgesonderte Fragmente zerteilt, eine verkrüppelte (mutilata) Erkenntnis. Jedes Ding ist wesentlich das Ganze, das im Erkennen modifiziert worden ist ; wie in einer Linie keine Punkte in actu existieren — sie sind Durchschnitte, keine Teile — so sind die vermeintlichen Konkreten des empirischen Wissens tatsächlich nützliche Fiktionen. Nach Spinoza ist das Mass, d. h. die Quantität, nur eine Denkweise, eine subjektive Operation ; nur im Resultate unserer eigenen Eingriffe wird den Dingen eine Quantität, eine Begrenzung, zugeschrieben, in der Realität stecken sie ebensowenig, wie die Sinnesqualitäten.

Gibt es überhaupt für Spinoza so etwas wie ein principium individuationis innerhalb der ausgedehnten Substanz ? Es scheint, als ob Spinoza ein solches Prinzip vorschwebt, wenn er, auf herkömmliche kartesianische Weise, Bewegung und Ruhe als diese (einzigen) Eigenschaften namhaft macht, die die besonderen Körper auszeichnen. Sonst aber scheint diese Ausflucht mit der Behauptung unvereinbar, nach der die Teile in der Natur nur subjektiv unterschieden werden können, da die Natur an sich keine Teile kennt.

Es gibt keine Lösung für diese Inkonsequenz, keinen Ausweg, der, um den Spinozismus in inneren Einklang zu bringen, zugleich das Eigentlichste und das Eigentümlichste an ihm nicht vernichtete. Dreimal fragte in den Briefen an Spinoza Walter von Tschirnhaus, vielleicht der scharfsinnigste unter den damaligen Kritikern, wie man aus einer einzigen Substanz die Vielheit der Dinge ableiten könne, und endlich gestand der Philosoph, er wisse diesen Punkt — der doch eine Schlüsselbedeutung für seine Lehre hatte — nicht genügend zu erklären.

Gewiss haben einige Kommentatoren in diesem Zusammenhang auf den Begriff der *modi infiniti,* der vermittelnden Glieder zwischen der Substanz und den einzelnen Wesen hingewiesen ; dieses Zwischenglied reicht jedoch zur Behebung der Schwierigkeit nicht aus. Wie wenig wir auch von den *modi infiniti* wissen, wissen wir doch, dass sie geschaffen sind und als unendliche Zusammenfassung aller einzelner Dinge — innerhalb der beiden Attribute — gelten sollen ; der Übergang von dem zeitlosen und unteilbaren Gott zu dem *modus infinitus,* der teilbar und zeitlich (ewig, aber im Sinne von unendlich dauernd) ist, bleibt ebenso rätselhaft, wie zu den besonderen Dingen. Diese Kategorie erhellt die Frage des Verhältnisses zwischen Gott und Welt ebensowenig, wie — um ein etwas ungeschicktes Beispiel zu benützen — bei Descartes die *glandula pinealis* das Rätsel der Körper-Seele-Verhältnisse erledigt : wo immer auch die Seele ihren Sitz hat, bleibt ihr Verkehr mit dem Körper innerhalb der kartesianischen Metaphysik unbegreiflich. Vom Standpunkt der Substanz — und das ist der einzige Standpunkt, von dem aus sich die Wahrheit eröffnet — wird die Unterschiedlichkeit der Dinge bei Spinoza verwischt, sie muss als Täuschung, jedenfalls als etwas nur subjektiv gültiges betrachtet werden ; ist doch die empirische Erkenntnis, obgleich für das Leben unerlässlich, eine gebrechliche, *mutilata cognitio.* Andererseits gibt es aber den *conatus ad suum esse conservandum,* einen allgemeinwirkenden Trieb, der jedem einzelnen Ding innewohnt und als ein ebenso unerschütterliches Gesetz wie das Gesetz der Unteilbarkeit der Substanz erscheint. Diese zwei sind unvereinbar und schliessen einander aus und doch machen beide zusammen das Rückgrat der Philosophie aus. Dieser Widerspruch kann innerhalb Spinozas Gedankenwelt nicht beseitigt werden ; in allen Teilen seiner Konstruktion erscheint er immer wieder.

Auch war dieser Widerspruch wahrscheinlich dafür verantwortlich, dass die Ausstrahlung dieser Philosophie so zweideutig war ; das ersieht man, wenn man in rohen Umrissen zwei Hauptströmungen in der Rezeption Spinozas nebeneinanderstellt : die deutsche-pantheistische und die französisch-freidenkerische Strömung.

[182]

Das *principium individuationis* wird aber noch rätselhafter, wenn man es innerhalb des Attributes des Denkens erwägt — obwohl doch jedes Ding auch an ihm teil hat. Trotz den aufklärerischen, pan-psychistischen Deutungen, die auch einige Kritiker des 19ten Jahrhunderts (Kuno Fischer, Tönnies, Empiriokritiker) teilten, ist das allumfassende Attribut *cogitatio* keine universelle 'psyche' ; ebensowenig hängt es vom menschlichen Denken über Dinge ab. Es ist eine allgegenwärtige Intelligibilität der Welt, ihr Bestehen als Erkenntnisobjekt. Es ist aber keine relative, sondern eine absolute Eigenschaft der Welt, und sie besteht fort, unabhängig davon, ob jemand an sie denkt ; solche Interpretation würde doch etwas Mögliches, eine Potentialität, in Gott voraussetzen, was offenbar dem Begriffe Gottes als reiner Aktualität entgegensteht. Man könnte vielleicht diese gar nicht einfache Seite des Spinozismus dadurch einigermassen erklären, dass man sie mit Heidegger's Seinbegriff in Beziehung bringt. Das Sein ist bei Heidegger so verfasst, dass es sich uns eröffnet ; dass es sich aber eröffnet, gehört zu seiner eigenen Konstruktion und hängt von uns nicht ab. Dass für Spinoza jeder Körper auch eine Idee ist, bedeutet weder, dass jeder Körper mit Bewusstsein ausgestattet ist, noch, dass seine Existenz von unserem Wissen abhängt. Wir haben hier mit der Teilnahme an der objektiven Logik des Seins zu tun, mit etwas, was wir als ein Wissen ohne das wissende Subjekt bezeichnen können.

Das war für Spinoza vielleicht eine Weise, die Aporie des Kartesianismus zu vermeiden : wie ist es möglich, die Einwirkung der körperlichen Dinge auf die Seele in den sinnlichen Empfindungen und die umgekehrte Einwirkung des menschlichen Willens auf den Körper in freien Handlungen zu erklären, wenn wir sonst wissen, dass es zwischen beiden Substanzen keine gegenseitigen Einwirkungen gibt ? Die von Geulincx, Malebranche und anderen Okkasionalisten gebotene Lösung setzte voraus, dass, mangels solcher Einwirkungen, Gott allein der unmittelbare Urheber aller Veränderungen in der Seele sein kann und dass Er in jedem Fall die Bestände der Seele mit denen der körperlichen Welt in Einklang bringt. Auf solche Weise wurde freilich die kartesianische Substanzlehre gerettet, aber um den Preis eines Weltbildes, in dem Gott die einzige Umwelt der menschlichen Seele bildet, so dass es keinen natürlichen Verkehr zwischen der Seele und dem physischen Universum gibt. Die spinozistische Lehre von der allgemeinen Intelligibilität lässt uns derselben Schwierigkeit auf die genau umgekehrte Weise ausweichen : sie macht alle Dinge zu Teilnehmern desselben Attributes, das den menschlichen Geist ausmacht.

Gleichwohl erzeugte diese Lösung, anstelle der gerade beseitigten Schwierigkeit, eine neue und nicht weniger peinliche. Nicht nur die erwähnte Frage des *principium individuationis* innerhalb des Attributs *cogitatio* wird unbeantwortbar, sondern auch eine andere: wie kann man die spezifische Idee des menschlichen Körpers, die definitionsgemäss mit diesem Körper identisch ist, also die Seele, ontologisch identifizieren? In diesem Fall ist doch 'die Idee' nicht nur das 'objektive Wissen' von dem körperlichen Dinge, dessen Idee sie ist, sondern auch dessen bewusstes Erlebnis, eine Subjektivität; wir wissen doch, dass in *diesem* Sinne nicht alle Dinge 'Ideen' sind; wie ist also die Besonderheit der menschlichen Seele zu begreifen?

Darauf, dass die Subjektivität innerhalb der Philosophie Spinozas überhaupt unkonstruierbar ist, haben wiederholt mehrere Kritiker hingewiesen — unter ihnen Mendelsohn, Hegel und Maine de Biran. In der Tat unterscheidet sich die Seele von den Ideen anderer Körper nur dadurch, dass ihr Gegenstand, ihr Ideatum, der menschliche Körper ist. Sie ist also ein Wissen von dem Körper, es gibt aber keine Gründe, dass es ein 'Wissen' in einem anderen Sinne sei, als das Wissen eines Steines von ihm selbst und das heisst — die objektive Teilnahme an derselben subjektlosen Logik der Natur. Es hilft uns nicht, in diesem Kontext die andere Kategorie, die der 'Idee einer Idee', herbeizurufen, da sich diese Kategorie ebenso auf alle Dinge erstreckt. Und so haben wir bei Spinoza nur das freischwebende Axiom: "Der Mensch denkt", ohne aber zu wissen, was für einen Sinn das genau hat. Endlich ist nicht abzusehen, wie die spezifisch menschliche Form der "animatio", die an sich selber gerichtete Subjektivität, auf dem Boden dieser Metaphysik gerettet werden könnte.

Wenn es kein *principium individuationis* im Denkattribut gibt (und was ein solches Prinzip sein könnte, stellen wir uns noch weniger vor, als im Fall der Ausdehnung), finden wir auch keine konzeptuellen Werkzeuge, um im Einklang mit der Doktrin die Gegenwärtigkeit der subjektiven Welt anzunehmen. Wir dürfen nur vermuten, dass die Wahrnehmungs- und Erkenntnisprozesse nicht darin bestehen, dass in ihnen die Dinge ihrer Materialität beraubt werden, sondern darin, dass wir sozusagen mit der intelligibilen Seite der Wirklichkeit selber in Kontakt kommen.

Die Welt der Ideen kann bekanntlich in keinen ursächlichen Zusammenhang mit der der Körper gebracht werden, obschon in beiden dasselbe vorkommt, da die Ideenordnung das objektive Wissen von dem, was mit dem Körper geschieht, darstellt. Unter dieser Annahme scheint es aber klar, dass die menschliche Subjektivität nichts anderes sein kann als das Bewusstsein von dem, was mit dem menschlichen Körper vorgeht. So ist Spinozas Mensch, wie schon Jacobi richtig bemerkte, nur Beobachter seiner eigenen Bewegung, nicht aber deren Autor (der Mensch als denkendes Wesen ist nicht der Urheber von irgendetwas, was in der körperlichen Welt vorkommt). Eine solche Stellung als Beobachter ist jedoch innerhalb dieser Metaphysik nicht gerechtfertigt, da die Subjektivität selber völlig unerklärbar bleibt.

Spinozas Schwierigkeit ist, wie erwähnt, die Kehrseite derjenigen, die bei Descartes erscheint. Bei dem letzten handelt es sich darum, wie, unter der Annahme, dass in der Wahrnehmung nur der Wahrnehmende selbt direkt wahrgenommen wird, die Wirklichkeit der Welt hergestellt werden kann. Bei Spinoza ist die Frage, wie, wenn man als Ausgangspunkt die Ordnung der intelligibilen Natur angenommen hat, der Weg zur Subjektivität gefunden werden soll. In beiden Fällen ist die Herstellung dieser Verbindung künstlich. Vielleicht — ist man versucht zu schliessen — ist es so, dass eine philosopische Sprache, die diese beiden Gebiete gleichzeitig umfasse, schlechthin unmöglich ist.

Auch ist die Unsterblichkeit oder die Ewigkeit, die der Seele in Aussicht gestellt wird, gewiss für Spinoza kein ewiges Leben des persönlichen Selbstbewusstseins. Es handelt sich vielmehr um das ausserzeitliche Dauern jeder Idee — da jede an demselben ewigen Attribut des Denkens teilnimmt, so wenig auch abzusehen wäre, wie wir widerspruchslos von ihrer individuellen Existenz überhaupt reden dürfen. Unabhängig von der Frage, inwieweit Spinoza in diesem Punkte die Überlieferung des arabischen Neuplatonismus mit seinem Glauben an die Unsterblichkeit einer einzigen universellen Vernunft (nicht aber persönliches Geistes) fortsetzt, war gewiss für ihn die Vereinigung mit Gott durch die intellektuelle Liebe das höchste Ziel, dem der Mensch nachstreben kann und soll. Die Vernunft, deren Betätigung unser Hauptwert ist, erscheint sozusagen als ein Empfänger, der auf die Wellen der Ewigkeit eingestellt ist : liegt es doch in der Natur der Vernunft, dass sie die Dinge *sub specie aeternitatis* erkennt.

Diese Vereinigung mit Gott setzt den Verzicht auf Persönlichkeit voraus. Gleichzeitig ist aber Selbstbejahung, Bewahrung der Individualität des Körpers und der Seele, ihre Anerkennung als Werte an sich, ein natürlicher Trieb, der allen Dingen zugehört (und zwar deshalb, weil das Wesen des Dinges seiner Definition gleicht und die Definition die Existenz feststellt). Die Vernunft nimmt diesen Trieb als eine notwendige Komponente der Natur an, wie sie sonst alles

[185]

in der Natur annimmt. Selbstmord ist naturwidrig, stellt Spinoza ausdrücklich fest ; aber der geistige Selbstmord scheint auch natur-gegeben oder naturgemäss, insofern uns die Vernunft dazu bewegt, mit Gott eins zu werden. Wie ein besonderer modus — menschliches Individium — gleichzeitig seine Selbstbewahrung und sein Aufgehen im zeitlosen Sein begehren kann, begreifen wir nicht. Es kommt selbstverständlich oft vor, dass Menschen einander widersprechende Begierden hegen, Spinoza hat sich aber nie klargemacht, dass hier ein Widerspruch vorliegt, und noch weniger, dass dieser in dem Fundamentalwiderspruch seiner Metaphysik verankert ist. In der Tat liegen die Wurzeln dieser zwei Tendenzen : die Welt im Akt der mystischen Union zu überspringen und sich selbst in der Welt zu bejahen — in Spinozas Unfähigkeit, zwei Weltauffassungen in Überein-stimmung zu bringen : einmal erscheint die Welt als unteilbare, zeit-lose Substanz, in der jede Unterschiedlichkeit aufgehoben wird ; ein andermal wird sie als *modus infinitus,* als unendliche Menge der in der Zeit lebenden, endlichen und zerstörbaren Individuen begriffen. Es gibt keine Synthese dieser Welten und keinen Übergang von einer zur anderen ; darum gibt es auch keine Synthese zwischen der Ethik, die in der mystischen Selbstzerstörung gipfelt, und der Selbsterhal-tungsethik ; keinen Einklang zwischen der Einstellung eines Mystikers und der eines Freidenkers.

In diesem Sinne stellt Spinozas Philosophie ein Scheitern dar ; aber ein philosophisch höchst bedeutendes Scheitern, keine triviale Ver-wirrung. Es ist das Scheitern eines Mannes, der daran geglaubt hat, dass die absolute Wahrheit sich in der diskursiven Sprache aus-drücken lässt, oder dass das Absolute sozusagen intellektuell ge-bändigt, in derselben Sprache wie die empirische Welt ausgesagt werden kann. Dieser Widerspruch Spinozas ist ein philosophischer Widerspruch par excellence, und darum sind in der Philosophie nur die Fehlschläge wichtig. Was völlig kohärent ist, ist entweder trivial oder uninteressant oder einfach keine Philosophie im legitimen Sinne.

Vor 100 Jahren, 200 Jahre nach Spinoza's Tod, hat Ernest Renan eine diesem Jahrestage gewidmete Vorlesung in den Haag gehalten. Er schlug damals vor, diese Philosophie als ein Modell der sekularen rationalistischen Religion zu begreifen, einer Religion ohne das Über-natürliche ; sie könnte, sagte er, eine bedeutende soziale Rolle spielen, da sie für die gebildeten Schichten annehmbar ist und ihre Autorität verstärken könnte ; diese Autorität sei dadurch unterwühlt, dass diese Schichten immerfort im Volk die traditionelle Religion nähren, an die sie selber nicht mehr glauben.

Ich glaube nicht, dass Renan recht hat. Eine rationalistische Religion ist weder erwünscht noch möglich ; tatsächlich ist sie ein Widerspruch in sich selbst. Das Geschick der Philosophie Spinozas gab einen von vielen Beweisen — und nicht den geringsten — dafür, dass die Idee einer Vernunftreligion hoffnungslos ist, dass es nicht in unserer Macht ist, das Absolute und das Empirische, das Unendliche und das Endliche, innerhalb derselben Sprache zu beherrschen, beide gleichzeitig als unser intellektuelles Eigentum in demselben Sinne zu besitzen, kurz, sich Gott und Welt in demselben Akt anzueignen.

כינוס זה היה השלישי בסידרת מפגשי ירושלים בפילוסופיה, הנערכים מטעם מרכז
ש״ה ברגמן לעיון פילוסופי של האוניברסיטה העברית בירושלים

כתבי האקדמיה הלאומית הישראלית למדעים
החטיבה למדעי-הרוח

שפינוזה — הגותו וכתביו

כינוס המכון הבינלאומי לפילוסופיה

ירושלים, כג—כו באלול תשל"ז

ירושלים תשמ"ג

שפינוזה — הגותו וכתביו